FOUNDATIONS OF ACADEMIC INQUIRY
SIXTH EDITION

Editors:
Editor-in-Chief: Kathy A. Lynn, M.A.
Editor: Stephen W. Braden, Ph.D.

KENNESAW STATE UNIVERSITY

HAYDEN
HM
McNEIL

Hayden-McNeil Sustainability

Hayden-McNeil's standard paper stock uses a minimum of 30% post-consumer waste. We offer higher % options by request, including a 100% recycled stock. Additionally, Hayden-McNeil Custom Digital provides authors with the opportunity to convert print products to a digital format. Hayden-McNeil is part of a larger sustainability initiative through Macmillan Higher Ed. Visit http://sustainability.macmillan.com to learn more.

Printed in the United States of America

10 9 8 7 6 5 4 3 2 1

ISBN 978-0-7380-6070-5

Hayden-McNeil Publishing
14903 Pilot Drive
Plymouth, MI 48170
www.hmpublishing.com

Braden 6070-5 F13

TABLE OF CONTENTS

Strategies for Academic Success

Life Skills

Foundations for Global Learning

Welcome to Kennesaw State University!

Dear KSU Student:

You are embarking on a learning journey that will change your life, and we are pleased that you have chosen Kennesaw State as the university at which to do it!

This is a young university, chartered fifty years ago this year. It is also a fine university, on the verge of becoming nationally recognized. It prides itself on being learning-centered, on providing students with a diverse set of opportunities to learn, and, most importantly, on putting students first.

As you study at Kennesaw State over the next several years, you will learn and understand more about yourself, the world, and your relationship to the world than you ever did before. And when you graduate from Kennesaw State, you will have both learned and understood more than ever before, and you will have developed an understanding about how much more remains to be learned and understood.

This will be an exhilarating journey. At times, it will also be difficult. That is the nature of higher education, to stretch your mind in ways that it has never before been stretched. This will take hard work on your part, on the part of the professors and staff who are here to help you learn, and on the part of your fellow students, your friends, and your family, all of whom will be part of your learning journey.

This course is designed to help you succeed in the learning journey that you are beginning. It provides information about Kennesaw State and its history, about the terms and concepts that the university community uses, about learning strategies required for success, about managing your time and handling stress, about career planning and money management, about globalization and diversity, and about many other things that you will need to succeed—not only here at Kennesaw, but, for that matter, in life!

So once again, welcome to Kennesaw State! You can and will succeed here, and this course is an important one in your early steps along that journey toward success. I am hopeful that your learning experience at KSU will kindle within you a desire to learn and to understand that will stay with you for the rest of your life.

Sincerely,

Daniel S. Papp, President

As You Journey to the Future

Dear KSU First-Year Seminar Student:

Welcome to Kennesaw State University. Your enrollment and participation in this course are some of the first steps you will take on a long, and I hope rewarding, odyssey into your future. We at Kennesaw State University are happy to be a part of your journey and to help you successfully navigate the waters of a college education. As you progress through your college experience, you will be challenged. However, it is our intent to provide you with the tools you will need to meet those challenges, and this course helps us do that. Through your active participation in this course, you will gain insight into your own values and your goals for your education, your career, and your life. You will also learn about strategies for achieving academic success through an understanding of your learning style, and you will find ways to optimize your learning experience. We will provide you with tips for effective time management and becoming a prepared citizen.

As important as these tools and techniques are, of even greater importance are the academic experiences that will set you on the course for a successful college experience. Your assignments will develop analytical and critical-thinking skills that will serve you well in this and subsequent courses.

Many of you may be "exploratory" students who do not yet know what you want for your academic major. We will provide you with academic and career advice to help you make the best selection. For those of you who already know what you want, we will help you connect with faculty and students in that discipline so you can begin to explore the rich possibilities that your chosen field has to offer.

We will also help you connect with various student organizations, both academic and social. These connections are important because national studies as well as studies here at KSU have shown that students who are engaged with their university are more likely to be successful and, therefore, more likely to graduate.

It is our fervent desire that you will not only graduate with an education that will lead you to a satisfying and productive career but that you will develop a love of learning that will sustain you and lead you to a satisfying and productive life. I wish you success in all that you do. It has been said that "a journey begins with a single step," so once again, welcome to Kennesaw State and the first step of your journey to a rewarding future.

Sincerely,

Ralph J. Rascati

Associate Vice President for Advising, Retention, and Graduation Initiatives and Dean of University College

STRATEGIES FOR ACADEMIC SUCCESS

CHAPTER 1

Higher Education: The First Year and Beyond

STEPHEN W. BRADEN, Ph.D. AND KATHY A. LYNN, M.A.

Chapter Goals

- Realize the value of higher education

- Understand the significance of liberal education and general education courses

- Have increased knowledge of the role of university professors

- Describe the purpose of first-year programs and seminars

Chapter Overview

This chapter provides facts pertaining to college graduation rates and describes many of the benefits of obtaining a liberal arts degree. This information is presented to assist students in understanding and appreciating the significance of a liberal education and general education courses. Finally, the role of university faculty and of the Department of First-Year and Transition Studies in fostering student success is presented.

Introduction

After navigating through mounds of application information and the complexities of scholarships and financial aid options, registering for courses, figuring out whether to live on campus, and making a myriad of other decisions, your personal university odyssey is under way. Congratulations!

The transition to college presents incoming students with many opportunities. In high school you may have been popular or ignored, respected or bullied, admired for your athleticism or teased for being intellectual or a "nerd," revered for driving the "right" car or

College teaches me how to make a living and about living.

College is a fresh start, a Clean slate

ridiculed for not wearing the most fashionable clothes. None of that matters now. From this day forward, you have the opportunity to explore who you are, to be comfortable being who you are, and, if you choose to do so, to create a completely new image.

Whether it is an activity you have always wanted to try, a talent you wish to hone, or something you never dreamed of doing, you are now in the right place and time to achieve your goals. On campus, you can be a spectator or participant in sporting events and recreational activities, attend concerts in genres from Alternative to Zydeco, or become a member in one of hundreds of clubs. You can volunteer for a cause in your community, study abroad on another continent, or lead a social action campaign to end any number of humanitarian crises across the globe. You can serve in student government, write for

the school newspaper, or have your own show on KSU's Owl Radio. You could even perform with an improv group, learn to grow organic vegetables, or jump out of an airplane. Think of anything you would like to do or try and chances are it is available to you here and now. And if it is not, opportunities exist for students to start a new organization or activity. Take advantage of this time to pursue your interests, explore new avenues, and engage with those who may share your interests as well as those who may challenge you to discover new pursuits.

This exciting time of transition is not without challenges. Many students entering college make it through, but some do not. Research reveals that in 2009, the six-year graduation rate of bachelor's students in the U.S. was barely one-half—55.5%, to be exact (NCHEMS, 2009). It may be helpful to ask yourself, what

6 years is normal now, Jobs effect this

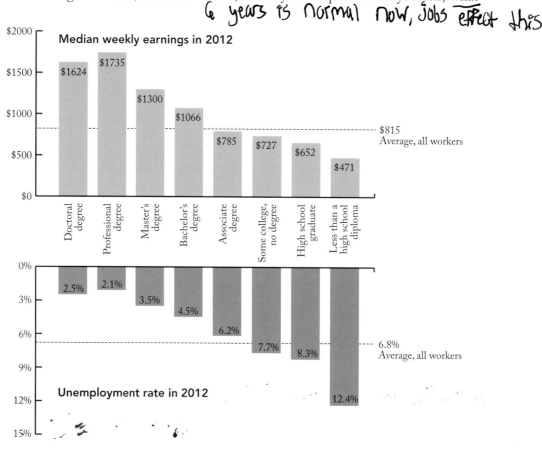

Figure 1-1. Source: Bureau of Labor Statistics, Current Population Survey (January 28, 2013)

My degree may be different than what I end up doing

do you hope to get from the university experience? There is an age-old debate about whether "college is to teach you about living" or "college is to teach you how to make a living." Obviously, "making a living" is part of "living." If finances are a motivator (as they are to most of us), consider the Bureau of Labor Statistics Survey in Figure 1-1.

With challenges often come rewards. Based on these figures, the median annual wages for a person holding a Bachelor's degree is more than $21,000 higher than that of a high school graduate. Notice, too, education pays not only in greater earning potential but in decreased unemployment rates. And there are other, perhaps less obvious, benefits awarded to those who attain a college degree. Research indicates that college graduates enjoy better health, volunteer more, and contribute more to society in general than those who fail to attain a college degree. Furthermore, graduates exhibit more confidence, are less likely to smoke, much less likely to live in poverty, and less likely to spend time in prison than their less-educated peers. Researchers say the benefits extend beyond the graduates themselves: Their children will be smarter as well (Wiles, 2004). Appreciating the benefits of an education, and more specifically a liberal education, can play a key role in one's motivation to achieve academic success.

A degree has countless rewards

Liberal Education and General Education Courses

Kennesaw State University (KSU) is a comprehensive university that offers a liberal education. In this context "liberal" has nothing to do with political or social ideology. Liberal education is taught in an environment in which both faculty and staff teach, research, and express their opinions through free inquiry without fearing retribution. This education can provide students with a better understanding of their world and an increased ability to think and analyze from a critical perspective. The Association of American Colleges and Universities (n.d.) notes the importance of a liberal education:

> Liberal Education is an approach to learning that empowers individuals and prepares them to deal with complexity, diversity, and change. It provides students with broad knowledge of the wider world (e.g., science, culture, and society) as well as in-depth study in a specific area of interest. A liberal education helps students develop a sense of social responsibility, as well as strong and transferable intellectual and practical skills such as communication, analytical and problem-solving skills, and a demonstrated ability to apply knowledge and skills in real-world settings. (n.p.)

The liberal education will affect you long after you leave KSU. It will help to prepare your mind for a lifetime of learning and you for productive, meaningful participation in the workplace and society. In "Only Connect...The Goals of a Liberal Education," William Cronon (1998) suggests that liberal education "aspires to nurture growth of human talent in the service of human freedom," and that, "liberally educated people have been liberated by their education to explore and fulfill the promise of their own highest talents" (p. 74).

how to think analytically

A liberal education includes studies in liberal arts, science, and math. It is, in great part, the broad knowledge attained through this general education that cultivates the personal qualities common to most liberally educated people. It is these personal qualities that enable one to deal with complexity, diversity, and change, to develop their highest talents, and to enjoy a broader and deeper appreciation of the world and people around them. This is why all students are required to complete general education courses at KSU.

> Perhaps the answer to that age-old question, "Does college teach you about living?" or "Does college teach you how to make a living?" is very simply, "Yes!"

How does all of this tie into the desire to "make a living" and the statistics that support the idea that those who attain a university degree are likely to enjoy higher income levels and lower unemployment rates? A recent study, *Raising the Bar: Employers' Views on College Learning in the Wake of the Economic Downturn*, indicates that "Employers want their employees to use a broader set of skills and have higher levels of learning and knowledge than in the past to meet the increasingly complex demands they will face in the workplace" (Hart, 2010, p. 1). Again, it is through the general education curriculum that students develop this broad set of transferable skills employers seek, skills such as effective written and oral communication, critical and analytical thinking and problem-solving, the ability to generate original thoughts and synthesize multiple concepts, a deep understanding of cross-cultural competency, and the social responsibility for citizenship and ethical leadership in our continually changing, globally expanding workplace and society.

Additionally, studying general education is an excellent opportunity for students who have not yet declared a major to explore several disciplines and for students who have declared a major to confirm that they are indeed pursuing a degree that will lead to a satisfying career path. When students begin to take major discipline courses, they will then study the in-depth concepts and applications necessary for their specific area of interest. But remember that it is the broad base of knowledge gained in the general education studies that supply the foundation for this in-depth learning.

KSU Understands the Importance of General Education

An American Council of Trustees and Alumni study on the state of general education ranks KSU among a select group of 19 colleges and universities in the nation that scored an "A" for its high-quality core curriculum, placing KSU in the top 2 percent among the 1,007 major public and private four-year institutions surveyed (Kennesaw State, 2011).

Kennesaw State University is not a trade school; rather, it is a place of higher learning. Students have opportunities to immerse themselves in the teaching of some of the world's great minds: Shakespeare, Mozart, Van Gogh, Maya Angelou, William Faulkner, Flannery O'Connor, Helen Keller, Albert Einstein, Bill Gates, Coretta Scott King, Leonardo Da Vinci, and countless others. Study great minds—their successes, failures, obstacles overcome, world-changing events—and how the world will be when your children and even your grandchildren are your age. While you are immersed in an environment of facts, ideas, theories, research methods, and analyses, you are also surrounded by individuals who are awed by all that is available to learn and who appreciate the vastness of knowledge. The faculty and staff at KSU want you to share this awe and appreciation.

general ed courses give me a wider skill set

Faculty Support

Some of you have been taught that college faculty members do not care about their students. This is not the case at KSU where effective teaching and learning are institutional priorities. After all, students are a reflection of what faculty do here at KSU. That said, there are differences between university faculty and high school educators. Job responsibilities for university faculty extend beyond teaching courses to include engaging in scholarly pursuits, actively involving in professional service on campus, contributing to their discipline associations, and serving as leaders in their communities. As such, while it is common for high school teachers to remind students of approaching due dates, offer make-up assignments, and approach you when your grade is below average, it is unlikely that your professors will be willing or able to do this. University faculty members are willing to challenge and be challenged by, support, enlighten, and assist you, but your success is ultimately your responsibility. However, many resources are available to assist you in this first year of college. You are enrolled in a class within a department that was created to assist first-year students with the transition to higher education.

profs will help, but I must initiate

College Faculty Members Do Care

While it is true that your professors are busy with teaching, service, and scholarly pursuits, know that they do care about their students. They care about you. Particularly in this first-year transition, students face many challenges adjusting to university life, connecting with others, and handling new responsibilities. Do not hesitate to approach your KSU professors with any concern you have. They do care and are here to help you succeed academically, socially, and personally.

Department of First-Year and Transition Studies

The first-year seminar course was first offered at KSU in 1983. The learning outcomes for the seminar (Fig. 1-2) are designed to broaden student skills in four major areas: (1) acquiring knowledge of the life skills necessary to succeed in college and post graduate life; (2) acquiring knowledge of the strategies necessary for academic success; (3) appreciating the importance of campus and community connections; and (4) articulating the importance of the foundations of global learning. In 2007 this department was established as one of several programs on campus developed to promote student success and increase retention, progression, and graduation (RPG) rates. The department's curricular initiatives are designed to improve student learning and transitions into and through the initial college experience. These initiatives include first-year and transition seminar courses (i.e., transfer student seminars, etc.), common reader

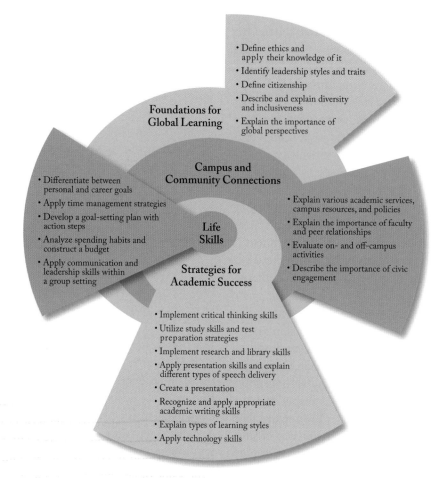

Foundations for Global Learning
- Define ethics and apply their knowledge of it
- Identify leadership styles and traits
- Define citizenship
- Describe and explain diversity and inclusiveness
- Explain the importance of global perspectives

Campus and Community Connections

Life Skills
- Differentiate between personal and career goals
- Apply time management strategies
- Develop a goal-setting plan with action steps
- Analyze spending habits and construct a budget
- Apply communication and leadership skills within a group setting

- Explain various academic services, campus resources, and policies
- Explain the importance of faculty and peer relationships
- Evaluate on- and off-campus activities
- Describe the importance of civic engagement

Strategies for Academic Success
- Implement critical thinking skills
- Utilize study skills and test preparation strategies
- Implement research and library skills
- Apply presentation skills and explain different types of speech delivery
- Create a presentation
- Recognize and apply appropriate academic writing skills
- Explain types of learning styles
- Apply technology skills

Figure 1-2. **Learning Outcomes for the First-Year Seminar**

programs, and learning communities as well as co-curricular initiatives such as First-Year Convocation and New Student Orientation. The department has jointly appointed faculty, includes innovative seminars focusing on global issues and civic engagement, and is the only academic department in the University System of Georgia and one of only two departments in the country with tenured and tenure-track faculty dedicated to teaching first-year seminars.

The Department of First-Year and Transition Studies not only offers nationally recognized first-year seminars and learning communities to thousands of entering students each year, but it is also a structural model for institutions preparing to either launch or enhance their comprehensive approach to first-year students' needs. The accomplishments of the department are recognized internationally, nationally, regionally, and within the state:

- KSU was named by *U.S. News & World Report* as one of the top institutions in the nation for a First-Year Experience program in its 2013 "America's Best Colleges" edition. This is the tenth consecutive year that KSU has been honored by this publication. KSU is the only Georgia institution to receive this recognition.

- KSU's Department of First-Year and Transition Studies and the Center for Student Leadership received the top national award from NASPA (Student Affairs Administrators in Higher Education) for making a positive impact on student learning through KSU's Thrive Program for HOPE Scholars. Thrive was recognized as a creative and collaborative program that successfully addressed student needs as well as critical campus issues.

- First-Year and Transition Studies was honored to receive the 2010 Georgia Board of Regents' Teaching Excellence Award for a Department/Program.

- KSU is also a recognized leader in first-year learning communities. The institution is a member of a group of six institutions that plans and hosts the annual National Learning Communities Conference.

- The University College Dean and an Associate Dean (the former First-Year and Transition Studies Department Chair) have been recognized nationally as Outstanding First-Year Advocates by the National Resource Center for The First-Year Experience and Students in Transition®.

- The Department of First-Year and Transition Studies has hosted visitors from colleges and universities interested in learning more about our first-year programs. Visitors include, but are not limited to, Auburn University, Utah Valley State University, and Northwest University (South Africa). In January 2013, a group of guests from Kansai University of International Studies, including the university's president and the Director of the National Institute for Educational Policy Research, traveled from Japan to meet with faculty and staff in the department.

KSU is an awesome school for freshman

This list of achievements is illustrative of this department's qualifications in the discipline of First-Year Experience and the faculty and staff's commitment to first-year student success. Furthermore, their research has been presented at international, national, regional, and state conferences, and has been published in book chapters and peer-reviewed research journals. KSU's First-Year and Transition Studies faculty continue to engage in the Scholarship of Teaching and Learning regarding first-year students in an effort to improve the effectiveness of current and emerging curricular initiatives.

Department of First-Year and Transition Studies Mission Statement

The Department of First-Year and Transition Studies at Kennesaw State University provides first-year students a foundation in academic and life skills to be further developed as these students progress toward graduation. In collaboration with other academic units and student success units, the Department of First-Year and Transition Studies assists students in the transition to college life by reinforcing the value of general education, by exposing students to the concept of global citizenship, by expecting students to engage in critical thinking, and by promoting personal growth through academic and social opportunity (Kennesaw State University, 2010).

Summary

Appreciate the opportunity to earn a university degree. Embrace all elements of higher education and get involved, be committed, and revel in the joy of learning. Take advantage of the resources available to you. Envision yourself learning, growing, and participating in your college, local, and global communities. Know that what you do here at KSU will have a profound impact on every day of the rest of your life. Enjoy the journey!

References

American Association of Colleges and Universities. (n.d). *What is liberal education?* Retrieved from http://www.aacu.org/leap/what_is_liberal_education.cfm

Bureau of Labor Statistics. (2010). *Education pays...* Retrieved from http://www.bls.gov/emp/ep_chart_001.htm

Cronon, W. (1998). Only connect: The goals of a liberal education. *American Scholar, 67*(4), 73.

Hart Research Associates. (2010). *Raising the bar: employers' views on college learning in the wake of the economic downturn.* Washington, DC: Hart Research Associates. Retrieved from http://www.aacu.org/leap/documents/2009_EmployerSurvey.pdf

Kennesaw State University. (2010). *First-Year Programs Mission Statement.* Retrieved February 18, 2012 from http://www.kennesaw.edu/fyp/faculty_staff/mission.html

Kennesaw State University. (2011). *Kennesaw State scores at top in nationwide curriculum study.* Retrieved February 16, 2012 from http://web.kennesaw.edu/news/stories/kennesaw-state-scores-top-nationwide-curriculum-stud

NCHEMS Information Center. (2009). *Progress and Completion: Graduation Rates.* Retrieved from http://www.higheredinfo.org/dbrowser/index.php?submeasure=27&year=2009&level=nation&mode=graph&state=0

Wiles, R. (2004). *College degree pays off big—not just in income, study concludes.* Retrieved from www.azcentral.com/families/education/.../1019collegebenefits19ON.html

Critical Thinking Questions

1. How can a degree in higher education benefit (a) you, (b) your employer, and (c) the global community?

2. What does a liberal education provide above and beyond vocational or professional skills?

3. List the job responsibilities for university faculty. What is the significance of each of these?

4. List the learning outcomes for the first-year seminar course and describe how each can aid students in achieving academic success.

EXERCISE 1-1
The Personal Qualities of Liberally Educated People

Name _____ Date _____

In William Cronon's article, he describes many personal qualities of liberally educated people. Consider the qualities in the following list. Provide a brief description (your own interpretation) for each and explain its importance in the workplace and society.

1. They listen and they hear.

2. They read and they understand.

3. They can talk with anyone.

4. They can write clearly and persuasively and movingly.

5. They can solve a wide variety of puzzles and problems.

6. They respect rigor not so much for its own sake but as a way of seeking truth.

7. They practice humility, tolerance, and self-criticism.

8. They understand how to get things done in the world.

9. They nurture and empower the people around them.

Next, retrieve the full article and read Cronon's explanation for each of the personal qualities. How is your interpretation of each of the qualities similar to/different from that of Cronon's?

The article was published in 1998 in *The American Scholar* (Volume 67, No. 4) and can be found through the GALILEO portal and in the Chapter 1 resources on the textbook website.

CHAPTER 2

Understanding Yourself as a Learner

STEPHANIE M. FOOTE, Ph.D. AND RUTH A. GOLDFINE, Ph.D.

Chapter Goals

- Understand academic expectations and skills that are key to college-level learning

- Learn how to become a self-directed learner

- Become aware of the different theories of learning

- Identify learning preferences and styles

- Understand Bloom's Taxonomy and the critical inquiry process

Chapter Overview

This chapter introduces many theories and ideas about the process of learning. The first part of the chapter explains the academic expectations and responsibilities of college students. Next, general education and the learning process are introduced, followed by dimensions of learning preferences and styles. Finally, Bloom's Taxonomy and the critical inquiry process, two other important aspects of thinking and learning at the college level, are presented.

Academic Expectations

College is vastly different from high school, and many of those differences might be enjoyable to first-year students, such as fewer hours spent in the classroom, the ability to select the days and times of classes, and fewer exams. However, one of the biggest differences between high school and college is the shift in responsibility for learning. High school teachers often tell students which key points from a lecture to write in their notebooks, keep track of each student's missing assignments, and frequently remind the class of project due dates. In college, the student is responsible for all of this—and more.

Teachers aren't going to hold my hand in college

learning is proactive & my responsibility

To be successful in college, students must develop and consistently use several "key learning skills and techniques" throughout the college experience, such as time management, study skills, goal setting, self-awareness, persistence, collaborative learning, ownership of one's learning, technology proficiency, and retention of factual information (Conley, 2011). These skills underscore the fact that, at the college level, learning is the responsibility of the student. To succeed in higher education, students must do more than just go to class; they must manage themselves and their learning. To begin to take responsibility for learning, students should:

- Ask questions when they don't understand

- Read, save, and consult the syllabus throughout the semester

- Know that the class lecture may *complement* the readings, not reiterate them

- Learn information independently, which may involve taking meaningful notes that will be useful during future study sessions

- Recognize when they are struggling in a class and seek help

Many first-year students may have assumed some—even many—of these responsibilities. However, it is important for students to integrate all these responsibilities into their academic routines in order to become self-directed learners and succeed in college.

Becoming a Self-Directed Learner

Self-directed learners are those students who take responsibility for their studies. Generally, these students also demonstrate an intellectual curiosity or a "drive to pursue, enjoy, and engage in learning opportunities" (University of Minnesota, 2012, p. 1). While an important first step in becoming a self-directed learner is to analyze the syllabus for every class and

Understand how I learn

create a study plan at the start of each semester, self-directed learners also keep track of their academic progress throughout the term so they always have a clear picture of how well they are doing in each class. Although instructors are ultimately responsible for maintaining an official record of student grades, students should personally track the grades they have earned so that at any given time in the semester they can calculate their class average based on the grades that have been returned. Some colleges and universities use early warning or alert systems to inform students that they are at risk of not successfully completing a course. Although these systems are useful, it is always best for students to learn to recognize the "red flags" or cues that indicate they are struggling academically. This type of personal monitoring or self-awareness is a key learning skill (Conley, 2011) that is essential to becoming "an effective self-directed learner" (Ambrose, Bridges, Lovett, DiPietro, & Norman, 2010, p. 191). Self-directed learners use metacognitive[1] skills such as reflecting and self-evaluation strategies to determine what they are learning and how they may apply that new knowledge (Zimmerman & Schunk, 2001). Similarly, they use these skills to identify personal strengths and weaknesses related to learning. Because they are regularly monitoring their learning, self-directed learners recognize when they are struggling with an idea or concept in a class and seek help before a test or exam.

To become a self-directed learner, you should:

- Evaluate your own learning to identify gaps in your understanding of course material. Often, you can observe gaps in your knowledge when you find yourself confused about a concept or idea even after you have completed the assigned readings and homework.

---

1 Zimmerman and Schunk (2001) define metacognition as "…the use of higher order thinking, reasoning, and learning skills during learning." This concept is also known "as thinking about thinking" (p. 83).

- Seek help to fill those gaps by meeting with your instructor, using campus resources (i.e., tutoring and Supplemental Instruction[2]), and finding additional readings or examples to help your comprehension of an idea or concept.

- Monitor and record (in a notebook, for example) your grades in each of your classes.

- Be honest with yourself and with your academic advisor about your personal strengths and weaknesses. Sometimes you may find that you continue to struggle in a class even after using all of the resources on campus. At that point, it may be necessary to work with your academic advisor to identify possible alternatives.

Academic Expectations for Classes Taught Online

The U.S. Department of Education (Radford, 2011) reported that from 2000 to 2008 the number of undergraduate students taking one or more courses offered through distance education rose from 8 to 20 percent, and many of those courses were offered online (*The Chronicle*, 2011). Hybrid or blended courses—taught as a mix of face-to-face and online class meetings—are also becoming more common. Even students

who do not choose to take online courses or hybrid courses may find that many of their classes that meet face-to-face involve some aspects of online learning.

Although the academic expectations for online courses are often similar to those of courses taught face-to-face, any student considering an online class must be aware that such a class may involve additional expectations. For example, some online courses are conducted in real-time or synchronously, while other online courses are self-paced or asynchronous. Students who plan to enroll in asynchronous online classes should conduct an honest self-assessment of their motivation to learn independently and their ability to set goals and meet deadlines without prompting from an instructor. Similarly, learners considering online classes that implement synchronous methods must be prepared to assess their ability and willingness to be online at specific times. Courses taught online or in a hybrid format can be a wonderful alternative for many students, but it is important to consider personal motivation, learning preferences and styles, and the individual course expectations before determining if these courses are a good option.

General Education Courses and the Learning Process

First-year students often begin with general education (or core) courses, which are the foundation of all upper-division courses. These classes touch on most, if not all, disciplines represented at the university, and they vary greatly in size, from intimate 25-student courses (e.g., English composition) to large lecture classes of 150 students or more (e.g., economics). Because these classes differ in size and content, generally they incorporate a wide variety of assignments and tests. For example, a composition course may require students to write a five-page paper. The midterm and final exams in a large economics class may be multiple choice, with responses recorded on Scantron answer sheets.

---

2   Supplemental Instruction (SI) is described more fully in the following chapter.

Online courses are a good option for the right person.

A speech class might demand two 10-minute oral presentations. And most classes will likely require students to use some form of technology. Clearly, general education courses are quite diverse, not only in content but also in structure and academic expectations. Consequently, there is no secret formula—no single correct way—for students to successfully complete all the assignments and pass the various exams they will face during the first year of college. Therefore, students should arm themselves with the learning strategies necessary to succeed and with an *understanding* of these strategies and how they might be adapted to various courses and assignments.

Of course, there is one significant complicating factor: YOU. Each student has specific learning preferences and styles that suggest how he or she best gathers and processes information. Thus, students must not only master the various learning strategies, they must also master them in a way that complements their individual style of learning.

An additional factor for consideration is that professors often have different teaching styles. Like learning styles, teaching styles can differ greatly and may be influenced by the professor's background or the subject matter covered in the course (see chapter 3 for more about teaching styles). Other variables related to one's personality and previous knowledge can also impact learning styles. Because learning is a process that involves changes in an individual's "knowledge, beliefs, behaviors, or attitudes" (Ambrose, Bridges, Lovett, DiPietro, & Norman, 2010, p. 3), learning styles should be adapted to facilitate the learning process. There is much to consider related to learning, but a good way to begin is by developing an understanding of your learning preferences and styles.

Gen ed courses are diverse, I need to understand myself first

Identifying Individual Learning Preferences and Styles

Learning preferences and styles can explain how an individual receives different types of information, how that information is perceived, and the rate at which the information is processed (Felder, 1993). One dimension of learning styles involves the ways students gather and process information; a preferred learning style is the one a learner relies on the most. Although the existence of learning styles is not universally accepted, nor are there universal learning styles, understanding that there are different ways of receiving and processing information can assist students in developing their own, individualized study strategies and in planning their study sessions.

Personal and environmental characteristics also impact how individuals receive and process information. Assessments based on Jung's Theory of Psychological Types[3] and Gardner's Theory of Multiple Intelligences can help provide students with a better understanding of how they learn.

The Myers-Briggs Type Indicator (MBTI) is based on Jung's Theory, and the four indices in the assessment—extrovert/introvert, sensor/intuitor, thinker/feeler, and judger/perceiver—explain preferences in a person's perception and judgment (CAPT, n.d.). These preferences can help us identify the environments in which we are most comfortable learning. For example, students who are introverts may prefer to study by themselves, whereas extroverts may prefer to study with a group.

In addition to the MBTI, there are inventories that measure Multiple Intelligences (MI). Gardner (1993) explains that these intelligences

---

3 Jung's Theory of Psychological Types contends that individuals may be categorized according to attitude type and function type. The MBTI is one of several instruments that have been developed from Jung's "simple schema of personality types" (Hopcke, 1999, p. 51).

Find your learning style

represent "the kinds of abilities valued by human cultures" (p. 62), but no one intelligence is superior to another. MI can help explain our natural abilities as learners, but it does not imply that we cannot develop intelligences in other areas. For example, a student might have a greater level of logical/mathematical intelligence, but he or she can still develop skills as a verbal or linguistic learner.

By examining how they receive and process information, the environments in which they are most comfortable learning, and their natural abilities, students can create a comprehensive picture of who they are as learners. It is through the analysis of their abilities and preferences that students are able to truly begin the process of thinking and learning at the college level.

Bloom's Taxonomy[4] and Critical Thinking and Inquiry

The learning process is also affected by how we think or the levels of thinking at which we operate. Bloom's Taxonomy, as depicted below, identifies and orders the levels of thinking from the most basic (lower levels) to the most sophisticated (higher levels). Most high school assignments and exams focus on lower levels of thinking that typically require students to memorize information and reproduce it—or merely recognize it—on an exam. This strategy can be referred to as shallow processing, which generally involves short-term memory (STM). In college, professors expect this *as a minimum*. In other words, students who do not advance beyond this level are not likely to master the course material and excel in their classes. Operating at the higher levels of Bloom's Taxonomy when learning new material requires deeper processing that engages long-term memory (LTM). The next chapter presents a number of learning strategies to help

---

4 The information on Bloom's Taxonomy has been informed by Mayer, R. E. (2002).

Bloom's taxonomy- levels of learning

students achieve deeper, more meaningful learning for college-level courses by learning to operate at those higher levels of thinking.

Bloom's Taxonomy

Bloom's Taxonomy, which categorizes and describes the levels of thinking at which a learner can operate, can be a useful tool for students as they develop the study strategies necessary to succeed in college. Specifically, students who are aware of the levels in Bloom's Taxonomy can make more informed decisions about what and how to study for each of their courses. Ultimately, what and how you study makes a tremendous difference in how successful you are in class, in turn affecting your GPA, which is crucial in maintaining scholarships that may be essential to your ability to remain in and graduate from college.

In Bloom's Taxonomy, the levels build upon one another, starting with the most basic and advancing to the most complex. According to this taxonomy, there are six different levels of thinking, presented below from the least to the most complex:

- Remembering (level 1)
- Understanding (level 2)
- Applying (level 3)
- Analyzing (level 4)
- Evaluating (level 5)
- Creating (level 6)

Has 6 levels; helps me know how to study

Figure 2-1. Bloom's Revised Taxonomy of Thinking and Learning (Coffey, n.d.)

Remembering

The lowest of the six levels, remembering, involves the retrieval of information from long-term memory. Being able to recall basic information is essential for meaningful learning and is necessary in the completion of complex tasks. Essentially, this is simple memorization—remembering a phone number, the correct spellings of common words, key events in history, the teachings of significant philosophers, and so on. If the goal of learning is to promote retention of knowledge, **remembering** is the most important cognitive process; however, it does not promote learners' ability to put information in context or to apply that information to more complex tasks.

Understanding

When students operate at the second level, **understanding**, they are able to construct meaning from what they have learned and to build connections between new information and prior knowledge. At this level, students are able to interpret, explain, and classify information. In addition, this knowledge can be used to formulate comparisons, develop examples, and make inferences.

Applying

Once learners have mastered the skills of recalling information (remembering) and restating it (understanding), they must develop the ability to apply it. At the applying level, an individual employs the knowledge he or she has acquired to new situations in order to execute familiar procedures or apply familiar procedures to unfamiliar tasks. When learners reach the **applying** level, they must draw on the abilities developed at the lower levels of Bloom's Taxonomy, first remembering (level 1) the needed knowledge and understanding (level 2) that information in order to apply it to a new situation.

Analyzing

At the **analyzing** level, learners break materials or concepts into their components and use analytical-thinking skills to examine those components, determining how they are related to each other and the overall structure/concept. Students operating at this level are able to distinguish the relevant from the irrelevant (differentiate), to determine how elements fit or function within a structure (analyze), or to ascertain the bias or intent of that which has been presented (organize). For example, learners might be asked to speculate about the cause(s) of a trend or phenomenon, to distinguish between one or more processes, or to identify the potential pitfalls of a proposed solution.

Evaluating

Students operating at the **evaluating** level make judgments based on criteria and standards. They are able to examine information, a product, or a process and formulate their own judgment about it. For example, is a Mac better than a PC? Is a large lecture class better than one with small group discussions? While some evaluations might seem fairly easy, students will be expected to support those evaluations with valid, verifiable, documented evidence.

Creating

When learners operate at the sixth and highest level of Bloom's Taxonomy—the **creating** level—they demonstrate the ability to generate ideas, alternatives, and hypotheses; to create procedures for the completion of a project or task; or to produce an original product, such as a play, essay, or presentation. Clearly, in order to create, they must first remember and understand the information needed to create an assigned (or desired) product, possess the ability to apply what has been learned, and analyze and evaluate the situation or circumstances to ensure they proceed in the most logical and efficient manner. In brief, students will need to invoke levels one through five of Bloom's Taxonomy before they can successfully operate at the sixth level.

Critical Thinking and Inquiry

Similar to Bloom's Taxonomy, higher-level thinking and learning (levels 3–5) involve aspects of the critical inquiry process. Thinking about something critically involves examining a problem or situation, gathering and evaluating information about that problem, and then devising and testing a potential solution. This process is similar to the scientific method used in many science classes. In its simplest form, inquiry or inquiring involves asking questions. Engaging in inquiry helps students take ownership of what they are learning (McKeachie & Svinicki, 2006) because they have an opportunity to prove or disprove something based on information they have gathered, evaluated, and applied.

In college-level courses, professors expect students to think critically about information presented in lectures and readings. It is often through thinking critically that students develop diverse perspectives about problems and issues. Professors generally want students to express and defend these perspectives because it is through this progression that real learning occurs. In his essay *Only Connect*, William Cronon (1998) describes how the process of learning at the college level allows students to become more broadly educated, which, in turn, helps them "… to see the connections that allow one to make sense of the world and act within it in creative ways" (p. 77). higher levels of thinking are used at the college level

Summary

This chapter has explored how students learn, introduced theories on learning preferences and styles, and examined how the different levels of knowledge are acquired and used. The following chapter will provide opportunities to apply this information to the development of an individual plan for academic success.

References

Ambrose, S. A., Bridges, M. W., Lovett, M. C., DiPietro, M., & Norman, M. K. (2010). *How learning works: 7 research principles for smart teaching.* San Francisco: Jossey-Bass.

Center for Applications of Psychological Type (CAPT). (n.d.). *Jung's theory of psychological types and the MBTI® Instrument.* Retrieved from http://www.capt.org/mbti-assessment/mbti-overview.htm

The Chronicle of Higher Education. (2011). *Online learning trends.* Retrieved from http://chronicle.com/article/Charts-6-Online-Learning/129634/

Coffey, H. (n.d.). *Bloom's taxonomy.* Retrieved from http://www.learnnc.org/lp/pages/4719

Conley, D. T. (2011, November). *The continuum of college and career readiness.* Presentation made at the Creating Successful Transitions to Postsecondary Education Symposium. Retrieved from https://www.epiconline.org/files/pdf/20111117_PSU.pdf

Cronon, W. (1998). Only connect: The goals of a liberal education. *American Scholar, 67*(4), 73.

Felder, R. (1993). Reaching the second tier: Learning and teaching styles in college science education. *Journal of College Science Teaching, 23*(5), 286–290.

Gardner, H. (1993). *Frames of the mind: The theory of multiple intelligences.* New York, NY: Basic Books.

Hopcke, R. H. (1999). *A guided tour of the collected works of C.G. Jung.* Boston: Shambhala.

Mayer, R. E. (2002). Rote versus meaningful learning. *Theory into Practice, 41*(4), 226–232.

McKeachie, W. J., & Svinicki, M. (2006). *McKeachies' teaching tips: Strategies, research, and theory for college and university teachers.* New York, NY: Houghton-Mifflin.

Radford, A.W. (2011). *Learning at a distance: Undergraduate enrollment in distance education courses and degree programs* (NCES 2012-154). Washington, DC: U.S. Department of Education. Retrieved from http://nces.ed.gov/pubs2012/2012154.pdf

University of Minnesota. (2012). *Is intellectual curiosity a strong predictor for academic performance?* Report prepared by the Research & Evaluation Team in the Office of Information Technology. Retrieved from http://www.oit.umn.edu/prod/groups/oit/@pub/@oit/@web/@evaluationresearch/documents/content/oit_content_395365.pdf

Zimmerman, B. J., & Schunk, D. H. (2001). *Self-regulated learning and academic achievement: Theoretical perspectives.* Mahwah, NJ: Lawrence Erlbaum Associates, Inc.

Critical Thinking Questions

1. In addition to the list of academic expectations at the beginning of this chapter, what are some other differences you have observed between high school and higher education?

2. Why is understanding your learning preferences and styles, Bloom's Taxonomy, and the critical inquiry process important in developing your learning strategies?

3. Identify the six levels of Bloom's Taxonomy. What types of assignments and exams might require you to operate at each of these levels?

CHAPTER 3

Learning Strategies for Academic Success

RUTH A. GOLDFINE, Ph.D. AND STEPHANIE M. FOOTE, Ph.D.

Chapter Goals

* Recognize the resources and responsibilities associated with academic success

* Foster strategies for reading and understanding college textbooks

* Enhance listening and note-taking skills

* Improve study strategies

* Develop test-taking strategies

Chapter Overview

This chapter demonstrates how you can apply knowledge of the learning process, learning preferences and styles, critical thinking process, and Bloom's Taxonomy, presented in the previous chapter, to develop or enhance your study skills.

Preparing for Academic Success

The preceding chapter explored how individuals learn by examining different theories related to the learning process. While an understanding of these theories is valuable, the knowledge they offer must be applied in order for them to have any real impact. Furthermore, it is important to understand that while instructors can *teach*, it is only students themselves who can actually *learn*. This simple fact is significant because it highlights the importance of taking responsibility for your own academic success. The first step in assuming this responsibility is to develop the appropriate attitude—a positive attitude—toward college and your studies at Kennesaw State University. Specifically, you must assume the attitude that you are a capable scholar and that:

¡DO THE READING!

- You are responsible for learning the material presented in your classes.

- You can successfully meet the challenges of your classes.

- You will make the most of your learning experience at KSU.

- You will graduate.

In addition to adopting a positive attitude, students must also divest themselves of any misconceptions about learning that might inhibit their academic success. Stephen Chew, a cognitive psychologist and faculty member at Samford University, refers to these misconceptions as the "beliefs that make you stupid." In his video, *Beliefs that Make You Fail…Or Succeed*, Dr. Chew presents four misconceptions about learning: learning is fast, knowledge is comprised of isolated facts, being good at a subject is inborn, and multitasking can be effective. Students who hold these mistaken beliefs must adopt a new perspective on learning, begin to think differently about who they are as learners (as discussed in Chapter 2), and use that knowledge to make decisions about the strategies for academic success that will be most beneficial to them.

Campus Resources

There are many on-campus resources and services available to students to help them achieve academic success. Typically, these are provided at no cost to students and can include:

- Tutoring (e.g., Math Lab, Writing Center)

- Supplemental Instruction (SI)

- Counseling Services

- Information Technology Services

- Academic Advisors/Advising

Attitude is half the battle

The Instructor as a Resource

A sometimes overlooked campus resource is the instructor. Students may be uncomfortable approaching their instructors for assistance, but sometimes even a brief conversation with the instructor can clarify a complex concept covered in a class lecture or clear up confusion about an assignment. Instructors can also put students in contact with other campus resources.

Differences Between Tutoring and SI

Although tutoring and SI share a similar goal—helping students to improve their academic performance in a course or courses—these two forms of academic support are quite distinct. Tutoring is generally conducted one-on-one or in a small group (with the tutor and tutees). Often, the tutoring session is focused on a concept or idea that the student has brought up specifically during the session.

SI sessions are open to students in a designated class and are led by other students, SI Leaders, who have taken that course before. Unlike tutors, SI Leaders sit through the class a second or third time so they know exactly what a professor is covering in class lectures and assignments. This information from class is important to SI Leaders because they use it to develop the content or lesson plans for their SI sessions. During these sessions, SI Leaders will review concepts taught in the course.

SI Leaders and tutors generally work closely with instructors to ensure they are covering concepts and ideas in ways that are consistent with classroom instruction.

The Anatomy of a Syllabus

One of the best and most important resources for students is the course syllabus. The syllabus is essentially a contract between instructors and their students, detailing what students can expect during a semester and what will be expected of them. A syllabus for each class should be distributed or made available (e.g., online) to students at the start of the semester. Each syllabus should include important details and information about the instructor and the course. It should also provide students with a general description of what they can expect to learn in the course and what they are expected to do, relevant university policies (e.g., academic integrity), and specific policies for the class that have been established by the instructor. At the start of every semester, students should carefully examine the syllabus for each of their classes. In particular, they should be aware of the following:

- Instructor's name, contact information, and office hours

- Necessary prerequisites

- Required textbook(s)

- Class schedule (often a day-by-day list of readings and activities)

- Course requirements (e.g., papers, exams, assignments, etc.)

- Grading system

- Attendance policy

- Due dates for assignments and exams

While students should consult the syllabus throughout the semester to ensure they are keeping pace with reading assignments and when they have questions about the course or an assignment, the syllabus is particularly valuable at the start of the semester when students are developing a semester study plan. Armed with a knowledge of key due dates, as noted in the syllabus of each of their classes, students can devise a semester plan that allows for sufficient time throughout the semester to study for exams and complete their assignments—hopefully preventing the need to cram or pull all-nighters. The ability to understand a syllabus and use the information it provides greatly contributes to academic success and facilitates students' efforts to become self-directed learners.

The syllabus is my friend; make a plan to manage my time

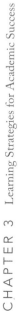

Reading and Understanding College Textbooks

Self-directed learners take responsibility for learning both in and outside of the classroom. In college and university classes, most of the learning outside of the classroom begins with reading and understanding material presented in textbooks. Because some instructors may not lecture directly from the textbook yet expect students to know the information in it, completing assigned readings can be crucial to a student's academic success.

To get the most out of reading college textbooks, students must become active readers skilled in identifying key information, noting material about which they have questions, and recognizing relationships between what they are reading and what they have already learned. Therefore, in addition to reading the material, active readers also interact with it by writing notes in their textbooks, highlighting passages in the readings (using different color pens or highlighters), or commenting in the margins

Actually read; study from books

of the textbook—whichever method best suits their personal learning preferences and styles. Additionally, consideration should be given to how the textbook will be used in future study sessions. Some students prefer to review information highlighted in a textbook or written in the margins of their books, while others choose to study from notes they have taken on the readings either in a notebook or on their computers.

To become efficient at reading actively, consider using the following strategy to become acquainted with the content of an assigned reading:

- First, become familiar with the material. Start by examining chapter headings, tables, graphs, and charts.

- Next, consider what the instructor has said in class. Knowing this can help determine what is most important in the reading.

- Finally, read the chapter summary and any questions at the end of the chapter. This material can provide an idea of important topics, concepts, or information included in the chapter.

While this strategy affords students with an overview of the assigned reading, it is still important to thoroughly and actively read the material in its entirety. While reading, mark the text or take notes in a manner that will be most useful in future study sessions.

When reading, students may at times struggle with identifying the key information that should be highlighted in their textbooks or included in their notes. To help isolate the most important material in a reading, consider using the following strategies:

- Locate the topic sentence in each paragraph. This sentence tells the reader what the paragraph is about and will likely contain one of the key concepts in the reading. A topic sentence should be supported by all of the other sentences in the paragraph.

- Review the examples provided to illustrate key concepts. Textbooks and instructors generally provide examples to illustrate key points. Sometimes the example itself is significant; other times it may be one of many that could illustrate the point being made. The ability to identify the examples that demonstrate a particular concept is useful—understanding a concept so well that you can cite an example of your own is even better.

- Make notes in the margins of the textbook. These notes may summarize a passage, indicate questions you have about the reading, or take the form of key words that can help you more easily locate specific material in a textbook during a study session.

- Locate key words (sometimes bolded) in a reading and ensure you understand not only the meaning of the words but how the concepts and ideas they represent fit in the context of the reading.

- Closely examine footnotes, tables, charts, diagrams, and other illustrations to identify any new information they provide and/or to determine how they add to the discussions presented in the reading. Quiz and exam questions may be based on information provided in these often-overlooked elements in a reading.

- Summarize or restate the reading in your own words. Practice this strategy by breaking readings into manageable and logical sections. After reading each section, write a short paragraph summarizing or paraphrasing the information in that section.

Students who would like to refine their reading skills may choose to employ a formal reading system, which offers a structured way to approach college reading assignments. One such system is SQ3R: Survey, Question, Read, Recite, Review. Examples of this system can be found on a variety of websites.

Take notes, highlight, and summarize what I read

Footnotes: An Underused Study Resource

To best understand the information presented in readings, students should read ALL the material—even the footnotes. Footnotes are exactly what their name suggests—notes at the foot (i.e., bottom) of a page. They are linked to their corresponding material in the main body of the text by a structured system of numbers that appear superscripted[1] or in brackets [2], or symbols—such as an asterisk (*) or dagger (†). When a numbering system is used, the numbers begin with one and continue consecutively throughout the entire chapter or document. Symbols may repeat in a document, but in such cases, it is understood that the symbol corresponds only to the footnote that appears on that same page.

Footnotes can serve a variety of purposes. They might (a) provide bibliographic information to cite the source of borrowed material, (b) direct readers to additional useful information pertaining to the main text or a topic contained therein, or (c) offer additional or detailed information to supplement or elaborate on what is stated in the main body of the text.

Footnotes that provide bibliographic information can guide students to the original source from which the footnoted material was derived. Often, this source provides information that affords readers a more in-depth understanding of a topic and may suggest new directions of exploration for those conducting research. Similarly, footnotes that direct readers to additional useful information also offer the opportunity to delve more deeply into the material discussed in the main body of text.

1 That is, raised, as in the example you just looked at to find this footnote.

Footnotes that offer supplemental information provide readers with explanations, definitions, and additional facts that elaborate on a topic. Such footnotes might provide synonyms or definitions of unusual words or jargon. They may offer additional explanation of a topic that, while not essential to the main body of text, may enhance students' comprehension or appreciation of a text. At other times, these footnotes may offer facts that help put the reading into context, as in the case of annotated editions of literary works, which often make extensive use of elaborate and lengthy footnotes.

Some texts may use endnotes rather than footnotes. Endnotes are essentially footnotes listed at the end of a chapter or document rather than at the bottom of the page on which each was referenced. The choice between using footnotes versus endnotes is generally determined by the documentation style required for the text (e.g., MLA, APA, CMS, etc.).

Listening and Note Taking Strategies

Much like the process of actively reading textbooks, listening requires students to be actively involved. *Hearing* is a passive activity, but *listening* requires involvement. That is, successful students do not simply hear what a professor says during a lecture; rather, they actively listen to the lecture. Active listening in the classroom requires that students focus their attention on the speaker and what is being said. To be an active listener in the classroom, students must:

- **Attend class regularly.** Sometimes students do not think attending class is critical because they can borrow notes from a classmate. What they fail to consider is that people receive and process information differently; therefore, notes that aid

Be an active listener.

one student's understanding of the course material may not be as beneficial to another student. Going to class and listening to a lecture is really the only way to ensure that you record the information presented in a way that you can effectively and efficiently process and understand.

- **Be attuned to the lecture.** Sit where you can clearly see and hear the speaker and any presentation material, and make eye contact with the professor as much as possible. Sitting near the front of the room (and, thus, closer to the speaker) may increase your ability to remain focused on the lecture.[2]

- **Engage your learning preferences and style.** Use whatever means of recording information best suits your learning preferences and style, and in a manner that will facilitate learning during future study sessions. For example, you may choose to take notes in a notebook, in the margins of your textbook, or on your computer. Alternatively, you may prefer to record the lecture and listen to it again when you review the material.

Taking Notes in Class

Taking notes *during* a lecture promotes listening skills because the note-taking process requires students to closely attend to what the speaker is saying. Consequently, taking notes during a lecture can foster retention of the material presented because students must actively process what they hear and transfer it to paper (or a computer). Therefore, even if you plan to make an audio recording of a lecture to listen to again during a study session, taking notes during a lecture can still be beneficial. Below are strategies to assist you in both preparing for a lecture and taking notes during a lecture.

---

2   In fact, students who sit in the front of the classroom are more likely to earn A's (Benedict & Hoag, 2004; Giles et al., 1982).

Before the Lecture

To take effective notes *during* a lecture, it is important to prepare *before* the lecture:

- Use a different notebook for each class or use colored dividers in a three-ring binder.

- Identify the topic for the day from the syllabus. Write the date and topic at the top of a new page in your notebook or binder.

- Create a note taking format for each class—what works well for one course might be inefficient for another. Some methods include Cornell and mind mapping (see Figures 3-1 and 3-2).

- Review the notes from the previous class before arriving at the lecture.

- Complete any assigned readings and review any supplemental materials the instructor may have made available to you (e.g., prepared notes, skeleton outlines, presentation materials, etc.) to provide background knowledge that will enhance your understanding of the lecture.

During the Lecture

The lecture style of instructors may vary greatly. Some will use PowerPoint presentations, others may reference the textbook when discussing key concepts, and still others may simply write a few ideas on the chalkboard or whiteboard. Consequently, self-directed learners must become proficient in adapting their note taking skills to an instructor's style of teaching. However, some general strategies can prove useful in a wide variety of situations:

- To identify the key points in a lecture that you will want to include in your notes, look for cues from your instructor that suggest specific information is important. Some of these cues might be when the instructor:

  - Writes words or phrases on the whiteboard or chalkboard

  - Provides an outline of the lecture or uses/provides a PowerPoint slide presentation

  - Alters the tone or volume of his or her voice to emphasize specific terms or examples

  - Restates the same material in a variety of ways

  - Asks if everyone understands what has just been presented

  - Reviews or summarizes certain material

  - States "This is important" or "You will need to know this"

- At times, instructors will use "signal words" that let you know something important is to follow. If a professor says, "There are three key stages in this process" or "Five variables were examined in this series of studies," be sure to record the correct number of stages or variables in your notes.

- Don't write on every line on the paper. Skip lines so that material can be added later and to make the notes easier to read.

- Write neatly the first time. Although recopying or retyping your notes can be an effective study tool, this should be an *option*, not a necessity.

- Develop a personal version of shorthand using abbreviations and symbols that will help record information quickly yet clearly convey the intended meaning during future study sessions.

- If you have already taken notes on the assigned readings or you have made marginal notes in the textbook, bring these to class so that important information from the lecture can be added to them. This will ensure you have all your notes on a given topic gathered in one place.

- Consider taking a voice recorder to class (with the instructor's permission) if you have trouble keeping up during class lectures.

After a lecture, it is a good idea to review class notes and identify topics that seem to recur in the instructor's lecture. The repetition of a key concept suggests its importance, so students would be wise to ensure they understand those concepts completely. Also, take note of examples demonstrating key concepts and ideas; these examples may appear in both the lecture and the textbook. Because examples often demonstrate the application of a concept, the ability to recognize a concept in use in an example that has been provided *and* to develop the ability to generate examples of your own will ensure you thoroughly understand the material.

Cornell Method of Note Taking

The Cornell method of note taking is a systematic way of organizing notes that facilitates future study sessions. All notes are written on 8 ½" × 11" pieces of loose-leaf paper in either a notebook or a three-ring binder. Each page is divided into three sections (see Figure 3-1): (A) a two-and-a-half-inch wide column at the left side of the paper that begins at the top of the page and ends two inches from the bottom of the page, (B) a six-inch column at the right side of the page that begins at the top of the page and ends two inches from the bottom of the page, and (C) a two-inch row at the bottom of the page that runs the entire width. Cornell paper, which includes the vertical line between Sections A and B, can often be found at campus bookstores and some office supply stores.

In the Cornell method of note taking, each area of the paper serves a distinct purpose. In Section B, notes written in paragraph form should include general ideas, not illustrative ones, and lines should be skipped only to indicate the end of ideas or thoughts. Section A is the recall or cue section. As soon as possible

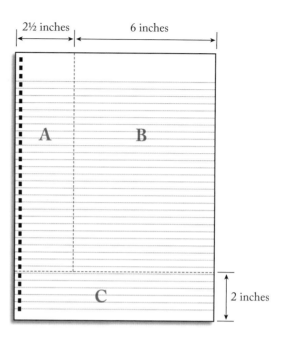

Figure 3-1. **Cornell Method**

after taking the notes in Section B, students should review them and write cues in Section A in the form of questions or key words to prompt recall of the information during study sessions. Any questions about the material should be included in Section A for future clarification. Finally, at the bottom of the page in Section C, students should write a summary of the information contained on that page. This will provide a means for quickly and efficiently locating information during study sessions.

The Cornell method of note taking offers a structured way to organize notes in a format that facilitates study and review. For example, when studying from notes taken using this method, students can cover the notes (Section B) and use the prompts in Section A to test themselves on the material. Additionally, reviewing the summaries in Section C will provide a quick overview of the key topics. Several websites offer guidelines for creating and printing Cornell paper.

There are different concrete methods for note-taking or study strategies

Mind Mapping and Concept Mapping Methods

The mind mapping and concept mapping methods of note taking can be used to visually organize information and ideas (Novak & Cañas, 2008). The key difference between these two forms of note taking is that concept maps are hierarchical—beginning with the key concept at the top of the map—whereas in mind mapping the most important concept is at the center of the illustration. Both forms of note taking use connecting lines to illustrate relationships between concepts and ideas. Students who prefer information presented in a structured, linear fashion may choose to create concept maps, while students who learn more easily from figures and drawings may prefer the less structured format of mind maps. To create a mind or concept map, begin with a central concept from which main points or supporting material branch (see Figure 3-2). Print the central concept—perhaps the topic of the lecture—at the top or in the middle of a blank sheet of paper. This concept can be written within a circle or box. It may also be useful to include an image of the central concept if there is one that is memorable. As main points related to that concept are presented, use lines to connect them to the central concept and use key words (not sentences) to record the main points. Any material or arguments presented to support these main points are then recorded on lines branching from them.

The following strategies can help to make mind mapping efficient and useful:

- Print using lower and uppercase letters so that the text is varied, clear, and readable.

- Add images and color where possible.

- Use consistent coding (e.g., circles around central concepts, boxes around main points).

- Print neatly and clearly.

- Focus on recording ideas; don't worry about organization.

While mind mapping and concept mapping are often quite effective for visual learners, all learners can benefit from the visual overview these strategies provide for specific concepts and topics presented in class readings and lectures. Finally, students who want to create a mind or concept map but prefer to do so using the latest technology can check out the various computer and smartphone applications that are available.

Study Strategies

Studying or independent learning occurs any time students perform academic-related activities outside the classroom, and self-directed learners know they must master study strategies that help them achieve academic success. Specifically, self-directed learners will develop a plan that includes protected study time, spend sufficient time studying to ensure they fully understand the subject matter, and maximize their learning through highly focused study sessions. Of course, each student's study plan and study sessions will vary depending on his or her academic strengths/weaknesses and learning preferences and styles, the course content, the instructor's teaching style, the way(s) in which the learning will be assessed, and the time needed to study. For example, an economics class may require that a student devote a study session to reading the textbook and reviewing lecture notes, whereas a study session for an English composition course may demand extensive time researching and writing. Consequently, when preparing to study, students need to consider several factors: how their study sessions will be structured; the time needed to study; how, when, and where to study; their personal study plan; and their instructor's teaching style.

Planning to Study

When students create a study plan for their academic success (see "Anatomy of a Syllabus" in this chapter), a primary consideration should be

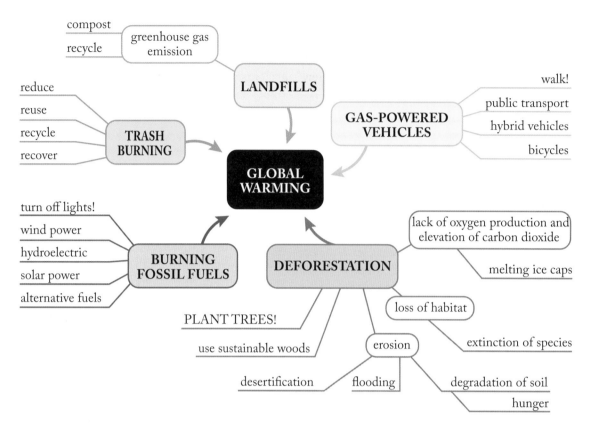

Figure 3-2. **Mind Mapping System of Note Taking**

allowing ample time for studying. In order to ensure they allow sufficient time, self-directed learners will develop a plan that takes into account the demands on their time that are fixed (e.g., dates/times of classes, work schedule, etc.) and those that are discretionary (e.g., time spent on Facebook or socializing); dates of exams and due dates of assignments; and any other major events that might impact the time they have available for studying. Once these factors have been allowed for in their schedules, students will be able to identify blocks of time that can be reserved for studying as well as the times of peak activity in the semester that might require extra study sessions to prepare for exams or complete projects. Based on these considerations, students should schedule study sessions for the semester, identifying the date, time, and length of each session.

Once students have scheduled their study sessions, they will need to consider the structure of those sessions. Specifically, students can spend a study session reviewing material alone or with a group of peers. However, students who decide to participate in study groups must choose their study partners with care. While it is important to get along and enjoy one another's company, the group must be able to remain focused on the reason they have met: to study. If study sessions digress into social hour, a study group will likely provide little academic benefit to its members.

Finally, the structure of a study session will be influenced by the goals of that session. Self-directed learners recognize that in order to maximize their efforts, each of their study sessions must be guided by specific goals, and those goals will often dictate the best format for the

Take time to Study

session. For example, a student might prefer to work alone if the goal of a study session is to complete a draft of an essay, whereas a group study session might be better suited to a review of class lecture notes. The more specific the goals for the study session, the more productive the session is likely to be.

Determining How Long to Study

Educators generally agree that students should study at least two hours independently for every hour they spend in the classroom (Piscitelli, 2004). To determine how much time should be spent studying, consider that a typical 3-credit hour class meets for one hour and fifteen minutes twice a week, for a weekly total of two and half hours of class time. Multiply those two and half hours of class time by two (the recommended hours of study time) for a total of five hours of studying per class each week. Therefore, a student who is taking four classes should be studying 20 hours per week. When added to the amount of time spent in class, the total hours devoted to academics should be 45–50 hours a week.

	Calculation of Study Time
2.5	hours in class weekly (for a typical 3-credit hour course)
× 2	recommended hours of study time for each hour spent in class
5.0	weekly hours of study time per course
× 4	number of classes
20	total recommended hours of study time per week

Twenty hours of independent studying per week may be a greater investment of time than most students anticipate and may prove impossible for some. In reality, the actual number of hours students spend studying outside of class each week will likely vary, depending on each student's learning preferences and styles as well as the courses he or she is taking. Students would be wise to allot more of their available study time to those courses that they anticipate will be difficult or challenging and adjust that time as needed during the semester.

Deciding How, Where, and What to Study

To maximize the time spent studying, it is essential to have a strategy for how you will study—and this may vary widely depending on factors such as the course, the instructor's teaching style, and the goals of that particular study session. However, individual considerations, such as learning preferences and styles, are important as well. Furthermore, students often have an idea of what has worked for them in the past (e.g., reviewing notes, using flashcards, quizzing themselves, etc.). In determining how to conduct a study session, students should examine the material they will be studying, consider their learning preferences and styles, and reflect on the study strategies that have worked well for them in the past. In particular, those study strategies that appear at the intersection of a student's learning preferences/styles and his or her previously successful study techniques are strategies that should be applied in future study sessions.

Learning conditions are another factor students should consider when making a decision about how to approach studying or learning new information. These conditions include the physical environment (i.e., quiet vs. noisy) but more importantly refer to the application or implementation of a particular learning technique (Dunlosky, Rawson, Marsh, Nathan, & Willingham, 2013). Specifically, learning conditions should model the ways in which a student's learning will be assessed. For example, in classes where students are asked to demonstrate a broad understanding and application of a concept on their exams, elaborative interrogation during study sessions could be an effective learning technique. Elaborative interrogation involves asking and answering the simple question "Why?" When students use this technique, they are integrating the new information into their existing knowledge about a concept or topic (Dunlosky, Rawson, Marsh, Nathan, & Willingham, 2013), thereby engaging their long term memory and allowing for a deeper level of learning.

Studying for Deeper Comprehension and Understanding

Often, intensive study sessions or brief periods of time when a student focuses on learning a single concept or idea can facilitate initial or shallow learning. However, such study sessions may not promote the deeper comprehension and understanding necessary for students to build associations between various concepts and ideas, and to firmly fix the newly acquired knowledge as part of their cognitive abilities. To achieve this level of comprehension and understanding, students need to engage in effective learning techniques that increase memory, comprehension, or both aspects of cognitive development. These techniques should also be tailored to the objective of the study session and the ways in which learning will be evaluated. While learning techniques can and should vary, a recent study by Dunlosky et al. (2013) found that the following five strategies had a positive effect on students' learning: elaborative interrogation, self-explanation, practice testing, distributed practice, and interleaved practice.

Elaborative interrogation, described earlier in this chapter, involves integrating new information into an existing base of knowledge about a particular concept or idea. Students can use consistent prompts, such as "Why does X exist?" or "Why is Z true (or untrue)?" to begin the process of relating new information to what they already know. Similarly, **self-explanation** also involves integrating new information but without the use of consistent prompts. With this technique, a student may be asked to solve a problem for "X." Following his or her attempt

at solving the problem, the student would be asked to explain the steps taken to solve the problem and then relate those to his or her prior knowledge. **Practice testing** is another strategy that may involve explaining a particular answer or approach to solving a problem. As the name implies, students who use this technique practice problems, develop and answer questions, or quiz themselves on information that may be included on a test or exam. In **distributed practice**, students attempt to learn new information (using any of the study techniques or a combination of approaches) over a prolonged period of time. Unlike the previously described techniques, distributed practice does not describe a specific technique or approach to learning; rather, it refers to a "schedule of learning episodes" (Dunlosky et al., 2013, p. 36). In other words, this strategy encourages students to learn or study something new in study sessions that are spread out over a period of time rather than scheduled back-to-back. The fifth strategy cited by Dunlosky et al. is **interleaved practice,** which involves varying the type of material a student studies in a single session. Doing so will allow the brain to more fully absorb the information and build associations, which will eventually become a new body of knowledge (Ambrose, Bridges, Lovett, DiPietro, & Norman, 2010). In a study conducted by Kornell, Eich, Castel, & Bjork (2010), college-aged students and retired adults who repeatedly viewed paintings by different artists were able to determine patterns in the painting styles. Conversely, participants in the study who viewed one artist repeatedly were less likely to observe the differences in styles.

Although the research demonstrates the potential learning that can occur when students study two or more subjects in a single session, interleaving is often considered a more complex learning technique. However, by interleaving different subjects or ideas, students begin to make personal connections or applications to the information they are learning, which reinforces the new knowledge. For example, concepts like Bloom's Taxonomy (for this class), the

writing process (for English composition), and the scientific method (for biology) are different yet share skills like questioning, analyzing, and creating. If these processes were studied together, students may begin to see the similarities between these processes and, in turn, experience a deeper and more profound level of learning. Also, practicing the skills in each of these processes helps to reinforce new knowledge and helps students see the connections between ideas that may span diverse disciplines.

The following steps can help you begin to interleave the concepts presented in several of your courses during a single study session:

- Look for classes/subject matter that might share similar content (i.e., history and geography).

- Identify classes that require similar skills (i.e., math and chemistry).

- Find subject matter or theories that involve similar processes (like the example described above).

Similar to varying information studied in a single study session, varying study location can also enhance learning. Students have traditionally been advised to designate a single location specifically for studying and to study in that location consistently, but research demonstrates

just the opposite.[3] In fact, simply alternating the room in which they study can improve students' rate of retention. It is believed that when the study location is varied, information is enriched, thereby helping students to better retain what they have learned (Carey, 2010).

Developing a Study Plan

Chapter 2 discussed several theories related to the process of learning and presented the idea that there are personal and environmental characteristics that impact learning. To put those learning theories into practice, it is important to consider personal learning preferences and styles. Results from inventories such as the MBTI can indicate, for example, whether a student is more likely to study successfully alone or in a study group. When students study alone, they can focus on the material with which they are unfamiliar, and they can study at their own pace, at whatever time they choose and wherever they choose. On the other hand, study groups bring together several different perspectives on the material and different levels of comprehension. Therefore, students in study groups can help each other by teaching one another what they have learned well and learning from others the material about which they are unclear.

Once you have determined whether studying alone or in a group is more beneficial to you, use what you have learned about Bloom's Taxonomy to identify the levels of thinking needed to complete your homework and assignments when you are establishing goals for individual study sessions. For example, a multiple choice exam may suggest the need for memorization since you will need to recognize the correct answer when taking the test (level 1). However, to prepare for a debate on whether KSU should have a football team, you must be able to understand

---

3   A classic 1978 experiment of college students revealed that those who studied a list of 40 vocabulary words in two different rooms did far better on a test than students who studied the words twice in the same room. Later studies have supported this finding (Carey, 2010).

the information you have found through your research (level 2), demonstrate how that information applies to your particular position and argument (level 3), and break down your opponent's argument in order to counter the discrete elements he or she is using to make the opposite case (level 4). Be aware that one goal of college is to foster your ability to operate at the highest levels of Bloom's Taxonomy. Therefore, if an assignment seems to demand only remembering and understanding (levels 1 and 2), check to ensure you did not misunderstand the assignment.

Table 3-1 illustrates how the various levels might apply to how you approach studying. The key words offer clues as to the instructor's expectations (e.g., if you are asked to *critique* a news article, know that you must operate at level 5, evaluating).

To maintain good study habits, you must make studying a routine.

One Final Consideration: Teaching Styles

The methods instructors use in the classroom and to assess student learning can also affect how students study for a course. Therefore, students need to become aware of the different teaching styles and the implications of each. For example, instructors teaching large, general education courses may choose to lecture, while professors teaching smaller classes may incorporate more class discussion and in-class activities. Additionally, some instructors will assign readings and discuss those readings in class, whereas other instructors will introduce a concept in class and then assign readings that supplement that information. What the instructor does (or does not do) will offer clues as to what students should study (see Table 3-2).

Clearly, the many factors to consider when planning a study session—study material, goals of the session, learning preferences and styles, Bloom's Taxonomy—demonstrate that there is no single answer to the question of *how* to study. Rather, students must plan a study session tailored to the goals of the session and to their specific learning preferences and styles.

Test Strategies

Performing well on exams is the result of hard work and successful study habits in the form of regular attendance in class, effective listening skills, proficient note taking abilities, and regular study sessions. However, this careful and deliberate preparation can be augmented by test strategies that ensure that preparation is put to efficient and effective use on test day.

Preparation

Students should begin preparing for exams on the very first day of class by examining the syllabus they received in each of their classes to identify exam dates. These dates should be considered when developing a study plan. Specifically, to prepare for exams, students should:

- Mark all exam dates on their calendar or student planner.

- Schedule study sessions prior to those exam dates to allow ample time to review before each exam.

- As much as possible, coordinate other assignments and personal activities to avoid being overwhelmed with other projects or obligations immediately prior to exam time.

- Review class notes frequently—daily, if possible.

Table 3-1. Practical Applications of Bloom's Taxonomy

LEVEL	SKILL	ACTIVITY
1. REMEMBERING	Recognize and recall what you have learned without necessarily understanding it. **Key Words:** recall, list, state, define, recognize, retrieve, identify	• Define vocabulary words. • Recall important historical dates. • Recognize appropriate equations.
2. UNDERSTANDING	Explain and demonstrate an understanding of the information you have acquired. **Key Words:** summarize, restate, infer, paraphrase, classify, explain, compare, exemplify	• Summarize readings from your textbook. • Restate the professor's lecture in your own words. • Explain the relationship between warring nations.
3. APPLYING	Apply the concepts, ideas, and skills that you have learned in a new but similar situation. **Key Words:** practice, apply, use, carry out	• Use mathematical skills and principles to solve word problems. • Use correct grammar skills in writing a paper.
4. ANALYZING	Use critical thinking skills to examine the discrete components of a concept or item to gain in-depth understanding of it. **Key Words:** differentiate, deconstruct, analyze, discriminate, categorize, distinguish	• Make a flowchart to show the critical stages in a process. • Construct a graph to illustrate the information you have gathered from a student survey.
5. EVALUATING	Check or critique knowledge, products, or processes. **Key Words:** check, evaluate, critique, test, monitor, detect, judge, assess, appraise, ascertain	• Write an argumentation paper in which you take a position on an issue and defend it. • Participate in a debate on a controversial topic. • Propose a solution to a problem on campus.
6. CREATING	Produce a process, idea, product, alternative, or hypothesis. **Key Words:** create, generate, develop, devise, come up with, design, construct, produce, compose	• Produce a painting or sculpture. • Devise a marketing strategy to increase student participation in campus activities. • Develop an in-class presentation.

Table 3-2. Teaching Styles Decoded

IF YOUR PROFESSOR...	YOU SHOULD...
Assigns readings from the text, then discusses them in class	Complete the reading before class, then note the items from the text that are emphasized in the professor's lecture.
Assigns readings from the text, then lectures from notes that complement rather than reiterate what is in the textbook	Read the textbook and take careful notes in class. Your professor will likely assume you have read the text and will offer additional information in class. You can expect to find questions from both the text and the lectures on your exams.
Offers numerous examples to illustrate a concept	Note some of these examples, then try to develop some of your own. The professor will likely expect you to illustrate or recognize the concepts you are learning through examples on your exams.
Offers outlines or copies of presentation materials	The materials will give you an idea of some of the key concepts your professor will expect you to know. Obtain these before their associated lecture or class discussion, if possible, and add notes from the text and class lectures to these outlines or bullet points.
Gives copious homework that is never graded	Do it all! This will indicate to you what you have mastered and what you still need to work on. Armed with this information, you can ask appropriate questions in class and/or seek one-on-one assistance from the professor or a tutor.

- Participate in group study sessions, attend in-class reviews for exams, and take advantage of any other available resources.

- If possible, find out the format of the exam and how it will be administered (e.g., multiple choice vs. essay, Scantron vs. on a computer, etc.).

Test-Day Strategies

The style or format of an exam will differ based on the instructor's preference, the content of the course, and the size of the class, to name a few. For example, students in large lecture classes will likely be given multiple-choice exams rather than essay exams. The final exam in a composition course may be an impromptu essay. While the format and style of the exams students face will differ—and therefore require a different approach to both studying for and taking each exam—several test-day strategies are applicable in most instances:

- Arrive early.

- Listen carefully to the instructions given by the professor.

- Read the instructions printed on the exam thoroughly and completely; ask for clarification if any part of these is confusing or ambiguous.

- Review the entire exam and develop a plan for completing it. This plan should consider:

  - The time available to complete the exam

  - Which questions can be answered quickly and correctly

  - The point value for each question/section

  - Your individual test-taking strengths and weaknesses

Taking the Exam

While each student's test-taking plan should be tailored to his/her strengths and weakness, the following are some suggestions that may be useful in most circumstances:

- Consider the point value attached to each section of the exam and decide how much time you will spend on each of those sections.

- Answer the questions that seem easy to you or that you are sure you can answer correctly. This will build your confidence and may offer clues to the answers for the more challenging questions.

- If you find you are having trouble with a particular question, move on and come back to that question later.

- Do not spend an inordinate amount of time on a problem or question that is worth only a few points.

- Trust yourself. Often, students second guess themselves on tests and exams. As tempting as it can be to go back and change an answer, generally, your instinctive response (i.e., your first response) is correct.

- Learn from the test. As you progress through the exam, be alert for key words or phrases that may provide clues to the questions with which you are struggling.

- Carefully review the test and your answers. Before submitting a test, re-read the directions, questions, and your answers to make certain you have adequately and appropriately responded to the test questions.

Post-Test Strategies

In order to learn as much as possible from the test and the test experience, consider implementing the following post-test strategies:

- Attend class the day the exam is returned and discussed.

- Review any comments the instructor has made on your exam.

- Make note of the style of the exam so you can better prepare for future tests.

Test Anxiety

Test anxiety can interfere with your ability to focus during study sessions and on exams. If you suffer from test anxiety, consider some of the following strategies to ameliorate your stress:

- Ensure you know the material.
- Arrive early.
- Avoid students who seem to be panicking.
- Begin with the questions you can answer easily.
- Visualize yourself doing well on the exam.
- Practice positive self-talk.

If you think you can or you think you can't, you're right.[4]

4 This statement was paraphrased from a quotation credited to Henry Ford.

Summary

This chapter presents numerous strategies that can aid students in achieving academic success, but attempting to incorporate them all may seem like a rather daunting task. Therefore, rather than trying to adopt them all at once, try one technique at a time and evaluate its benefits to you. Does reading the footnotes aid in your understanding of a text? If so, continue doing that until you have integrated it into your personal approach to studying. Does sitting in the front of the classroom help you to better focus on the lecture? Make sure you arrive early to each class so that you can claim a seat front and center. Repeatedly engaging in those learning strategies that are most effective for you will firmly establish them as a regular part of your study habits and lead to success throughout your academic career.

References

Ambrose, S. A., Bridges, M. W., Lovett, M. C., DiPietro, M., & Norman, M. K. (2010). *How learning works: 7 research principles for smart teaching.* San Francisco: Jossey-Bass.

Benedict, M. E., & Hoag, J. (2004, Summer). Seating location in large lectures: Are seating preferences or location related to course performance? *The Journal of Economic Education, 35*(3), 215–231.

Carey, B. (2010, September 6). Forget what you know about good study habits. *New York Times.* Retrieved from http://www.nytimes.com/2010/09/07/health/views/07mind.html?pagewanted=1

Chew, S. (2011). *How to get the most out of studying: Part 1 of 5, beliefs that make you fail…or succeed.* Retrieved from http://www.youtube.com/watch?v=RH95h36NChI

Dunlosky, J., Rawson, K. A., Marsh, E. J., Nathan, M. J., & Willingham, D. T. (2013). Improving students' learning with effective learning techniques: Promising directions from cognitive and educational psychology. *Psychological Science in the Public Interest, 14*(1), 4-58.

Giles, R. M., Johnson, M. R., Knight, K. E., Zammett, S., & Weinman, J. (1982). Recall of lecture information: A question of what, when and where. *Medical Education, 16,* 264–268.

Kornell, N., Eich, T. S., Castel, A. D., & Bjork, R. A. (2010). Spacing as the friend of both memory and induction in young and older adults. *Psychology and Aging, 25*(2), 498–503.

Novak, J. D. & Cañas, A. J. (2008). *The theory underlying concept maps and how to construct and use them.* (Technical Report IHMC CmapTools 2006-01 Rev 01-2008). Pensacola, FL: Institute for Human and Machine Cognition. Retrieved from http://cmap.ihmc.us/Publications/ResearchPapers/TheoryUnderlyingConceptMaps.pdf

Piscitelli, S. (2004). *Study skills: Do I really need this stuff?* Saddle River, NJ: Pearson.

Critical Thinking Questions

1. Why is an understanding of your learning preferences and styles important in developing your learning strategies and designing study sessions?

2. What function does a syllabus serve? Why is it important? How can you best use it?

3. How much time should you devote to your studies?

4. How can you become a more active listener?

5. What purpose do footnotes serve?

6. Is it better to take notes on a reading or use a highlighter to mark important passages in the material? Why?

7. What reading strategies can you use to facilitate your understanding of the assigned readings?

CHAPTER 4

Undergraduate Research and Creative Activity:
Beginning to Think Like a Scholar

DAVID R. THOMPSON, Ph.D.

Chapter Goals

- Introduce students to the value of undergraduate research

- Introduce students to common outcomes of undergraduate research

- Help students understand the research process

- Encourage students to apply a model of systematic inquiry

Chapter Overview

This chapter introduces students to undergraduate research and its impact on academic success, development of life skills, and connecting with the campus through collaborative research with faculty and other students. Especially appropriate for first-year students, an easy-to-follow model of systematic inquiry is presented as a series of "decision points" that mark phases of the research process.

Undergraduate Research: A Trend in Teaching and Learning

Undergraduate research is defined by the Council on Undergraduate Research as "an inquiry or investigation conducted by an undergraduate that makes an original intellectual or creative contribution to the discipline." Four basic characteristics on undergraduate research have been identified (Hakim, 1998): "mentorship, originality, acceptability, and dissemination" (as cited in Description of undergraduate research, 2007, p. 6–7):

Many things were discovered on accident

Mentorship involves substantial interaction with faculty and students. Hakim indicated that the focus of the mentor relationship is on student outcomes as opposed to the outcomes of research and teaching. Originality assumes that the student takes an active part in the creation of new knowledge through active participation in the research project.... The student learns the acceptable methods of inquiry related to his or her field of study. A research project should conclude with the production, dissemination, and critique of a final project. This product could be in the form of a research paper presented at a conference or symposium, a poster session at a conference, or a manuscript submitted for publication in an academic journal.

In the late 1800s, German universities challenged the status quo that called for conveying "information in as direct a manner as possible"—rote memorization without question, often in Latin (Description of undergraduate research, 2007, p. 13). "German higher education embraced the concept of discovery" and welcomed students in laboratories and intellectual entanglements. "Teaching through research activity meant that students not only learned faster but also learned the process of discovery through their involvement" (p. 14).

As the United States embraced higher education for the masses in the twentieth century, "the rapid increase in the numbers of students enrolled in undergraduate education meant the likelihood of students' engaging in individual conversations with faculty or even in small groups for discussion would become difficult, if not impossible." As a result, some students feel disengaged from the process of learning. Especially in the first year or two of college, these students may "find higher education a meaningless and vacant experience" (Description of undergraduate research, 2007, p. 15). "Countering

Research is not reserved for graduate students

the impersonalization of mass higher education are the smaller classes and opportunities that can be found, even at large research universities, in undergraduate research experiences" (p. 15).

Helm, Bailey, McBride, and LaBianca (2011) say, "Undergraduate research is part of a major active learning reform movement in American undergraduate education (DeHaan, 2005; Ishyama, 2002; Kinkead, 2003). Instead of students passively obtaining knowledge about their discipline, research stimulates active participation of students (Ishyama, 2002; Healey & Jenkins, 2006). This activity not only increases the student's analytical abilities, but also enhances oral and written communication skills (Ishyama, 2002, Kardash, 2000). Therefore, a growing number of academics 'see undergraduate research as the pedagogy for the twenty-first century' (Dotterer, 2002, p. 81)" (p. 93).

Learning Outcomes for Undergraduate Research and Creative Activity

Seven common categories of "the intended outcomes for undergraduate student engagement in research and creative activities" have been identified (Description of undergraduate research, 2007, p. 8):

1. Enhance undergraduate education through hands-on learning activities that cultivate students' analytical, logical, and creative thinking, problem solving, curiosity, written and oral skills, and self-reliance;

2. Provide concrete examples of how theories and principles are applied to find solutions to problems;

3. Introduce students to the methods of inquiry in their disciplines and foster appreciation of the research process;

4. Stimulate students' interest in pursuing academic or research careers;

5. Help socialize students to their respective professions and academic fields;

6. Prepare students for advanced graduate or professional education;

7. Sufficiently train students to compete in an increasingly global market as future leaders.

First-year students are asked to engage in experiences that further develop their "analytical, logical, and creative thinking, problem solving, curiosity, written and oral skills, and self-reliance" (Description of undergraduate research, 2007)—including perhaps involvement in undergraduate research. Such involvement may be structured progressively, especially in science, technology, engineering, and mathematics (STEM). For example, early in the undergraduate experience, instructors may teach students the research process, basic research skills, and simple, hands-on research techniques. After a year or two, students may be given low-skill roles as technicians in their professors' research projects. Finally, a student may contribute as a co-researcher or independent researcher at a high level of involvement (p. 9).

First-year students need to understand that an isolated research assignment may not be designed to integrate students' findings into the existing body of knowledge. "Graff (2006)… suggested that a key characteristic distinguishing undergraduate research from other intellectual activities is the notion of 'entering the current conversation of a particular field in a significant way.'… A key component of undergraduate research should include the process of framing the results of a study in response to a current discussion in the field as opposed to simply presenting findings of a study in a vacuum outside this context. A more meaningful process for students is to discuss their findings in light of what others have written on the topic" (as cited in Description of undergraduate research, 2007, p. 7). This is one reason development of information-gathering skill is important for first-year students. By evaluating ideas against existing work, students learn the context that surrounds their questions.

Helm, Bailey, McBride, and LaBianca (2011) say, "Undergraduate research yields benefits for student motivation and self-efficacy (Kardash, 2000), which are necessary precursors to persistence in learning (Bandura, 1977; Zimmerman, Bandura, & Martinez-Pons, 1992; Zimmerman, 2000)" (p. 94). This may be of particular importance for first-year students who may be at risk of failing or withdrawing from college because of a low level of confidence in successful completion of college work. In the context of Helm et al.'s article, "persistence of learning" means working through the research process to completion. In the language of the First-Year Experience, persistence refers to the will and ability to continue to make progress toward graduation.

Related to the idea of persistence in college is retention. As universities often use the term, retention refers to a student remaining in college during consecutive semesters. First-Year Experience programs are especially interested in retention of students from the first to second year of college. Jones, Barlow, and Villarejo (2010, p. 87) say,

"Theoretically, involvement in academic or social programs and increased faculty and peer contact, regardless of major, have been identified as important for institutional integration and for retaining students in college" (Tinto, 1993). Tinto suggests that social and academic integration strongly impact institutional commitment and the subsequent decision to persist or withdraw from the institution. Tinto defines integration as a process in which the "individual establishes membership in the institution through involvement in its academic or social life" (p. 87).

Given this meaning of "integration," some studies document benefits of undergraduate research for minority students. For example, Prince, Felder, and Brent (2007) say, "Some studies show that research involvement improves student retention (notably that of African-Americans) in academic programs and influences students to pursue graduate study" (p. 290). And Jones, Barlow, and Villarejo (2010) say, "We find that introducing students to undergraduate research early on and for an extended period of time are beneficial for the retention and performance of all students, but that underrepresented minorities may have the most to gain from such strategies" (p. 110).

Other reported benefits of undergraduate research experiences have little to do with academic acuity, even in disciplines known for their scholarly rigor. Howitt, Wilson, Wilson, and Roberts (2010) say, "Surprisingly, given the research-intensive nature of this [science] degree, the learning gains students report relate to both an appreciation of what research is like and life skills, such as time management, rather than scientific skills" (p. 405).

A study by Craney et al. (2011) supports the idea that benefits of undergraduate research "reflect personal and professional growth." The study "confirmed that undergraduate research is a 'powerful affective, behavioral, and personal-discovery experience' (Seymour et al., 2004, p. 531) that benefits all students regardless of their discipline or career directions" (p. 110). Yet other studies, such as that reported by Caccavo

(2009), find that "today's students are increasingly focused on learning practical information that will help them choose a career path and succeed professionally. Providing freshmen with opportunities to do inquiry-based science facilitates this process" (p. 12).

Ultimately, a student's goal is graduation. Jones et al. (2010, p. 110) say, "We found that participating in as little as one to three terms of research and initiating that research during the first two years has strong positive associations with graduation outcomes, which provides some indication that undergraduate research may be beneficial even among those who are not highly committed to the major to begin with" (p. 108). Snow, DeCosmo, and Shokair (2010) say, "Many studies have shown that students who participate in research are more satisfied with their education and more likely to complete their degrees than those who lack this experience (Nagda et al. 1998; Hathaway, Nagda, & Gregerman 2002; Russell, Hancock, & McCullough 2007; Kuh 2008). Furthermore, whether they are doing research themselves or learning about it from

peers, students benefit from understanding the essential links between research and learning" (p. 19). Falconer and Holcomb (2008) say, "Kuh (2003) has firmly established the notion that the more effort students devote to educationally purposeful activities, the more they learn. Independent (out of class) scholarly activity is one way this happens, by enabling students to engage in inquiry beyond the classroom setting. Haworth and Conrad (1997) complement the idea of engagement with the term 'ownership,' which reflects the shift in responsibility for learning from the professor to the student. Students who are engaged and feel ownership enter situations as active participants seeking knowledge, rather than passive consumers. This theory suggests that students who engage in independent research not only have an opportunity to integrate and apply knowledge, but gain more from subsequent coursework" (para. 7). This existing research presents evidence that students who actively engage in undergraduate research, compared to those who do not participate in undergraduate research, are more likely to be retained from year to year, to persist along a degree path, and to graduate.

Research Process

Lee, Matthews, Cucina, and Tritschler (2011) have defined a 12-stage approach for teaching an undergraduate research course during a 14-week semester. Their 12 stages are: "(1) selecting a topic, (2) identifying and reading published research, (3) writing the Introduction section, (4) designing the methods, (5) developing the Methods section, (6) applying for Institutional Review Board (IRB) approval, (7) scheduling appointments with participants, (8) collecting data, (9) analyzing the data, (10) writing the Results section, (11) writing the Discussion section, and (12) presenting the final product" (p. 69).

This 12-stage approach is designed for upper-level undergraduates—juniors and seniors—who enter the course with knowledge of discipline-specific research methodologies,

ethical treatment of human subjects (thus the need for IRB approval), data collection procedures, and statistical analysis. There may be some first-year students who are ready for such a 12-step research process, in particular, those first-year students who understand the following and are able to paraphrase it for use in a daily local newspaper:

> Short oligonucleotides including siRNA and micro-RNA used to degrade mRNA transcripts, and therefore suppress protein translation, and antisense oligonucleotides to manipulate splicing are of high potential for therapeutic applications. Using this methodology we were able to show that the harmful 17.5-kDa GH- variant causing the autosomal dominant GH-deficiency (IGHDII) can be blocked and, therefore, the disorder rescued. (Lochmatter & Mullis, 2011, p. 68)

To the author of this chapter, who was trained in social science—rather than natural science or "the hard sciences" (in this case, "hard" probably means both observable and difficult), this summary means little. However, once the title of the article and name of the publication are known, it is possible to use Sherlock Holmes-like detection skills to get a sense of the topic. The title is "RNA interference in mammalian cell systems," and the name of the publication is *Hormone Research in Pediatrics*. Therefore, this article probably has something to do with discovering a way to improve treatment of childhood hormone disorders. But only a trained scientist can say why it might be a good idea to "rescue" a disorder.

This may be an example of a professor's research project that used graduate and undergraduate research assistants for identifying published research (known as a literature review), collecting data, analyzing the data, writing a portion of the paper that reports this study, and/or presenting this research at an academic conference.

Perhaps still out of reach for many first-year students is this study by Emily Vraga, "Dealing with Dissonance: Responding to an Incongruent Test Result in a New Media Environment," published in 2011 by *Cyberpsychology, Behavior, and Social Networking*:

> The data were collected using two experiments embedded in Web-based surveys of undergraduates at a large Midwestern university in the United States. The respondents were contacted via e-mail and were offered extra credit for their participation. Study 1 took place for 2 weeks in May 2008 and had 248 respondents; Study 2 occurred during 2 weeks in October 2008 and included 487 respondents.
>
> Both experiments used a 2 × 2 design manipulating (a) whether individuals were exposed to a confirmation or refutation of their party affiliation, followed by (b) either a congruent or incongruent political message. On the basis of their pretest political affiliation, subjects were randomized into two groups. All subjects took a simulated implicit attitude test, asking them to match the Democratic and Republican parties in conjunction with "good" or "bad" words.
>
> This test purportedly measured unconscious preferences by testing reaction time when matching the valenced words with the groups. After the simulated test, respondents received one of two statements, which claimed they had a "moderate preference" for either the Democratic or Republican party. This response was randomized: half of the respondents viewed a result that was congruent with their party affiliation and the other half viewed an incongruent result (48.6% exposed to an incongruent result). After viewing the test result, subjects saw a second type of political message—bolstering political

> advertisements in the spring and news coverage of negative advertising in the fall—which was either congruent or incongruent with their party affiliation (52.5% exposed to an incongruent political message). Because congruence depends on party affiliation, Independents are excluded from all analyses, leaving 735 respondents. (p. 690)

With the help of a trained scholar, perhaps a faculty mentor, an untrained "young scholar" (regardless of age) may begin to identify elements of Vraga's research by talking through some of the 12 phases of the research process spelled out by Lee, Matthews, Cucina, and Tritschler (2011). The passage above is a summary of Vraga's methodology, step #5: Designing the methods. This study appears to be an experiment because Vraga uses a 2 × 2 design that involves manipulation of variables—spelled out above as "(a)" and "(b)." Because data are collected from "undergraduates at a large Midwestern university," the researcher would be required to comply with U.S. federal standards for the ethical treatment of human subjects. Thus, the researcher would have needed to obtain approval from her university's Institutional Review Board (IRB) before collecting data. It looks like research subjects are randomly assigned to a treatment condition—meaning different sets of respondents see different stimulus material. The research is administered through an online survey, which suggests data are collected electronically in digital form. The researcher probably designed data collection to be compiled in a format that may be readily run through a data analysis program. That cuts weeks off the research process—especially since useable data are collected from 735 individuals. Also, the researcher tells the reader data collection is done shortly before the 2008 presidential election.

This kind of "dissection" takes practice. It becomes easier once a student acquires some basic knowledge of research methods. Compared to the first example, Vraga's write-up looks more like "plain English." Yet there is a "researcher's code" to decipher.

The next example of a research summary should be even more comprehensible to the untrained researcher. Bembenutty's 2011 study titled "Meaningful and maladaptive homework practices: The role of self-efficacy and self-regulation" has been published in the *Journal of Advanced Academics*:

> The main objective of this article was to examine the role of self-regulation of learning on assigned homework. The findings reveal positive relationships between homework activities and self-efficacy, responsibility for learning, and delay of gratification. This review shows a positive relationship between homework and a range of self-regulation skills that facilitates academic achievement and performance. This review also found support for the notion that homework assignments can enhance the development of self-regulation processes and self-efficacy beliefs, as well as goal setting, time management, managing the environment, and maintaining attention. (p. 469)

In this description of findings of a "review"—probably a synthesis of existing, published articles about students' approach to homework, an untrained researcher needs to know that, in short, a "positive relationship" means "the more this, the more that." So, the more a student engages in doing homework, the more confidence the student has in completing homework effectively, the more the student plays an active role in learning, and the more the student displays patience in seeing a benefit from doing homework.

Because Bembenutty's article is a review, not much "technical" information is presented. A newbie undergraduate researcher may find Bembenutty's article a reasonable entry point for practicing the reading of scholarly writing.

Academic writing varies by academic discipline and by the purpose and tone of the publication in which it appears.

To begin to think like a researcher, read research articles. For first-year students, the author of this chapter recommends this approach to reading a scholarly article:

- Quickly read the abstract (a brief summary) to get an idea of the topic and findings of the study.

- Read the first few paragraphs. Look for phrases like: "The purpose of this study is…" and "For the purpose of this article, [this key term] is defined as…" Also look for phrases like: "This study extends the work of [this scholar] by…" That is the clue that this article contributes to the body of knowledge by advancing existing research just one step. As stated early in this chapter, this is what Hakim (1998) refers to as "originality," "the creation of new knowledge" (as cited in Description of undergraduate research, 2007, p. 6–7).

- Browse the section that describes how the study was designed just to get a sense of the researcher's approach to this project.

- Read the last few paragraphs. This may be a section labeled "Discussion" or "Conclusion." Here the reader usually finds a wrap-up of the purpose of the study, the findings, and the importance or possible impact of this research.

Novice researchers should feel free to avoid "discipline-speak," the jargon of scholars in a specific academic field. Novice researchers also should feel comfortable skipping over large sections of text while "reading" research articles. Just get a sense of the study and its results. It is okay to stop at this point. Seeing the big picture may be enough for a novice researcher. Details come later when more has been learned about research methods.

An important skill for a first-year student beginning to think as a researcher is inquiry. Research is a process of discovery based on time-tested methods for seeking answers. Inquire. Ask questions. Then question the answers. Research is a process of systematic inquiry.

For example, in this brief item titled "Texting tops smelling" from *AARP The Magazine*, Leslie Quander Wooldridge (2011–2012) says:

> Given a choice, about half of the world's young people ages 16 through 22 say they would give up their sense of smell if they could keep a tech item (often a laptop or cell phone), per a new poll. (p. 11)

What questions come to mind?

Researchers, whether novice or expert, may want to know the answers to questions like these:

- What poll?

- Who did the research? Were they trained researchers? What was their motivation to conduct this research?

- Was this research funded? If so, by whom or by what organization or company?

- What was the research question—the basis for the study? Was it, "How obsessive-compulsive are young people about their gadgets?" Or was it, "To what extent do young people value their sense of smell?"

- How many young people are there in the whole world between the ages of 16 and 22? Did every one of them respond to the poll?

- Was smell the only option for a sense to "trade" for keeping technology? Or were other senses included as well? If other senses were included, did the researchers discover why smell would be the one to give up?

- Who is Wooldridge? Is there a connection between Wooldridge and the poll?

- Where did the headline come from? The one-sentence summary of the poll results says nothing about texting, does it?

- Can we see a copy of the survey questions?

- Are there any published studies of the perceived value of technology devices? If so, is 16–22 a commonly used age range?

- Are there any published studies of the self-reported value of human senses—smell, touch, taste, sight, and hearing?

- What was the theoretical foundation for this study?

Again, ask questions; then question the answers. Research is a process of systematic inquiry.

It is reasonable for instructors to ask their first-year students to write a research paper. In some cases, the assignment may call for students to engage in undergraduate research, as defined early in this chapter, and to contribute to projects that result in original contributions to the body of knowledge. In other cases, instructors may ask first-year students to demonstrate college-level "research" skills by writing an informative or argumentative (persuasive) paper using primary sources, secondary sources, or both.

Table 4-1. Examples of Research Sources

PRIMARY	SECONDARY
Memoir	Biography
Speech	Textbook
News footage	Journal/Magazine article

Visit the textbook website chapter 4 resources for additional examples and activities.

"Primary sources provide first-hand testimony or direct evidence concerning a topic under investigation," according to the Yale University library website (Primary sources, 2008). "They are created by witnesses or recorders who experienced the events or conditions being documented. Often these sources are created at the time when the events or conditions are occurring, but primary sources can also include autobiographies, memoirs, and oral histories recorded later. Primary sources are characterized by their content, regardless of whether they are available in original format, in microfilm/microfiche, in digital format, or in published format." A Google search restricted to ".edu" sites with the search term "primary sources" retrieves web addresses for sites that collect links to actual primary sources or to institutions at which primary source materials are archived.

According to McMullen and Dube (2011), "Secondary sources provide information indirectly, through authors who have made judgments about the quality of the primary and secondary information they have used. You must evaluate how well-informed and unbiased these judgments were. A historian's recounting of research on the process of change in government or a psychologist's use of Freudian psychology to analyze Hitler's personality would be examples of secondary sources."

Model of Systematic Inquiry

The author of this chapter has modified the 12-stage approach to somewhat advanced undergraduate research spelled out by Lee, Matthews, Cucina, and Tritschler (2011, p. 69). The modified 9-stage model is appropriate for first-year students because it does not assume prior knowledge of methodology and the ethical treatment of human subjects.

This model of systematic inquiry has been proven to work well when an assignment calls for a first-year student to demonstrate college-level "research" skills by writing an informative or argumentative (persuasive) paper using primary sources, secondary sources, or both. The model has been followed by students writing research papers and by students preparing speech presentations for class. Evidence of the value of this model includes these accomplishments of first-year students who applied this model of systematic inquiry: Several first-year students have presented single-authored research papers in an open division (not a student category) at a national academic conference, and students have placed in the top three of a public speaking competition—ahead of juniors and seniors.

Figure 4-1 illustrates this easy-to-follow model of systematic inquiry. Think of each stage of this research process as a "decision point." At each

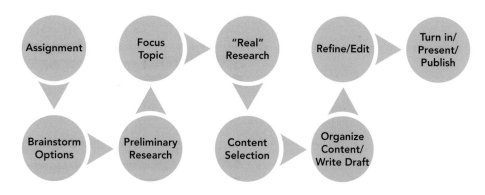

Figure 4-1. **9-Stage Model of Systematic Inquiry**

decision point, the researcher is asked to perform tasks related to that research phase, to evaluate the decisions made in completing those tasks, and to remain in that phase or on that decision point until satisfactory progress has been made.

As presented here, the decision points are intended to be sequential. Do one; then move on to the next. Do not skip phases. At each decision point, stop and think. Ask: "What are my options here? What do I have to work with? What can I do with it? What is the best choice at this point in the process?"

Assignment

In the context of a course for first-year students, the assignment is likely to include:

- Description of the task. For example:

  - Write a 10-page paper about one time management strategy.

- Parameters or guidelines. For example:

  - Use theory(s) or model(s) from psychology as a basis for the paper.

  - The assignment may specify use of a specific approach, such as 1) informative or 2) argumentative.

  - Use a minimum of 25 reliable sources.

  - Use American Psychological Association (APA) Style for both in-text citation and for full citations on a References page.

- Formatting guidelines. For example:

  - The paper should be printed on 8-1/2" × 11" paper; use 1-inch margins on all sides; use 11-point Times New Roman typeface; and double space. Include a running head and put page numbers in the footer.

- Due dates. For example:

  - There may be multiple due dates, including topic approval, review of a "good" draft, and deadline for turning in the final version of the paper.

- Grading guideline—spells out how points may be earned (or deducted) for various elements of the paper.

In some cases, the assignment may include a head start, such as a choice of topic or even a choice of specific topic worded as a Specific Purpose. For example:

- Specific Purpose: To inform the audience about one time management strategy.

Brainstorm Options

In this phase of systematic inquiry, the "researcher" plays with possible ways to develop a paper topic. If the task is to write a 10-page paper about one time management strategy, the researcher needs to find a starting point.

The author of this chapter uses what he calls the Frankenstein Method—first, assemble the pieces, then bring the project to life. Take five minutes to make note of any- and everything related to "time management." The trick is to avoid making judgments about ideas and concepts. Just get the ideas on paper. In classroom brainstorming exercises, the author's students often generate 60–80 ideas in five minutes. The next step is to cross off silly ideas like "buy a bigger clock." At this point, workable ideas should begin to emerge. Select what seem to be the best four or five ideas and move on to Preliminary Research.

Preliminary Research

Basically, preliminary research refers to using keywords related to the best four or five ideas discovered by brainstorming to test for adequate and sufficient source material.

This is not the time for a simple Google.com search. Go to the website of an academic library and find the databases. Search the databases—a productive starting point often is Academic Search Complete. Limit the search to retrieve "full-text" articles, rather than sources that provide only an abstract and citation information.

If Academic Search Complete returns no "hits" for one search term or if the hits do not seem to relate to the topic of the assignment, go to the next "best idea." It is likely that a search may return a huge number of hits. In that situation, refine the search by using the Advanced Search function of the database. If 50–200 hits are returned, it may be a good idea to read the titles and abstracts of these articles to check for relevance. This may seem time consuming, but it saves time in the long run.

Preliminary research is a phase of the research process that seems to be overlooked. Lee et al. (2011, p. 69) go directly from "selecting a topic" to "identifying and reading published research." At first glance, this seems efficient. However, if the topic is not yet focused it will be difficult to search for "the right" published research. And, if there is inadequate source material available for the selected topic, the researcher may be more likely to reach for connections between the topic and available literature that have the potential to misdirect or weaken the research. In a worst-case scenario, the researcher may follow through to the end with a faulty premise. Or a researcher may realize—after wasting valuable time—the study must be re-conceptualized.

Be open to changes in strategy at this point in the research process. If a favorite idea does not turn up related literature, put it aside and try another idea.

Test the waters here. If the well is dry, go try another well.

Focus Topic

For any researcher, in particular a novice, there is a need to focus the topic before moving to the literature review (identifying and reading published research related to the topic). Focus takes shape through creation of a specific purpose and thesis statement.

If the assignment is "write a 10-page paper about one time management strategy" and preliminary research has revealed quite a few good sources for goal setting, overcoming procrastination, and the role of health and fitness in successful time management, then there are some decisions to make. Is one of these topics a subset of another? In other words, can something that first appears to be a main topic become support material within another topic? Given the sources found already, is there enough to write a strong thesis statement?

The thesis statement will differ by approach. For an informative paper or presentation, material is presented as though the author or speaker were simply offering information. The audience may do as it pleases with that information.

If the 10-page paper assigned is to inform the reader about one time management strategy, the specific purpose may look like this:

> Specific Purpose: To inform the audience about one time management strategy.

From there, a thesis statement may be created:

> Thesis Statement: One time management strategy is dealing with procrastination which involves recognition of counterproductive stalling behavior, identification of the probable cause(s) of procrastination, and employing a coping strategy to overcome procrastination.

For an argumentative paper, the writer or speaker has a purpose. In the context of a first-year seminar, it may be likely that the purpose would be to convince the audience to accept a judgment. To focus a topic for an argumentative (or persuasive) paper, begin with the statement of judgment—called a claim or proposition. Using the proposition as a starting point, the specific purpose and thesis statement are written.

> Proposition: People should recognize dealing with procrastination is the most important time management strategy.

> Specific Purpose: To convince the reader that dealing with procrastination is the most important time management strategy.

> Thesis Statement: Dealing with procrastination is the most important time management strategy because there are recognizable causes of procrastination, those causes may be self-identified, and coping strategies for overcoming procrastination have been developed.

Notice how both approaches may use many of the same sources. Also notice each statement builds upon the previous statement. Wording is consistent from one to the next. That helps establish focus. And focus is expressed through the specific purpose and thesis statement. Think of this as a simple formula:

Informative approach
Thesis Statement =
[Specific Purpose] + [List of main points].

Argumentative/Persuasive approach
Thesis Statement =
[Proposition] + [because] + [List of main arguments].

"Real" Research

Once the thesis statement has been created, the researcher begins a focused search for relevant source material. This is the "Real" Research phase of this model of systematic inquiry. In discipline-specific research courses, this phase is called the literature review. The goal is to find as much existing literature about the topic at hand as possible. Scholars take what is known in a given body of knowledge and advance it one step at a time. In the context of a first-year seminar, young scholars apply existing literature to support their points with citable evidence. This takes many students beyond familiar opinion-based writing to a more academic approach that relies on carefully crafted, well-reasoned application of analytical and critical thinking.

Use the thesis statement to stay on track. Without a thesis statement as a guide, it is very easy to lose sight of the direction this research is taking. And that makes it very easy to overlook meaningful, useful source material, as well as making it easy to capture tangential material that cannot be used productively in the assigned paper.

Given the topic already introduced—overcoming procrastination, the researcher begins a focused, deliberate search to locate and "capture" scholarly sources. Researchers have fun at this stage. Information location is like a professor's version of a scavenger hunt at a six-year-old's birthday party. The fun comes from discovering one or two (or more) directly relevant sources that can anchor the research project at hand as well as uncovering sources that can be connected to the research topic through well-organized writing.

Gather quickly during this phase. Avoid agonizing over whether to "grab" this material or not. Make a snap decision and move on. Save or "capture" what may be used later. Ignore the rest.

The trick, of course, is locating "the right" sources. A college library is a labyrinth. It takes experience to navigate its complex passages productively and efficiently.

Today's first-year students are fantastic at online search and retrieval. However, when it comes to locating specific, highly credible, scholarly sources, new college students may not be experts. As an anonymous quote says, "The Internet is like the world's largest library. But all the books are on the floor."

Hahn and Zitron (2011) conducted a study in which they observed first-year students locate a specific source in a university library. The purpose of the study was to gather data about "wayfinding" or "navigation" through the library that may be used to improve library design—to make the library more user-friendly. Students who were successful in their search reported using these navigation strategies: following library signs;

asking staff for assistance; using the library's classification system (such as the Dewey Decimal Classification, a.k.a. Dewey Decimal System); recognizing how the library's shelving is arranged; applying new knowledge to find sources in an unfamiliar setting; and applying prior knowledge of library arrangement to the current situation. The majority of students who failed the task and did not locate the assigned item reported problems trying to understand the library's classification system and inability to comprehend the arrangement of the stacks (p. 31).

Take time—long before an impending deadline—to learn the layout of the campus library. Learn about resources available in the library, including special collections, government documents, maps and atlases, and highly trained reference librarians. Become familiar with services like Inter-Library Loan (ILL), information literacy workshops, and seminars that offer tips for conducting library research for specific academic disciplines, majors, or even courses. This chapter has introduced electronic databases as productive sources for finding and retrieving high-quality scholarly sources.

In this author's experience, there is a marked difference in quality of student work. In general, first-year students who use scholarly sources, often retrieved from a combination of database searches and "hard copy" finds of materials from library stack holdings, do better work.

For a good summary of factors to consider in evaluating the quality and credibility of print and online sources, visit the textbook website chapter 4 resources for links to informative KSU Library Subject Guides and the Purdue University's Online Writing Lab (OWL). In general, according to the OWL web page, "Some sources such as journal or newspaper articles can be found in both print and digital format. However, much of what is found on the Internet does not have a print equivalent, and hence, has low or no quality standards for publication."

For a college-level research assignment, frequent use of source materials with "low or no quality standards for publication" is not acceptable.

"Capturing" information during the "Real" Research phase is a skill in itself. Document full bibliographic information for each piece of information captured or saved for later use. "Full bibliographic information" means everything needed to write a complete citation on a References page. This will be covered in more detail under the heading Organize Content/Write Draft. Also, be sure to indicate what information—some of which may have been copied and pasted—is a direct quote. Proper documentation of saved source material is critical for two reasons: (1) Bibliographic information will be required for proper citation. Collecting that information here saves a great deal of time, compared to backtracking to the original source later. (2) Use of direct quotes without quotation marks is considered plagiarism—a violation of the intellectual property rights of the original author. Students who plagiarize may find themselves suspended or even dismissed from school. An institution's policy on plagiarism may be found in the Undergraduate Catalog under a heading like Academic Integrity, Academic Honesty, Intellectual Property, or Plagiarism.

Content Selection

By making snap decisions during the "Real" Research phase, the researcher probably captured too much material. That is good. In the Content Selection phase of this model of systematic inquiry, the researcher begins to align content with the thesis statement.

Read the source material for items of relevance that support the main points listed in the thesis statement. Tag material to be quoted or paraphrased. If using a print source, a small adhesive sticker can mark the spot. For electronic material saved to the researcher's computer important material may be highlighted with bold, or underline, or add a "New Comment" with MS Word's Review features.

Deliberately decide what material to use and what to exclude. Do not delete anything. It may be needed later.

By the time the Content Selection phase is complete, the researcher has a feel for whether or not enough information has been gathered for each main point. And the paper begins to take shape in the mind of the researcher.

Organize Content/Write Draft

By writing a thesis statement, the researcher has identified the basic skeletal structure of the paper. For example, for the informative approach spelled out above, the researcher has created:

> Thesis Statement: One time management strategy is dealing with procrastination which involves recognition of counterproductive stalling behavior, identification of the probable cause(s) of procrastination, and employing a coping strategy to overcome procrastination.

The basic outline for this informative research paper could look like this:

Introduction

Body

I. recognition of counterproductive stalling behavior

II. identification of the probable cause(s) of procrastination

III. employing a coping strategy to overcome procrastination

Conclusion

References

For an argumentative approach, the researcher begins with:

Thesis Statement: Dealing with procrastination is the most important time management strategy because there are recognizable causes of procrastination, those causes may be self-identified, and coping strategies for overcoming procrastination have been developed.

So, the basic outline for this argumentative research paper could look like this:

Introduction

Body

I. recognition of counterproductive stalling behavior

II. identification of the probable cause(s) of procrastination

III. employing a coping strategy to overcome procrastination

Counterargument (to acknowledge an alternative point of view which further strengthens the author's argument)

Rebuttal (to refute the alternative point of view)

Conclusion

References

In his book, *The Transition to College Writing*, Keith Hjortshoj (2001) spells out a writing "recipe":

- Figure out what to say and make an outline.

- Compose a draft according to your outline.

- Revise your draft.

- Edit the revised draft.

- Turn in the finished product. (p. 56)

The basic outlines and the writing recipe presented here are simply tools for beginning the writing process. But some first-year students—especially those who procrastinate—may have some trouble getting started. The writing process for some of those students may look like this:

- Begin the assignment the night before the due date.

- Turn it in, hoping the instructor may overlook the hurried, unpolished writing.

Unlike these procrastinators, students who follow a model of systematic inquiry find it relatively easy to "fill in" the outline with solid source material. Following the principle of advancing the body of knowledge one step at a time, researchers carefully identify information that comes from an outside source with proper in-text citation (a cross-reference in the body of the paper to the full citation on the References page) and proper citation at the end of the paper. Usually, an instructor will specify in the assignment a preferred citation style.

Citation Style

Although several citation styles have been defined, the two most frequently used by first-year students are Modern Language Association (MLA) style and American Psychological Association (APA) style. Learn about both styles. They are similar in that they both require full bibliographic information—enough for anyone to find the article used as a source in the research paper. However, the styles differ in format. For example, the same book written by one author may be cited as:

MLA

Gleick, James. *Chaos: Making a New Science.* New York: Penguin, 1987. Print.

APA

Gleick, J. (1987). *Chaos: Making a new science.* New York: Penguin.

Citation style is a technical aspect of writing. Style must be precise. Accurate. One misplaced period or comma could mean a point deduction during grading.

Here is the trick to precise MLA or APA style: Do not learn it. Instead, become familiar with the Purdue Online Writing Lab (http://owl. english.purdue.edu/owl/). Follow the link to either style. Find the example for the type of resource for which an in-text citation or citation is needed and make yours look like the example.

Some students choose to use online style converters. Almost always, there is a flaw in the output of these converters. These students are in no position to challenge point deductions for citation style.

On the other hand, students who use the Purdue OWL site can print pages that show the examples used as models for citation in the paper. An instructor may say, "You're right. It looks like APA has updated its style since I learned it. I'll adjust your grade." Or an instructor may say, "You're close. But the source you used is actually an 'article from an online periodical' rather than an 'article from a scholarly journal in print.' I can see you are learning how to use APA style, and I think you handled this question about the point deduction in an appropriate manner. You're doing well."

Refine/Edit
This stage is listed as a separate part of the process to remind students that revisiting a draft after a day or two is a productive strategy. Technical aspects of revising, editing, and proofreading are beyond the scope of this chapter.

But think about refinement as several steps—working from the "big picture" toward fine detail. Look at structure first. Is this a well-organized paper? Then move to content. Would the paper be improved by removing or adding any content? Now look for details like material that should be attributed to a source. Does the format satisfy the guidelines spelled out in the assignment? For example, "The paper should be printed on 8-1/2" × 11" paper; use 1-inch margins on all sides; use 11-point Times New Roman typeface; and double space. Include a running head and put page numbers in the footer." Are all citations precise and accurate for the required style? Finally, double-check grammar, spelling, and punctuation.

For a speech or presentation of a research project, this is the rehearsal phase. Polish to perfection.

Turn In/Present/Publish
The final phase of this model of systematic inquiry is moment others see. It may have taken several weeks or months to reach this point. No one else knows the time and effort required to work through the research process. But the quality of the paper or presentation should demonstrate an understanding of and an ability to accomplish college-level work.

Scholars take what is known in a given body of knowledge and advance it one step at a time. They are expected to share this advance through dissemination of their work. In the context of a first-year seminar, sharing work by turning it in to the instructor or by making an in-class presentation may be enough. In addition, there are opportunities for undergraduate researchers to reach a broader audience by presenting their work at local, regional, national, and international academic conferences. Undergraduate researchers also may consider publication of their work in academic journals and scholarly newsletters.

Think ahead to graduate school. Publication of research conducted as an undergraduate helps pave the way to admission to a graduate program.

Summary

This chapter has provided an overview of the value of undergraduate research in terms of improving the overall college experience and building a sense of self-efficacy. The model for systematic inquiry presented differs from existing descriptions of the research process in that it does not assume prior knowledge of research methods or statistical analysis. For the first-year student, the practice of systematic inquiry is a key to beginning to think like a scholar.

From here, the student may choose to engage in research efforts on a higher level. "The real benefit [of undergraduate research] is the engagement of students with faculty in the process of discovery and learning. To have the benefit of a tutorial experience with faculty in a small group or even one-on-one has long been the ultimate learning experience" (Description of undergraduate research, 2007, p. 16).

Faculty who work with undergraduate researchers are looking for talented students. To be recognized as a worthy research partner or assistant, students should demonstrate scholarly thinking, write thorough, well-reasoned literature reviews, and be precise with citation and attribution.

Kennesaw Journal of Undergraduate Research (KJUR)

According to the website for the *Kennesaw Journal of Undergraduate Research* (http://digitalcommons.kennesaw.edu/kjur/):

The *Kennesaw Journal of Undergraduate Research (KJUR)* is a peer-reviewed scholarly journal dedicated to promoting scholarship among undergraduates at Kennesaw State University. The journal seeks to develop a spirit of inquiry among undergraduate students by providing them an avenue for dissemination and exchange of knowledge.

Undergraduate research is defined as "an inquiry or investigation conducted by an undergraduate student that makes an original intellectual or creative contribution to the discipline" (Council on Undergraduate Research, http://www.cur.org/about.html).

Guided by this inclusive definition, *KJUR* welcomes submissions of diverse work across disciplines. Here is a partial list of the works that the journal will accept:

- Research articles
- Fiction
- Business models
- Historical analyses
- Book reviews
- Film analyses
- Photography
- Artwork

KJUR accepts scholarly or creative work conducted by an undergraduate student or a team of undergraduate students at Kennesaw State University. The work must have at least one faculty mentor as a collaborator.

References

Bandura, A. (1977, March). Self-efficacy: Toward a unifying theory of behavioral change. *Psychological Review, 84*(2), 191–215.

Bembenutty, H. (2011, Spring). Meaningful and maladaptive homework practices: The role of self-efficacy and self-regulation. *Journal of Advanced Academics, 22*(3), 448–473.

Caccavo, F. (2009, Winter). Teaching undergraduates to think like scientists. *College Teaching, 57*(1), 9–14.

Collins, L. H. (2001). Does research experience make a significant difference in graduate admissions? *Eye on Psi Chi*, Chattanooga, TN.

Craney, C., McKay, T., Mazzeo, A., Morris, J., Prigodich, C., & de Groot, R. (2011, Jan/Feb). Cross-discipline perceptions of the undergraduate research experience. *Journal of Higher Education, 82*(1), 92–113.

DeHaan, R. L. (2005). The impending revolution in undergraduate science education. *Journal of Science Education and Technology, 14*(2), 253–269.

Description of undergraduate research and creative activities (2007). *ASHE Higher Education Report, 33*(4), 5–17.

Falconer, J., & Holcomb, D. (2008, September). Understanding undergraduate research experiences from the student perspective: A phenomenological study of a summer student research program. *College Student Journal, 42*(3), 869–878.

Hahn, J., & Zitron, L. (2011). How first-year students navigate the stacks: Implications for improving wayfinding. *Reference & User Services Quarterly, 51*(1), 28–35.

Hathaway, R. S., Nagda, B. A., & Gregerman, S. R. (2002). The relationship of undergraduate research participation to graduate and professional educational pursuit: An empirical study. *Journal of College Student Development, 43*(5), 614–631.

Haworth, J. G., & Conrad, C. F. (1997). *Emblems of quality in higher education.* Needham Heights, MA: Allyn and Bacon.

Healey, M., & Jenkins, A. (2006, Fall). Strengthening the teaching-research linkage in undergraduate courses and programs. *New Directions for Teaching and Learning, 107*, 45–55.

Helm, H. W., Bailey, K. G. D., McBride, D. C., & LaBianca Ø. S. (2011). Creating a research culture in a small non-selective department. *Psychology Journal, 8*(3), 93–101.

Hjortshoj, K. (2001). *The transition to college writing.* New York: Bedford/St. Martin's.

Howitt, S., Wilson, A., Wilson, K., & Roberts, P. (2010, August). 'Please remember we are not all brilliant': Undergraduates' experiences of an elite, research-intensive degree at a research-intensive university. *Higher Education Research & Development, 29*(4), 405–420.

Ishyama, J. (2002). Does early participation in undergraduate research benefit the social science and humanities students? *College Student Journal, 36*(3), 380–386.

Jones, M. T., Barlow, A. E. L., & Villarejo, M. (2010, January/February). Importance of undergraduate research for minority persistence and achievement in biology. *The Journal of Higher Education, 81*(1), 82–115.

Kardash, C. M. (2000). Evaluation of an undergraduate research experience: Perceptions of undergraduate interns and their faculty mentors. *Journal of Educational Psychology, 92*(1), 191–201.

Kinkead, J. (2003). Learning through inquiry: An overview of undergraduate research. *New Directions for Teaching and Learning, 93*, 5–17.

Kuh, G. D. (2008). *High-impact educational practices: What they are, who has access to them, and why they matter.* Washington, DC: Association of American Colleges and Universities.

Kuh, G. D. (2003, March/April). What we're learning about student engagement from NSSE. *Change, 35*(2), 24–32.

Lee, A. N., Matthews, T. D., Cucina, I. M., & Tritschler, K. A. (2011, Jan–Mar). Promoting research writing in an undergraduate measurement course. *Measurement in Physical Education and Exercise Science, 15*(1), 67–84.

Lochmatter, D., & Mullis, P.E. (2011, January). RNA interference in mammalian cell systems. *Hormone Research in Pediatrics, 75*(1), 63–69.

McMullen-Light, M., & Dube, C. (2011). Primary vs. secondary sources. Retrieved from http://www.writing.ku.edu/~writing/guides/primary.shtml

Nagda, B. A., Gregerman, S. R., Jonides, J., von Hippel, W., & Lerner, J. S. (1998). Undergraduate student-faculty research partnerships affect student retention. *The Review of Higher Education, 22*(1), 55–72.

Primary Sources (2008). *What are primary sources?* Retrieved from http://www.yale.edu/collections_collaborative/primarysources/primarysources.html

Prince, M. J., Felder, R. M., & Brent, R. (2007). Does faculty research improve undergraduate teaching? An analysis of existing and potential synergies. *Journal of Engineering Education, 96*(4), 283–294.

Purdue Online Writing Lab (2012). http://owl.english.purdue.edu/owl/

Russell, S. H., Hancock, M. P., & McCullough, J. (2007). Benefits of undergraduate research experiences. *Science, 316*(5824), 548–549.

Seymour, E., Hunter, A. B., Laursen, S. L., & DeAntoni, T. (2004). Establishing the benefits of research experiences for undergraduates in the sciences: First findings from a three-year study. *Science Education, 88*(4), 493–594.

Snow, A. A., DeCosmo, J., & Shokair, S. M. (2010, Spring). Low-cost strategies for promoting undergraduate research at research universities. *Peer Review, 12*(2), 16–19.

Tinto, V. (1993). *Leaving college: Rethinking the causes and cures of student attrition.* Chicago: The University of Chicago Press.

Vraga, E. K. (2011). Dealing with dissonance: Responding to an incongruent test result in a new media environment. *Cyberpsychology, Behavior, and Social Networking, 14*(11), 689–694.

Wooldridge, L. Q. (2011–2012, Dec/Jan). Texting tops smelling. *AARP The Magazine,* 11.

Zimmerman, B. J. (2000). Self-efficacy: An essential motive to learn. *Contemporary Educational Psychology, 25*(1), 82–91.

Zimmerman, B. J., Bandura, A., & Martinez-Pons, M. (1992). Self-motivation for academic achievement: The role of self-efficacy and personal goal setting. *American Educational Research Journal, 29*(3), 663–676.

Critical Thinking Questions

1. How can participating in undergraduate research in the first year in college improve the likelihood that a student will continue through to graduation?

2. Why is IRB approval an important aspect of research?

Name _____ Date _____

The purpose of this exercise is to develop a plan for engaging in undergraduate research, defined as "an inquiry or investigation conducted by an undergraduate that makes an original intellectual or creative contribution to the discipline."

Complete these sentences, please:

If I could take part in any imaginable research project, I would want to help answer this question:

Research faculty involved in this project would be trained in the following academic discipline(s):

To "catch up" with the body of knowledge related to this research project, I would

As a first-year student, I would make myself noticeable to faculty involved in this research project by

Name _____ Date _____

The purpose of this exercise is to define a timeline for the sample assignment below to be completed using a model of systematic inquiry.

Sample Assignment: Write an 8–10-page paper that compares academic skills training and development in a first-year seminar to academic skills training and development in high school.

Given: The day the assignment is made is considered Day 1; the day the assignment is due is considered Day 18.

The Task:

1. Spell out each phase of the model of systematic inquiry and set "mini deadlines" for completing each phase.

2. Go back and fill in more detail about each step to be completed within each phase. Assign "mini deadlines" within each phase.

Name _____ Date _____

The purpose of this exercise is to practice precise citation style.

Note: All examples are direct quotes from http://owl.english.purdue.edu/owl/

Convert These from MLA Style to APA Style

An Article in a Scholarly Journal

Bagchi, Alaknanda. "Conflicting Nationalisms: The Voice of the Subaltern in Mahasweta Devi's *Bashai Tudu*." *Tulsa Studies in Women's Literature* 15.1 (1996): 41–50. Print.

Article in a Newspaper

Behre, Robert. "Presidential Hopefuls Get Final Crack at Core of S.C. Democrats." *Post and Courier* [Charleston, SC] 29 Apr. 2007: A11. Print.

Article in an Online-Only Scholarly Journal

Dolby, Nadine. "Research in Youth Culture and Policy: Current Conditions and Future Directions." *Social Work and Society: The International Online-Only Journal* 6.2 (2008): n. pag. Web. 20 May 2009.

A Page on a Website

"How to Make Vegetarian Chili." *eHow.* Demand Media, Inc., n.d. Web. 24 Feb. 2009.

An Article from an Online Database (or Other Electronic Subscription Service)

Langhamer, Claire. "Love and Courtship in Mid-Twentieth-Century England." *Historical Journal* 50.1 (2007): 173–96. ProQuest. Web. 27 May 2009.

Identify the Type of Source for These APA Citations

Wendy, S. W. (Writer), & Martian, I. R. (Director). (1986). The rising angel and the falling ape [Television series episode]. In D. Dude (Producer), *Creatures and monsters*. Los Angeles, CA: Belarus Studios.

O'Neil, J. M., & Egan, J. (1992). Men's and women's gender role journeys: A metaphor for healing, transition, and transformation. In B. R. Wainrib (Ed.), *Gender issues across the life cycle* (pp. 107–123). New York, NY: Springer.

Kernis, M. H., Cornell, D. P., Sun, C. R., Berry, A., Harlow, T., & Bach, J. S. (1993). There's more to self-esteem than whether it is high or low: The importance of stability of self-esteem. *Journal of Personality and Social Psychology, 65*, 1190–1204.

Brownlie, D. (2007). Toward effective poster presentations: An annotated bibliography. *European Journal of Marketing, 41*(11/12), 1245–1283. doi:10.1108/03090560710821161

National Institute of Mental Health. (1990). *Clinical training in serious mental illness* (DHHS Publication No. ADM 90-1679). Washington, DC: U.S. Government Printing Office.

CHAPTER 5

Communication for Academic Success

STEPHEN W. BRADEN, Ph.D.

Chapter Goals

- Describe proper communication skills in and out of class

- Understand how to develop a successful presentation

- Know how to properly deliver a presentation

Chapter Overview

This chapter describes how to become a competent communicator inside and outside of the classroom. Effective communication involves not only what is said, but how it is said. During class you might have to participate in a class discussion or give a presentation individually or as part of a group. This chapter will provide you with information on how to communicate with your professors and how to prepare for speech presentations.

Communication Inside the Classroom

College professors vary in their teaching styles. Some prefer to lecture the entire class time, while others prefer a combination of lecture and student interactions such as group activities or interactive discussions. Knowing how to effectively communicate in these environments will make the transition to the university classroom much easier.

In-Class Discussions

Communicating in the college classroom goes beyond raising one's hand to ask or answer a question. Effective classroom communication involves being an active participant and respecting one's professors and peers. Dallimore, Hertenstein, and Platt (2008) argue that students who speak up and engage in classroom discussions experience an improvement

in their oral and written communication skills. Their research also found that students' comfort with classroom participation is connected to preparation (i.e., reading the assigned material before coming to class) and regularity of participation. Participating in discussions and group activities can be a challenge for students who are apprehensive about speaking up in the classroom, but it can become easier through proper preparation and practice.

Effective communication in classroom discussions is more about *quality* than *quantity*. If the professor asks a discussion question, he or she expects you to contribute. Similarly, if the professor assigns a group activity, all students are expected to participate. Share in discussions by providing thoughtful, constructive, and succinct input and responses. Also, if you have a question about the lecture or assigned reading, ask, when appropriate, during class. If your comment or question does not pertain to the topic of discussion, save it for after or outside of class.

Nonverbal Communication

Nonverbal communication can be powerful. When you see a student slouching in his chair or laying her head on her desk, what does that communicate? It is a sign of disrespect and apathy to fellow students and to the professor. Sit up straight, make eye contact with the professor, and take notes; this communicates interest in the course. In some contexts, nonverbal communication communicates more powerfully than verbal communication (Patterson, 2010). And there are other examples of poor nonverbal communication: missing class, arriving late to class, texting during class, and misuse of computers and other electronics in class.

If you miss class, some professors consider it a common courtesy for you to send an email explaining your absence. If you are late to class, you may want to approach the professor after class and apologize and offer a brief explanation. In either case, do not ask the professor, "What did I miss?" Ask a classmate or, if available, post your question to the course online discussion board.

For many college professors, texting is one of the most disruptive behaviors in the classroom. Although you use it to communicate with friends or family, texting during class sends a different message to your professors. Professors spend time outside of class to prepare lesson plans, and their job is to present those lessons in class. Texting while the professor is lecturing communicates a message of disrespect. Many students argue that they can text during class and still perform well in the class. However, texting in class is a distraction to the student doing the texting, the students sitting around that student, and the professor. Rosen, Lim, Carrier, and Cheever (2011) examined the impact of text messaging in class and student information retention. They found that the students that received and sent 16 or more texts in a half-hour period earned scores at least one letter grade lower than students who received no or fewer than seven text messages.

Similarly, if you prefer to take notes on your laptop, netbook, or tablet, confirm that it is okay to do so in each class. First, check the syllabus for policies regarding electronics in the classroom. If this is not specifically addressed, ask your professor if he or she approves. If they do, know that this too can be distracting and disrespectful to those seated near you and to your professor if you choose to check emails, update Facebook, or surf the Internet during class. Use your computer for taking notes and, when it makes sense, for accessing a website being used during the lecture.

Communication Outside the Classroom

Contrary to popular rumor, most professors are very approachable, and they want you to communicate with them if you have questions or concerns. Perhaps you have a question about a grade on an assignment, or would like clarification on a concept covered in class, or you are in need of assistance choosing an appropriate research topic. Talk with your professors before or after class, write an email, or schedule an appointment to meet in their office. Be clear and concise, and always be courteous, respectful, and tactful. Remember that professors chose their careers because they are passionate about teaching and learning. When you have a sincere reason for communicating with your professor, you will likely find your professor is welcoming and happy to assist you. However, be certain that your purpose for speaking with your professor is appropriate. Below are some examples of comments and commonly asked questions that are generally not well received your professors:

* "I really need a 'B' (or 'A') in this class" or "Can I still get a B in this class?" or "I *cannot* fail this class!" Professors do not give grades;

students earn grades. Your professor wants you to focus on learning rather than simply on your grade point average. And if you do have a concern about your grade, approach your professor early in the semester.

* "Is this going to be on the exam?" Check your syllabus and course schedule; your professor will likely share the exam format with you, but you will soon learn to process the information presented and discern important concepts.

* "That assignment/exam was unfair!" While it is acceptable to state your case regarding an assignment or exam, do so respectfully and with strong evidence if you want your professor to seriously consider your argument.

Again, those comments and questions that do not pertain to the topic of discussion in the classroom are best reserved for outside of class—you may speak with the professor before or after class. If this is not possible, you should use email to schedule an appointment or ask a question.

Most first-year college students are familiar with email and have been using it as a way to communicate with friends, family, and teachers for years before stepping on to a college campus. However, many first-year students are unaware of how to use their email efficiently and correctly. Aguilar-Roca, Williams, Warrior, and O'Dowd (2009) found that students that are trained in professional email etiquette saw an improvement in their email communication with professors. Professional email etiquette begins with your email address. First, you should only use your assigned university email for any university correspondence. This is the primary address your professors (and university) use to communicate with you. Using a non-university email account could pose risks to your privacy and may result in the email being sent to the professor's spam folder. Aguilar-Roca et al. (2009) recommend that students do the following when emailing professors:

- In the subject line, place the course name.

- Start the email with Dr. or Professor and the professor's last name.

- Use proper punctuation and grammar and proofread your email before sending.

- Do not use text message/instant messaging abbreviations in the email.

- Close the email with your name.

Also take into consideration professors have many responsibilities on campus besides teaching. It may take a minimum of 24 hours before your professor responds to your email.

Verbal, nonverbal, and electronic communication are all important, but there is another very important aspect of communication in higher education, and that is delivering presentations. Students will likely be delivering individual speeches or may be part of a group presentation. The remainder of this chapter addresses classroom presentations, beginning with your responsibility as a speaker.

Speaker Responsibility

Anyone giving a speech has the responsibility of being ethical. Ethics is a "branch of philosophy dealing with values relating to human conduct" ("Ethics," n.d.). Ethics are important because words, either spoken or written, have the power to persuade, to do harm, and to affect society in general.

The speaker also has the responsibility to present information in an accurate manner and in the proper context. Words matter; they have done great things throughout history and have also done great harm throughout history. Consider not only *what* you will say but *how* you will deliver your message. Realize that verbal communication is irreversible; once a person says something, he or she cannot "un-say" that message. People may apologize, retract, or refute

their own words, but the words have still been spoken. Another consideration is that all verbal communication has persuasive qualities. Some statements are more persuasive than others, but because all communication is motive-based, there is always a persuasive context.

Listener Responsibility

Just as speakers have responsibilities, so do listeners. Audience members have the ethical responsibility to pay attention to the speaker. Listening and hearing are not the same. Hearing is passive. When people *listen*, they are cognitively engaged with the speaker's message, and that makes it an active process.

Sometimes people listen for appreciation, such as with music or television. Other times, such as in a classroom, students listen to comprehend/understand material. Finally, one may listen to evaluate or make a judgment. In some instances, one may listen to comprehend, then make a judgment about what was heard. The latter two types of listening require more attention to detail and are on a higher cognitive level.

Chapter 3 notes good listening behaviors, and applying them can help you perform better in college. In college, students will be called upon to make presentations in the classroom. As one would want the audience—classmates and professor—to be polite and pay attention, students have the responsibility to pay close attention to classmates when they are speaking in class. Dozing off or studying for an exam while a classmate is speaking is ethically unacceptable.

Speech Goals

Professors may assign a certain type of speech for classroom presentation, or students may have leeway in their topic selection. There are two basic types of speeches that can be prepared: informative and persuasive.

In an informative speech, the speakers may see themselves as *teachers* in that they give their audience information and let them decide how they will use that information. For example, a speech about statistics on seat belt usage correlating with auto injuries and deaths could be done in a straightforward, informative format. But this speech could also take on a persuasive quality if the speaker wanted to convince the audience of the important aspects of wearing seat belts. In the persuasive speech, the speaker is an *advocate* for a position.

Speech Topics

Again, students may be assigned a topic or may be asked to choose their own topic. Whatever the situation, give careful consideration to topic selection and how the material will be presented. First, the topic must be appropriate (McKerrow, Gronbeck, Ehninger, & Monroe, 2003). Never offend any member of the audience; doing this gets a speaker nowhere and will likely cause a reduction in a grade. Nearly all topics can be presented if done in a professional manner. If there is any doubt, check with the professor on what and how to discuss the information.

Second, chances are the topic will require research. Sources must be reliable, relevant, and current to the topic. Be wary of sources that are not credible, as the information may be false or unreliable. Also, make sure the source does not have an agenda.

Finally, it may be necessary to narrow the topic. A topic such as environmental issues is very broad, whereas a topic such as water pollution or air quality is more focused and will result in the speech having more depth.

Speech Parts

The speech should be broken down into three sections: introduction, body, and conclusion (Osborne & Osborne, 1994). And the speech needs balance. Use the following guidelines:

SPEECH PART	APPROXIMATE PERCENTAGE OF ENTIRE SPEECH
Introduction	10–15%
Body	65–75%
Conclusion	10–15%

The speech body is the first part to be developed because the introduction *sets up* the body.

Speech Body

The body is where the majority of your information is located. This information requires some facts. Facts are verifiable information. For example, one could present a speech about the growth of Kennesaw State University and claim that "KSU is the third largest university in the University System of Georgia." This is a true statement and can easily be verified through numerous sources. The speech body also needs **supporting materials** in the form of examples, statistics, and/or testimony (Lucas, 2004).

Examples humanize information and make abstract concepts come to life. It is one thing to state, "Parking is a problem for many in the KSU community," and another to state, "Parking is so bad at KSU that this morning it took me 25 minutes to find a place to park my car." This makes the situation real. An example could be **hypothetical**; that is, a fictitious event that could happen in real life, such as: "Let us suppose you are trying to find a place to park at KSU, you have an exam in 10 minutes, and the professor has a policy that anyone late to class on exam day gets a zero on that exam." This is fictitious but applies a real-life possibility to make the point. Another type of example is a **narrative** or brief story. For the most part, audiences appreciate hearing stories told properly. A word of caution, however, the narrative should be related to the topic and not take up too much time.

Statistics are numerical data and "the interpretation of numerical facts or data" ("Statistics," n.d.) that describe the magnitude of events. Think about how much of your life is explained through statistics: GPA, number of course hours, miles per gallon, consumer prices, cost of rent, increase in salary, etc. Statistics make a powerful impact on audiences but have limitations. Below are some guidelines for using statistics:

First, do not use too many numbers (Dobkin & Pace, 2003). Reading a large number of statistics will not only confuse an audience, but audience members may also become bored. In some cases statistics have to be explained. For example, is the audience aware of the difference between mean and median averages? Again, statistics are powerful but must be used appropriately and sparingly. Finally, incorporating statistics into your visual aids, to be discussed later in this chapter, may be an asset to you.

The last type of supporting material is **testimony** which is the words of others and comes in three varieties (Osborne & Osborne, 1994).

Peer testimony is the words of average people. Let us go back to the parking example: Suppose you talked with a classmate about his/her problems parking at KSU. The student's comments would be peer testimony.

Expert testimony is what it sounds like: a person who is an expert in the field of discussion. An expert on parking at KSU might be an administrator who studies and implements space issues, or a KSU police officer.

Prestige testimony is words the audience respects based upon the person's good name and reputation. Suppose Atlanta Falcons quarterback Matt Ryan came to KSU to promote education and talked about his college career at Boston College. No doubt, Mr. Ryan also had occasional parking woes as most university students do, and he might comment on student parking. However, he is certainly not an expert on the KSU parking situation.

Organizing the Speech Body
Informative and persuasive speeches have different organizational tools that can be used, but both types of speeches may implement strategies from the other type.

Informative Speech Design
In most classroom speeches you are going to be presenting an informative speech. In an informative speech you are a teacher—you are not advocating for a cause, you are providing the audience with information. The following are ways in which to organize your ideas for **informative speeches**:

The **historical/chronological** method examines change over time. Large events can be used as main points. For example, the history of the Civil Rights Movement could focus on issues such as *Brown vs. Board of Education*, Dr. Martin Luther's Kings famous "I Have a Dream Speech," and the 1964 Voting Rights Act. Suppose a student wanted to do a speech on the history of Kennesaw State University. Because it is important to break the speech body down into main points, a good way to structure the speech body would be to break the history down by major events:

- The first main point could be the reasons the school was started and the process of opening the school.

- The second main point could be about the growth leading the then two-year college to become a four-year institution.

- The third main point might be about the incredible growth of the 1990s and achieving university status.

- The fourth main point could focus on the year 2000 and after with emphasis on housing, athletics, and academic program development.

Each of these main points would have subpoints in them and cover a wide range of issues. There is no set number of main points for speeches. Analyze your topic and allow what works best for you to be your guide.

Spatial speech designs are how things are arranged and their relationships by space. A geography major might use a spatial design to inform the audience about the layout of KSU, or the city of Atlanta, or the design of the Convocation Center. Suppose a student wanted to deliver a speech on the layout of New Orleans:

- One main point could be the popular French Quarter.

- Another main point might cover the beautiful garden district.

- A third main point might cover the business district.

Process speeches can make good use of the order of sequence. Suppose a communication major with a media emphasis wanted to inform the audience how a newspaper story is created from beginning to end. Using the sequence of story selection and assignment, interviews and research, writing the story, sending it to the copy editor, forwarding it to the print department, and finally delivering the paper would be a logical way to organize ideas. As another example, if a student wanted to do a speech on the process of interviewing, it could be structured as such:

- The first main point would be about researching potential jobs.

- The second main point might cover creating a résumé and cover letter.

- The third main point might concern an actual interview.

Remember, main points have subpoints. Take the last main point on interviewing. The subpoints could be:

- Practicing/mock interview

- How to dress

- What to do and not do during the interview

- Following up afterward

Categorical organization is a good choice for topics that logically and naturally fall into certain categories. Different types of schools in the University System of Georgia would best be explained by noting that there are Research I schools, such as the University of Georgia, Georgia State University, and Georgia Tech; then there are state universities, such as KSU, Clayton State, and the University of West Georgia; and there are technical-based schools, such as Southern Polytechnic State University. Regional schools include Georgia Southern University and Valdosta State University ("Institutions map," 2007). In this categorical design there would be four main points, one for each category.

The **cause-effect** organization usually has two main points. For instance, a social work major might want to discuss teen drug use with the first main point as the cause of drug use focusing on issues of poor parental supervision, peer pressure, and poor grades in school. Then as the effect, the second main point, he would present truancy, sexually transmitted disease, crime, violence, etc.

The **effect-cause** design reverses the previous method. Suppose an economics major has the topic of inflation. If the first main point is the effect of inflation, then the second main point concerns what caused the effects.

The key factor to which of these two are used is what best fits a particular topic.

Persuasive Speech Designs

Persuasive speeches are of three primary varieties: (1) trying to influence the audience to agree with a particular position, such as advocating more troop deployment to Afghanistan; (2) calling on the audience to agree and then to act upon something, such as agreeing that Afghanistan needs more American troops but also acting by writing a letter to government officials in support of said position; or (3) refuting a stated position, such as arguing against American troop reduction in Afghanistan.

Ways to organize persuasive speeches include the following:

In the **problem-solution** design there are two main points. The first clearly details the problem, and the second provides a way to address the problem. For example, a social work major is going to present a speech on teen pregnancy. The first main point could note the personal and social problems that can occur due to teen pregnancy, then the second main point could cover programs and counseling to address these problems.

The **problem-cause-solution** method is an extension of the previous method with an added main point: cause. In problem-solution, the cause may be mentioned in the first main point but is not as detailed as the three-step process. After the problem is presented, a thorough examination of the cause of the problem is addressed.

As an example, suppose a student wants to deliver a speech about his or her university's parking woes. The first main point would note the issues (problem) of parking needs and availability on campus. The second main point could be about congestion, space issues, and peak parking demand. The third and final main point could offer solutions such as increased shuttle services, altering class scheduling during peak times, and offering online and hybrid courses.

Arguments

An **argument** takes a persuasive position on an issue and contains **claims**, supported by **evidence**, and tied together with **reason** ("Argument," n.d.). The claim is what/how you think things are or should be. A claim stating: "KSU needs to build more parking decks" could be supported by evidence, using supporting materials such as statistics noting need versus space, geographical factors, and student frustration, and connected with reason/logic. It is an easy connection to make, as the number of parking spaces and the increase in vehicle numbers are directly correlated with the claim. Arguments come in three basic types: **fact**, **value**, and **policy** (McKerrow, Gronbeck, Ehninger, & Monroe, 2003).

Arguments from **fact** are about whether something did or did not happen. For example, criminal jury trials are about questions of fact.

> Example: Did Fannie Mae and Freddie Mac directly affect the economic troubles that surfaced in 2008?

> Example: What was the actual amount of the Congressional stimulus bill in spring 2009?

Both of these examples have competing positions that can be taken.

Arguments from **value** are based upon the right and wrong of an issue or the goodness or badness of an issue and may use a moral argument platform.

> Example: Is Barack Obama a good or bad president?

> Example: Do Americans have a "right" to healthcare?

Policy arguments take the position that a course of action should or should not be taken.

> Example: Should a value added tax (VAT) be passed by Congress and the revenue it generates used to lower the national debt?

Example: Should the University System of Georgia allow KSU to cap enrollment?

Realize that each of these type of arguments will probably incorporate tenets of the other two. A policy speech could use facts as argument and support and use values to bring in what is right and wrong about the policy.

A topic can also be approached in different manners. In 2009, KSU initiated a mandatory meal plan policy for most students—a topic that could be argued from fact, value, or policy.

Example of arguing from fact: Students can eat cheaper at other places than The Commons and save money.

Examples of arguing from value: It is wrong to force KSU students to buy a meal plan, or it is a good thing that KSU has a good meal plan.

Example of arguing from policy: KSU should end its mandatory meal plan program concerning The Commons.

What determines the category is the goal or what is to be accomplished by the speech.

Reasoning

After the speech is prepared, go over it word for word and assess it for logic. How easy will it be for the audience to understand the points? Does it flow well? Ensure that it is easy to understand and will make sense to the audience. Once the body of the speech is organized, the speech introduction can be developed.

Speech Introduction

The speech introduction is an opportunity to make a good first impression. It should be carefully crafted and should interest the audience. Generally speaking, the speech introduction has six components. Each of these fulfills a vital function. The six functions are:

- To get the audience's attention

- To introduce yourself (if necessary)

- To announce the topic

- To justify the topic

- To establish your credibility

- To give the audience a preview statement

It is imperative to **grab the audience's attention** as the speech begins; this may be done in a variety of ways. One way is to provide shocking statistics. Suppose a social work major's speech topic was about teen pregnancy rates. A statement such as: "This year alone more than 1,000,000 teen girls in the United States will become pregnant. Of that 1,000,000, 95% are unintentional and one-half are 17 years old or younger." Also realize that you will need to cite a source for such information.

Another way to get the audience's attention is to use a narrative. If using the teen pregnancy topic, it might be wise to tell a very brief story noting the effects of teen pregnancy on specific individuals.

Also, questions or a series of questions, either real or rhetorical, cognitively engage the audience.

Another suggestion for grabbing the audience's attention is, depending on the topic, for the speaker to share a famous or profound quote as long as it matches the topic, or if appropriate to the topic, a joke or brief funny story. A word of caution—never joke about a serious and/or sad story or topic.

The second thing to do, if the audience is unfamiliar, is to **introduce yourself**.

Third, is to clearly **state the topic**. Do not keep the audience uninformed about your issue. For example, the speech on teen pregnancy might have a topic statement such as: "Today I am going to talk to you about the problem of teen pregnancy."

After introducing the topic, provide a statement or two to **justify** its importance. This is easily done by: "Teen pregnancy has an impact upon millions of mothers, children, our school systems, and our economy."

Next, ask yourself, "Where do I get the authority to speak on an important topic?" Establishing your **credibility** on the topic can be done in two ways: (1) By personal experience and/or (2) by revealing credible research. For example: "I have first-hand knowledge of teen pregnancy because I have a cousin currently in that situation, and I have thoroughly researched the topic."

Finally, make it easy for both you and the audience to know what is going to occur in the speech by providing a **preview statement** of your main points. Using our present topic, a good preview statement would be: "Today I am going to tell you the problems with teen pregnancy, then I will cover the causes, and finally I will offer several solutions to combat teen pregnancy."

The best speeches are simple to understand. Clearly letting the audience know what, why, and how you will present the material is imperative for a good speech.

Speech Conclusion

The conclusion is the last component of the speech and needs to be as carefully crafted as the other two speech parts. Remember, it is the last thing the audience will hear the speaker say.

When beginning the conclusion, **summarize** what was covered in the speech body, highlighting only the most important factors. After the summary, end the speech with a few words. These are **concluding remarks**. Here is an excellent chance to give your opinion, even in an informative speech. Finally, "end with a bang" by knowing exactly how you will finish your speech. End clearly and concisely. Do not end your speech by saying "that's it."

If the speech is persuasive in nature, this is where you make strong and compelling statements. If you want the audience to do something, it is where you give a call for action.

Transitions

Transitions are tools that let both the speaker and the audience know where you have been in the speech and where you are going by linking information together (Osborne & Osborne, 1994). Think of words that begin with the root word "trans-." Transport, transfer, transcribe, transmission, Trans-Atlantic, transmit, and transform. All these words show change, a shift in direction.

Transitions are imperative when leaving the introduction. For example, your preview statement, which is the last thing done in the introduction, might be "Today, I am going to discuss the causes of teen drug use and then the effects." The transition could simply be: "First, let's look at the cause of teen drug use."

You will also need a transition between main points. As you end the first main point (the cause), a statement might be, "Now that I have discussed the causes of teen drug use, let's delve into the effects of that use." This simple sentence lets the audience, and you, know that a shift is being made.

The other place a transition is required is when leaving the speech body; somehow, the audience needs to be alerted that the speech is nearing its end. After finishing the above-mentioned main points, a speaker might say something as simple as, "In conclusion" or might be more creative and declare: "Today I have discussed teen drug use causes and effects, and what can we conclude?"

Transitions are very important and should be used with regularity. Once the speech topic is selected and researched and the speech is logically organized with appropriate arguments, reasoning, and transitions, it is time to focus on delivering the presentation.

Communication Apprehension

Speech anxiety, formally known as communication apprehension, is a natural aspect of public speaking. Everyone has some apprehension, but on varying levels. Even people who like to speak still get nervous. Anxiety can be reduced and/or controlled by not procrastinating, by being organized, and by practicing the delivery of the speech. Also, speakers should not let the negative voice inside them, or spoken by others, cause them to doubt their ability. Everyone has the ability to properly deliver a speech. If anxiety is a concern, speakers cannot only prepare and practice but also use positive visualization for internal support by imagining giving a successful presentation. A self-fulfilling prophecy can be an aid, not a hindrance.

Speech Delivery

Delivery involves how you speak the words and how you convey the nonverbal aspects of communicating to an audience.

There are four primary delivery styles:

- Manuscript

- Memorizing

- Impromptu

- Extemporaneous

In **manuscript** style, the speech is written out word for word and read to the audience. This method is discouraged and in most public speaking classes not allowed. Reading sounds like reading; only professionals can use this style. Additionally, it is difficult to make good eye contact with the audience, which is imperative for a speech, while reading.

The second style is **memorizing** the speech. This is also discouraged because memory lapses can cause the speech to be a failure.

Impromptu delivery style is the most difficult delivery style for most people. In this style, the speaker is given a topic and a very brief, if any, time period of preparation. This does occur in some classroom settings when a professor asks for someone to defend or to refute a position.

Extemporaneous speaking occurs when the speaker carefully crafts, works off an outline, and practices the speech. This is the preferred method of speech delivery. Obviously there will be some memorization in extemporaneous style, but familiarity is different from memorizing word for word.

A note about extemporaneous delivery: Do not feel as if you have to use the same words each time you practice or formally deliver the speech. A professor may give the same lecture to several different sections; the words will not be exactly the same for each, but the content will be.

A final note about delivery: Lucas (2004) notes that "Good delivery does not call attention to itself" (p. 294). A magnificent delivery may call attention away from the importance of the topic. Speech delivery should have some attributes of conversation but be more formal and more energetic. Different topics and audiences require different delivery styles. A politician wanting votes is in a different situation than a friend delivering a eulogy at a funeral. Carefully assess the topic, audience, and context.

Eye Contact

Speakers usually glance at well-organized notes, but **eye contact** with the audience is imperative for success. Do not focus on one or two people, but scan the entire audience in a natural manner. In a normal classroom setting, say 25 to 35 students, you should be able to make sustained eye contact at least once with each person in the room.

Voice

The speaker's **voice** is the medium by which he or she delivers the speech message. Rate, pitch, volume, and vocal inferences are all components of voice.

The **rate** is how fast or slowly the speech is delivered. The average rate in the United States is 125–150 words per minute (Lucas, 2004). Sometimes, due to nervousness, people have the tendency to speak faster when standing in front of an audience. If you think this might be a problem, you might want to draw "slow down" or "stop" signs on your outline as a mental aid.

The **pitch** is voice tone, and most people have a natural rise and fall in tone. Try to avoid a monotone drone, but also be sure to sound natural.

Volume is the loudness of your voice. It is essential that every audience member be able to hear the speaker. Some people, especially those who are naturally shy, speak too softly; this is maddening for an audience. Fill the room with your voice, but do not shout at the audience members.

Saying "uh," "er," "hmm," and "duh" are all **vocal interferences**. To some extent they are natural and most everyone says them. But too many will distract and bore the audience. Being prepared and practiced should help reduce these sometimes annoying inflections.

Posture, Appearance, and Hand Gestures

How you present your body torso to the audience is posture. Stand up straight; do not lean on a table, chair, or podium. It is alright to walk around a bit during a presentation, but be cautious not to simply pace. Ask your professor how this will be evaluated.

Hand gestures are motions used to emphasize or to draw attention to certain aspects of the speech. Never put your hands in your pockets. Hands can be used to hold notes or some visual aid material. Hand gestures should accentuate important material but always appear as natural.

Appearance is the overall look the speaker presents in front of the audience, including dress, neatness, and personal grooming. How should you dress? First, discuss expectations with your professor. If the professor has no guidelines, you should dress neatly, appearing clean and wearing appropriate attire. Avoid being sloppy. Hair should be neatly groomed with no headwear, and, of course, personal hygiene is a factor. Also avoid wearing distracting attire such as gaudy necklaces, bracelets, rings, etc. Many students will play with these items during the delivery of their speech, which is distracting to the audience. Realize that these nonverbal concepts make an impact on how the audience sees you and your topic.

Visual Aids

Some speeches require **visual aids**, and your professor may have requirements. As always, ask for clarification. Visual aids are anything presented in a form that the speaker can see to supplement the information the listener hears (Hamilton, 2005). Possible visual aid material includes charts and graphs.

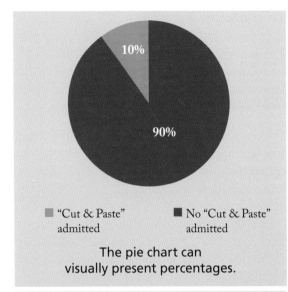

The pie chart can
visually present percentages.

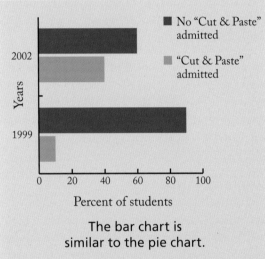

The bar chart is
similar to the pie chart.

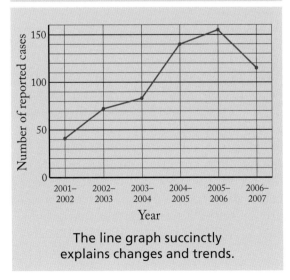

The line graph succinctly
explains changes and trends.

Figure 5-1. **Visual Aids Describing
Plagiarism on Campus**

Charts and **graphs**, similar to those shown in Figure 5-1, are tools that present complex data in a condensed manner. They are a valuable aid in detailing trends or portions of information, especially in statistics.

Delivery Methods

PowerPoint is a Microsoft Corporation software package that is popular today for both professors and students. As a visual aid, PowerPoint can present images, main points, and ideas in a colorful and pleasing manner. Two notes of caution: (1) Do not use PowerPoint slides as giant note cards and (2) you must still maintain eye contact with your audience. The slides are not your speech, but an aid to you. Do not merely read from the slides; supplement the speech by using bullet points on the slides. If you use PowerPoint or any other presentation software, ensure that you can still make eye contact with the audience and that equipment and room layout do not hinder this. Use the computer monitor to view your slides, and do not read from the screen as in most circumstances that means your back is turned to the audience.

Transparencies or materials displayed on document cameras are usually either drawn or photocopied materials highlighting important aspects of your speech. Prior to PowerPoint, transparencies were quite popular. Today document cameras are commonly used to project materials. As with all visual aids, slides and other projected materials should be neat, used solely as an aid, and presented such that all audience members can see them.

Models are used to present objects. Models may be smaller than what they represent, such as a physics major using a model airplane in explaining how a real airplane uses lift to take off, or they may be larger than the actual object, such as when a biology major uses a model to explain how the human eye functions.

Objects are tangible things used to assist in explaining material. Suppose a KSU club hockey player was delivering a speech about playing hockey and wanted to demonstrate all the equipment. Those pieces of equipment would be excellent visual aids to assist in delivering the speech.

Delivering a Group Presentation

In your college career it is likely that you will be assigned to a group to develop a project. In some cases, your professor will want your group to present this project to the class. Many times, groups of students do not consider transitioning between speakers. Further, group presentations have unique challenges in that different people have different speaking styles. The following are a couple of options for presenting group presentations.

Moderator Approach

Suppose a group moderator, Claire, wants to set up the situation so the audience will be able to easily understand the topic. Her group has researched the topic, "Has man caused global warming/climate change?" Claire opens with:

"We have all heard much about the debate about whether human activity is causing harm to our climate, and subsequently our planet. Today, our group will present evidence on both sides of the debate. First, Christine will present known data on Earth's temperatures and carbon emissions. Then, Jake will present evidence that human activity is causing temperatures to rise. Next, Heather will provide evidence that the change is natural and reasonable. Finally, Ryan will deliver what our group thinks about the issue. So, let's begin with Christine."

An easy way to transition between speakers would be for Christine to finish her report and then say: "Now, Jake is going to present another point of view." This serves as both a transition and a preview of the next speaker.

Bookend Approach

The bookend method can be approached in a similar fashion as the moderator approach, but in this method the first speaker is also the last speaker and presents the conclusion. This gives a nice sense of closure to the presentation. Transitions between speakers are, of course, necessary in this approach as well.

There are various other methods, such as panel or roundtable approach, to use in making a group presentation. Whatever the method, groups should schedule time to practice together in private and ensure smooth transitions. Say a group of five students is giving a presentation. The group should not view the presentation as five small speeches, but as one presentation with five speakers. Practice is essential for success.

Final Matters

Public speaking is one of the oldest art forms on Earth; it can be a pleasant and powerful manner of delivering a message. To succeed, you must prepare, organize, and practice.

Prepare

Preparing to speak is deciding on the topic by analyzing the audience and its expectation, and it is making a schedule to break down the information into sections.

Organize

To **organize** the speech means deciding how to get the main points across, researching those points, and creating the three-section speech.

Practice

Practice is going over the speech several times, standing in front of a mirror and/or delivering the speech to family members or roommates.

By following the prepare, organize, and practice method, or POP, you are more likely to give a successful speech.

Summary

Communication takes place inside and outside of the classroom; some modes are more obvious than others. Be willing to participate in classroom and group discussions, be aware of the messages you are communicating through nonverbal communication, and take advantage of the opportunities to develop and hone speech communication skills. Verbal communication skills are valued, even required, by many employers. Perhaps more importantly, throughout history, the ability both to speak in public and to evaluate what others say has been important. As members of a free society, it is our obligation to be **good consumers of information**. It is imperative to plan in advance for a classroom presentation. The purpose of the speech must be clear and the topic appropriate. The information in the speech needs to come from reliable sources, have supporting material, and be logical in nature. It is important to break the speech into three distinct parts, with transitions throughout. Some topics require visual aids. Finally, a pleasing delivery helps both the speaker and the audience.

References

Aguilar-Roca, N., Williams, A., Warrior, R., & O'Dowd, D. K. (2009). Two minute training in class significantly increases the use of professional formatting in student to faculty email correspondence. *International Journal for the Scholarship of Teaching and Learning, 3*(1), 1–15.

Argument. (n.d.). *Dictionary.com Unabridged* (v 1.1). Retrieved from http://dictionary.reference.com/browse/ethics

Dallimore, E. J., Hertenstein, J. H., & Platt, M. B. (2008). Using discussion pedagogy to enhance oral written communication skills. *College Teaching, 56*(3), 163–172.

Dobkin, B., & Pace, R. (2003). *Communication in a changing world.* New York: McGraw-Hill Publishing.

Ethics. (n.d.). *Dictionary.com Unabridged* (v 1.1). Retrieved from http://dictionary.reference.com/browse/ethics

Hamilton, C. (2005). *Communicating for results: A guide for business and the professions.* New York: Wadsworth Publishing.

Institutions map. (2007, January 12). *Colleges & Universities.* Retrieved from http://www.usg.edu/inst/map.phtml

Lucas, S. (2004). *The art of public speaking.* New York: McGraw-Hill Publishing.

McKerrow, R., Gronbeck, B., Ehninger, D., & Monroe, A. (2003). *Principles and types of public speaking.* Boston: Allyn &. Bacon.

Osborne, M., & Osborne, S. (1994). *Public speaking* (3rd ed.). Boston: Houghton Mifflin Company.

Peterson, M.L. (2010). *More than words: The power of nonverbal communication.* Madrid: Editorial Aresta S.C.

Rosen, L. D., Lim, A. F., Carrier, M., & Cheever, N. A. (2011). An empirical examination of the educational impact of text messaged-induced task switching in the classroom: Educational implications and strategies to enhance learning. *Psicologia Educativa, 17*(2), 163–177.

Statistics. (n.d.). *Dictionary.com Unabridged* (v 1.1). Retrieved from http://dictionary.reference.com/browse/statistics

The author would like to acknowledge and offer gratitude to Dr. Danielle Williams for her contributions to this chapter.

Critical Thinking Questions

1. What do you think students fear most about public speaking?

2. How could a sensitive topic, such as sexually transmitted diseases, be appropriately addressed as a topic? What would be some topics that are taboo?

3. Which of the three speech parts is most important, and why?

4. List four speech body organizational designs, choose a topic for each, and explain how you would elaborate that topic in your speech.

5. When are visual aids needed? When not?

Name _____ Date _____

1. What do you hope to accomplish in your speech?

2. What is your topic?

3. If you have apprehensions about delivering your speech, list them here.

4. Choose which organizational design(s) you will use in the speech body and list your main points.

5. What sources will you present?

6. Introduction
   a. How will you get the audience's attention?

   b. What is the topic's justification?

c. How will you establish your credibility?

d. Write a preview statement in one sentence.

e. Write out the transition to the body.

f. List the main points.

- Write out the first main point one in a single sentence.

- Note the subpoints in sentence form for this main point.

- Write out main point two.

- Note the subpoints in sentence form for each for this main point.

- Write out main point three.

- Write out the subpoints. (If you have another main point, list it as above.)

- Write out the transition to the conclusion.

7. Conclusion

    a.   Summarize the speech body.

    b.   What are your concluding remarks?

8. How will you finish strongly?

9. If using visual aids, what will they be and where in the speech will they be used?

LIFE SKILLS

CHAPTER 6

Motivation for Student Success

HILLARY HETTINGER STEINER, Ph.D.

Chapter Goals

- Recognize reasons for attending college

- Define and describe characteristics of intrinsic and extrinsic motivation

- Describe Maslow's Hierarchy of Needs

- Describe and apply the expectancy-value theory of motivation

- Recognize how students' attributions influence motivation

- Demonstrate elements of goal setting and goal orientation

- Explain the relationship between motivation, goals, and self-regulation

Chapter Overview

Dr. Smith's students have just received their graded tests and are talking with each other about the results. "I knew I wouldn't do well. I went to that concert last night instead of studying," says one. "I'm happy with my grade. I studied hard for this test so I deserve this A," says another. "I've never been good at her tests," shrugs a third student. "I don't know why they make us take all these GenEd classes anyway." Gather a group of students together to talk about their classes and you will likely hear a wide variety of statements like these. These statements all reflect student *motivation*, which is an important aspect of student success and influences many of the decisions college students make.

[handwritten annotation: explanation of why we do things]

[handwritten annotation: extrinsic= external stimulus- earn a reward/avoid punishment]

You might think of motivation as the driving force that urges you to put forth your best effort in a class, but it can also include how you react to successes and failures, the value you place on getting an education, and your confidence in your abilities. Because these aspects of motivation are tied to the goals we set for ourselves and the choices we make, it is necessary to understand how they influence us. This chapter will challenge you to take a careful look at how your own motivation is impacting your college achievement. Understanding the relationship between the various aspects of motivation and putting the ideas of this chapter into practice is essential to student success.

Introduction

> "People who are unable to motivate themselves must be content with mediocrity, no matter how impressive their other talents."
>
> —Andrew Carnegie

Many students complain that they lack motivation. What they really mean is that they lack *academic* motivation. In actuality, everyone is motivated to do *something*. The key for college students is developing the motivation to do what it takes to succeed in college. Ask any successful person what propelled them toward success, and one likely answer may be knowing what he wanted, having a desire to achieve, and

then setting goals to that resolve. This chapter will introduce you to several important aspects of student motivation, including the extrinsic/ intrinsic distinction, expectancy-value theory, Maslow's hierarchy of needs, and attribution theory. We will also discuss the relationship of motivation to your goals and goal orientation.

Intrinsic and Extrinsic Motivation

To be successful in college, it is important to be aware of why you are attending college. If you are attending for reasons other than your own, you probably will not be as motivated to graduate. While you might still succeed, success will be much more difficult because your motivation is coming from elsewhere—perhaps your parents, grandparents, or a spouse—rather than coming from within. Even if your primary motivation to succeed is internal, you may feel external pressures too, such as maintaining a scholarship, balancing your involvement in campus organizations, or keeping a part-time job. Students who maintain that inner drive to succeed in school despite all those external demands are usually the most successful.

In general, explanations regarding the type or source(s) of motivation can be categorized as either *extrinsic* (outside the person) or *intrinsic* (inside the person). Extrinsic motivations are motivational elements that come from outside stimuli. Extrinsic rewards can be in the form of material things, privileges, recognition, trophies, praise, or friendship. These are public ways of saying "good job." Extrinsic rewards are not necessarily unfavorable. In fact, basic learning theory teaches that one way we learn is by receiving incentives for positive behaviors. Striving for that A (which is an extrinsic reward) can be powerfully motivating. However, truly motivated people often have intrinsic motivation as well. Intrinsic motivation comes from within and is best observed when you are doing something you love. Many writers find writing a difficult process, but they do it anyway because it is

If intrinsically motivated, external motivation can be detrimental

personally rewarding. Many athletes describe the feeling of being "in the zone" when they are completely focused and performing at their best, even while pushing their bodies to the physical limit. Intrinsic motivation is what keeps these individuals going even when the going is tough. Often, intrinsic motivation is tied to (Daly, 2008):

- A perceived skill or competence in a given area

- An ability to take ownership, to be self-directing or autonomous

- The likelihood that you can connect or relate a specific situation to something of value

In other words, you are more likely to be intrinsically motivated to complete an assignment when you know you will do well, when you have some control over the assignment, and when the assignment has some value for you.

Are you in college because you want to be here? Have you set goals that will help you succeed while you are here? How do you recognize the intrinsic motivation that will truly make a difference? It all begins with *you*, knowing who you are and applying that understanding to selecting a major and ultimately a career. Completing Exercise 6-4 "Understanding You" at the end of this chapter may be beneficial in this effort and in understanding the relationship between intrinsic motivation and success.

Intrinsic - more effective

Self-Efficacy and the Expectancy–Value Theory of Motivation

At the heart of our intrinsic and extrinsic motivations are two important factors: our expectations of success and the value that success has for us. *Expectancy–value theory* states that we are motivated to do things that we think we will do well and that have some kind of value for us (Wigfield & Eccles, 2000). Reread the student conversations above and you will see how both of these things have an impact on motivation. If you predict you will get an A in a course, and an A gets you closer to your goal of graduating with honors, you will be motivated to do the coursework. You *expect* success, and you *value* the reward you will receive. Remember, though, that a grade is an extrinsic reward. If you also love the subject and the professor's teaching style, then you are receiving intrinsic rewards too, which increases the value the course has for you even more. What about the student who does not see the value in the course and does not think he will do well? Low value and low expectancy will result in low motivation for the course.

What is your favorite sport to play? Chances are you are probably pretty good at that sport. You expect to succeed when you play that sport, which is very motivating. Another term for this *expectancy* piece of motivation is *self-efficacy*. Your self-efficacy is your perceived competence in an area (Bandura, 1997). In other words, it is the confidence level with which you approach a task. Self-efficacy is domain-specific, that is, it is different for different tasks and subject areas. A math major may have high self-efficacy for solving calculus problems but low self-efficacy for writing poetry. A volleyball player may have high self-efficacy for playing volleyball but low self-efficacy for playing tennis.

Want to increase your academic motivation? Celebrate the small victories that lead you toward your goal, and pat yourself on the back when your hard work pays off. Identify the aspects of a course where you experience success and focus on those. This will increase your self-efficacy, and in turn, your motivation. Try also to find something of value in every course you take. Perhaps the course has extrinsic value for you—it is necessary to get into the major of your choice. Or perhaps it has intrinsic value—you really love the online debates you have been having with your professor and classmates. Increasing your expectation of success and the value it holds will increase your motivation.

Maslow's Hierarchy of Needs

What if other, "personal" distractions are impacting your motivation? One of the most influential writers in the area of motivation, Abraham Maslow, developed a hierarchy of human needs that describes basic human motivations (Maslow, 1971). He proposed that as humans we are unable to meet our higher-level needs until our lower-level, survival-based needs are met. In other words, we do not have the luxury of worrying about our grades if we

are hungry, lonely, or in physical danger. Once we meet the needs of a lower level, we are able to focus on the next level of needs. Trying to study in an un-airconditioned apartment during a heat wave just does not work well. Our bodies must focus on this lower-level need—trying to stay cool—before we can focus on trying to learn. This theory has implications for college students who are struggling financially, emotionally, or socially, as focusing on learning becomes much more difficult when these lower-level needs have not been met.

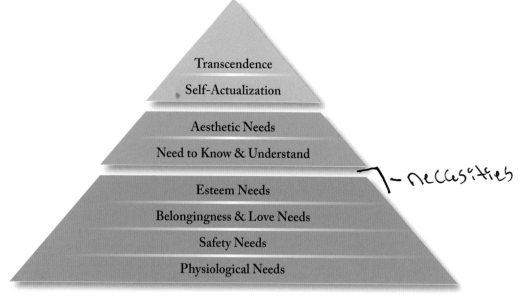

— neccesities

Figure 6-1. Maslow's Hierarchy of Needs

If we don't meet these needs, we won't get anything out of them

The first four levels of Maslow's hierarchy are called *deficiency needs*, and include:

1. **Physiological Needs**: Hunger, thirst, bodily comforts, etc.

2. **Safety/Security Needs**: Feeling safe and out of danger. *having order, stability*

3. **Belongingness and Love Needs**: Affiliating with others, being accepted. *more than us*

4. **Esteem Needs**: To achieve, feel competent, gain approval and recognition.

According to Maslow, a person is ready to act upon the next set, the *growth needs*, if the deficiency needs have been met. KSU has various campus resources available to make sure students' basic deficiency needs are met, such as Dining Services and a food bank for physiological needs, the Office of Student Success Services and numerous student organizations for social needs, Counseling and Psychological Services for mental well-being, and KSU Police for safety needs. The Student Financial Aid office also offers emergency loans to students whose basic needs are not being met by other sources. All of these are examples of resources that can assist students in moving beyond deficiency needs.

Maslow's original hierarchy chart included only one growth need—self-actualization. According to Maslow, self-actualized people 1) are problem-focused; 2) have an appreciation of life; 3) are concerned for personal development; and 4) engage in "mountain top" experiences. These are people who have reached optimal development in life. Later, Maslow added other growth needs that come before the self-actualization need:

5. **Cognitive Needs**: The need to know, to understand, and explore.

6. **Aesthetic Needs**: The need for symmetry, order, and beauty.

and a final need that comes after **self-actualization** (need #7):

7. **Transcendence**: To connect to something beyond the ego or to help others find self-fulfillment and realize their potential. Maslow acknowledged that very few people will ever reach this highest stage.

As an individual becomes more self-actualized and transcendent, he or she becomes better able to operate, function, and achieve in diverse situations and circumstances (Maslow & Lowery, 1998; Maslow, 1971). Moving beyond deficiency needs frees the mind to focus on cognitive needs, which ultimately leads to academic success.

Attributions and Learned Helplessness

Recall again the above student conversation about test grades. Did you notice that the students all gave reasons for the grades they received? One said that her grade reflected her choice of a concert over studying. Another said she got a good grade because she studied hard. And another blamed the professor, implying the tests were difficult to pass no matter how much effort was involved. The reasons that the students shared are called *attributions*, and because they come from the individual's point of view, they are not always accurate (Weiner, 1985). Are the professor's tests indeed unfair? Perhaps, but more likely the third student is making a faulty attribution. In fact, some students do this habitually, explaining away their failures as being out of their control.

When you experience something—for example, you take a shot at the free throw line on the basketball court—several mental processes occur immediately afterward. First, your mind labels that experience as a success or a failure. Likely, if you made the basket, it is a success; if not, it is a failure. Second, your mind tries to find a *reason* why you succeeded or failed. "I made the basket? It must be the result of all that practice." "I didn't make it? It is because the opposing team's fans distracted me with all that noise." These are attributions. Sometimes our attributions are correct, but other times they just reflect our need to protect ourselves psychologically. The same thing happens when students receive feedback in the form of grades, praise, or criticism. Some students will attribute their success to hard work; others will attribute it to an easy test. Some students will attribute their failure to their own flawed study habits; others will attribute it to a tough professor. As you might imagine, students who continually attribute successes and failures to forces outside their control have lower motivation. In fact, students who feel like they fail no matter what they do will eventually quit trying, a state of mind psychologists call *learned helplessness* (Dweck, 1975).

To prevent this from happening, become aware of your attributions. Be honest with yourself about why you think you failed that test or did so well on that paper. Ask for a friend's opinion of the situation to make sure you are seeing things clearly. And remember to congratulate yourself when your successes are the results of your own individual efforts.

Goals

A final important aspect of motivation is *goal-setting*. You have likely heard many times over about the importance of having goals. But do you know *why* goals are important? Do you know *what kind* of goals lead to success? And do you know *how* to put these goals into place? This section will assist you in understanding your academic goals and how they play a part in your motivation.

Goals can be categorized as short-term or long-term, and both are important. Long-term goals are necessary for defining your values and beliefs. Every college student should have a long-term goal in mind, whether it is achieving a degree in four years, being accepted to graduate school, or embarking on a fulfilling career. But goal-setting cannot stop there. Long-term goals can be intimidating and not as motivating because the focus is so far in the future. Short-term goals, on the other hand, help provide manageable steps to reaching long-term goals. They are less intimidating and aid in marking your progress toward your ultimate goal. Remember, goals will be most beneficial if they are SMART: Specific, Measurable, Achievable, Relevant, and Timed (Douglass, 1998, p. 60).

The goals that we set for ourselves are intimately related to our *goal orientations* (Schunk, Pintrich, & Meese, 2008). Some students worry excessively about how their grades compare to others in the class. This is an example of a *performance goal orientation*. Students who have performance goals focus on how they appear to others. They are motivated primarily by extrinsic rewards, and will often work hard only if the assignment is graded. These students may even be tempted to cheat in order to get a good grade. Other students are content to focus on their work without worrying what others think. Their primary goal is to learn. Psychologists say these students have a *mastery goal orientation*. Can you guess which goal orientation is best? Certainly, having a mastery goal orientation, which reflects intrinsic motivation, is preferable, but like extrinsic motivation, performance goals are not all bad. Competition is powerfully motivating for some people and may lead to higher achievement. Performance goals become dysfunctional, though, when they cause students to cut corners, cheat, or focus solely on the outcome of grades at the expense of true learning.

What are your short-term and long-term goals? Do you have a mastery or performance orientation? Take the time during this first year of college to reflect on your beliefs and determine a set of goals that will direct your achievement. Remember that flexibility is important; be willing to change your plans if necessary. Rarely do you set goals and follow through to completion without any problems. You might change your major, withdraw from a class, or experience unexpected setbacks. If this happens, reassess your plan for reaching your goal and revise it or make a new goal. There is nothing wrong with changing your goals if you make a mistake or decide to change your plans.

Successful College Students

First-year students from every college and university enter higher education with similar fears, concerns, energy, excitement, and enthusiasm. However, perhaps one differentiator of students who do and do not succeed, is being motivated enough to practice the concepts taught here. The following is a list of practical questions associated with high academic achievement and is an excellent checklist to help spark the motivation necessary for student success. Ask yourself the following questions:

- Do you have a written list of important goals that define your personal success?

- How do the goals that you have set align with your personal values?

- Do the goals reinforce or affirm your demonstrated personal strengths?

SMART

- Are you able to relate your current activities or goals to things that have short-term and/or long-term value to you?

- How invested are you in your current goals or activities? Have you set them, or has someone else set them?

- Do you believe you have the ability to do present activities or obtain future goals?

- Does the satisfaction of achieving goals seem to be too far in the future?

- Do your present activities relate to your goals?

- Do your seemingly important goals conflict with present activities?

- Are your extrinsic incentives low?

- Do your personal problems interfere with present activities?

(Valdosta State University, 2006)

Successful students tend to possess the following characteristics (Braden, 2005):

- **They have a definite reason for attending college.** Are you here because of your parents? Are you here because college is a ticket to a trade? Complete the "Why Are You Here" exercise at the end of this chapter, and think about your reasons for attending college.

- **They have selected a vocation and are pursuing this course.** Do not panic if you have not yet chosen a career. Spend this first year trying out several courses in a variety of fields and exploring general education requirements.

- **They realize the need for understanding the material in each class and envision the value of it.** Successful students do not study just to pass a test. Their goal is to learn the subject matter, not just memorize the information.

- **They have a desire to succeed**. They are internally motivated, self-directed, and intentional in their efforts.

- **They have the will to succeed**. Quitting is not an option, and they develop this will by accomplishing short-term goals.

- **They have developed good study skills.** They make efficient use of their time and their mind. They understand that study skills are learned, and they become independent learners.

- **They know they must set priorities.** They realize the time to learn is now and make studying a priority.

Ultimately, successful students are students who develop into *self-regulated learners* (Zimmerman & Schunk, 2008). Self-regulated learners have the skills for success and the motivation to put those skills into action. They do not need outside forces to motivate them; instead, their motivation is within their control. The college environment for learning is relatively unstructured and requires that you develop personal discipline and self-motivation. But to do so, you must be self-aware, have your basic needs met, know your potential, aspire to greatness, and set goals for your success. The synergy of these is the foundation for the motivation you need to progress academically, personally, and professionally. By understanding the relationship among the various aspects of motivation, goal setting, and achievement you are able to lay the groundwork for the exciting path your college career will take.

Popular Goal Quotes to Remember

Goals determine what you're going to be.

—Julius Erving

A goal properly set is halfway reached.

—Zig Ziglar

If you want to accomplish the goals of your life, you have to begin with the spirit.

—Oprah Winfrey

Goals help you channel your energy into action.

—Les Brown

What you get by achieving your goals is just as important as what you become by achieving your goals.

—Zig Ziglar

Goals that are not written down are just wishes.

—Anonymous

Summary

This chapter provided information on various aspects of student motivation. Fundamentally, motivation is either extrinsic—stemming from outside sources—or intrinsic—developed from within. Our motivation to achieve is affected by how well we expect we will do as well as how much we value the outcome. Our motivation is also heavily influenced by our needs as human beings and by the attributions we make regarding our successes and failures. Finally, our goals and goal orientations help focus our motivation toward a specific end. Understanding and improving these aspects of motivation are crucial to becoming a self-regulated college achiever.

References

Bandura, A. (1997). *Self-efficacy: The exercise of control*. New York: W.H. Freeman.

Braden, S., Matthews, K., & Mixson-Brookshire, D. (Eds.). (2005). *Knowledge, success, understanding: A text for the first-year experience* (129–137). Dubuque, Iowa: Kendall/Hunt Publishing Company.

Daly, J. A. (2008). Motivation and goal setting: Dancing to your own beat. In S. Piscitelli (Ed.), Rhythms of college success: A Journey of discovery, change, and mastery (pp. 24–45). Upper Saddle River, New Jersey: Pearson Prentice Hall.

Douglass, M. (1998). *ABC time tips*. New York: McGraw-Hill.

Dweck, C. S. (1975). The role of expectations and attributions in the alleviation of learned helplessness. *Journal of Personality and Social Psychology, 31*, 674-685.

Maslow, A. (1971). *The farther reaches of human nature*. New York: The Viking Press.

Maslow, A., & Lowery, R. (Eds.). (1998). *Toward a psychology of being* (3rd ed.). New York: Wiley & Sons.

Schunk, D.H., Pintrich, P.R., & Meece, J.L. (2008). *Motivation in education: Theory, research, and applications* (3rd ed.). Columbus, OH: Merrill.

Valdosta State University. (2006). *Academic Achievement Checklist*. Retrieved April 4, 2008, from http://teach.valdosta.edu

Weiner, B. (1985). An attributional theory of achievement motivation and emotion. *Psychological Review 92* (4), 548–573.

Wigfield, A., & Eccles, J.S. (2000). Expectancy-value theory of achievement motivation. *Contemporary Educational Psychology 25*, 68–81.

Zimmerman, B.J., & Schunk, D.H. (Eds.) (2011). *Handbook of self-regulation of learning and performance*. New York, NY: Routledge.

The author would like to acknowledge and offer gratitude to Dr. Kimberly Grimes Frazier for her contribution to this chapter.

Critical Thinking Questions

1. Who are you?
2. Why are you here at KSU?
3. What are your needs?
4. What motivates you?
5. What are your short-term goals?
6. What are your long-term goals?
7. What are your academic goals?
8. What are your personal goals?
9. What are your professional goals?
10. What will you do to be a successful student at KSU?
11. What areas, academically, do you feel you have successfully mastered?
12. What areas, academically, do you feel you need assistance?

EXERCISE 6-1

Analyzing Your Own Attributions

Name _____ Date _____

List the five most recent assignments or tests for which you received a grade. Did you perceive this grade as a success or a failure? For each assignment, describe, in one sentence, why you think you received this grade. This is your "attribution." For each attribution, decide: 1) Is this caused by something within, or by external forces?, 2) Is this something that has the potential to change?, 3) Is this something that is under my control?

ASSIGNMENT OR TEST	GRADE	ATTRIBUTION
1.		
2.		
3.		
4.		
5.		

ASSIGNMENT OR TEST	SUCCESS OR FAILURE?	EXTERNAL OR INTERNAL?	STABLE (UNCHANGING) OR UNSTABLE?	CONTROLLABLE OR UNCONTROLLABLE?
1.				
2.				
3.				
4.				
5.				

Do your attributions show a pattern?

Do you feel your attributions are mostly accurate?

What improvements could you implement for more accurate attibutions?

Life Skills

Maslow's Hierarchy of Needs

Name _____ Date _____

For each of the scenarios below, decide: 1) what lower-level need is currently requiring the student's attention, and 2) what higher need is being sacrificed in order to focus on this lower need.

A. A KSU freshman, recently diagnosed with diabetes, is making changes in her usual diet, causing her to be short-tempered with her best friends.

B. A KSU freshman who was physically assaulted over the summer is afraid to go to sleep at night, making it difficult for him to concentrate in his classes the next day.

C. A very talented student gives up on writing because a classmate made fun of her poem.

D. A talented athlete decides to give up soccer, something that gives him a great deal of pride, because his girlfriend threatens to leave him if he doesn't.

EXERCISE 6-3

Motivation Scenarios

Name _____ Date _____

Based on what you have learned in this chapter, what advice would you give to each of the following students? How can they increase their motivation?

A. Claudia: "How can I be motivated to get stuff done if graduation is four years away? I'm just a freshman! I don't see the point of making some big goal towards a career when all I want to do is enjoy college right now. I'm all about instant gratification. If I don't receive a reward for something right away, I don't want to deal with it. That's just my personality and I can't change it!"

B. Damon: "My freshman year I got a 1.8 GPA. Now I'm a sophomore, I've lost my HOPE scholarship and I'm on academic probation. I just don't see the point of trying. Obviously I'm not good at college. I mean, I guess it had something to do with the fact that I partied too much, but now I know I have to get serious because I'm in danger of getting kicked out, and I really do want a college degree. It just makes me unmotivated thinking about how horrible I did last year."

C. Nathan: "I really don't know why I'm here at KSU. All I want to do is lay around, hang out with friends, and play X-Box, and you don't have to go to college to do that. I like to learn stuff if it's on my own terms, but I don't like the thought of being graded. Maybe I'll just drop out."

D. Kim: "I'm finding it hard to be interested in my classes. I don't have a major yet, and I have to get one soon. Since I don't know where I'm headed in a career, I don't really care about the classes I'm in. I like learning things if I'm interested in the subject, but it's hard to stay focused when I don't know where I'm going."

Understanding You

Name _____ Date _____

I am happiest when:

When I am alone I am usually:

My favorite food is:

A situation that causes knots in my stomach:

My #1 pet peeve is:

The one thing that people who know me well would say about me is:

What I think deeply about is:

An academic goal for this year is:

A personal goal for this year is:

A professional goal for this year is:

My favorite sight:

My favorite smell:

My favorite taste:

My favorite sound:

EXERCISE 6-5

Why Are You Here?

Name _____ Date _____

Define college and what it means to you.

List five reasons you decided to come to college.

1.

2.

3.

4.

5.

What is your top concern about attending KSU?

List three strengths that you currently have that will assist you in succeeding in college.

1.

2.

3.

CHAPTER 7

Time Management

DAVID R. THOMPSON, Ph.D.

Chapter Goals

- Understand the rhythm of the semester

- Manage multiple assignments

- Consider the Myth of Multitasking

- Use time management strategies

- Overcome procrastination

- Take responsibility for incremental progress toward goals

Chapter Overview

This chapter presents a method of evaluating and adjusting use of time that will help one focus on succeeding as a college student. "Rhythms" of college life will be introduced, the Myth of Multitasking will be presented, time management techniques will be presented, and a few tricks for successful time management for students will be spelled out. At the end of the chapter, exercises are provided to help one identify specific ways to improve time-management skills.

Introduction

Hard work is often the easy work you did not do at the proper time.

—Bernard Meltzer, *Guidance for Living*

Students already know how to meet a variety of time-related obligations and commitments: turning in assignments on time, arriving on time for theater rehearsal or athletic practice, attending classes every day, participating in student organizations or student government, and meeting friends at the local hangout to enjoy each other's company.

But university students are in a new league. First-year college students face familiar challenges in a new context. More and tougher assignments may be expected. Longer and more challenging rehearsals and practices are common. It is easy to accept a leadership role in a student organization without realizing how much time and effort it takes to coordinate more people and bigger projects than in high school. Many college students need a job—or multiple jobs—to cover monthly expenses. And college lifestyles may offer opportunities to make more friends than ever.

How can a college student do it all? There are only 24 hours in a day.

"Time is a paradox: you never seem to have enough time, yet you have all the time there is," Douglass (1998) says. "The problem is not a shortage of time but how you choose to use the time available" (p. xi). Tullier (1999) says something similar: "We can't control time; all we can control is our behavior. We can conduct ourselves in a way that makes the most of the time we're given" (p. 55).

Notice the words "choose" and "control" and "conduct ourselves." One may not be able to "do it all." Time management may be thought of as an exercise in decision making.

Alexander (1992) says, "You can only manage *yourself* in relation to time. You cannot choose *whether* to spend it, but only *how*. Once you waste time, it's gone—and it cannot be replaced.... Even within structured time you have opportunities to select *which* tasks to handle at what priorities. In exercising your discretionary choices, you begin to control your time" (pp. 5, 7).

First-year college students find themselves in an environment in which time is relatively unstructured, compared to high school or a full-time job. The element of flexibility in time use sometimes contributes to poor academic performance by students new to university life. Reis et al. "found that poor time management led to underachievement: Students who did not know how to handle unstructured time tended to be less academically successful" (as cited in Balduf, 2009, p. 288). Balduf's (2009) study found poor time management was a contributing factor to underachievement by college students, even for students who had not needed "to do much to earn the success they wanted" in high school (p. 275).

Think of time management as a form of self-control or self-discipline—the deliberate process of discretionary use of time.

Rhythm of the Semester

Much like the ecosystems studied in biology, a 15-week semester has a life of its own. The semester has periods of vibrant growth, during which students will be very busy with tests, group projects, lab assignments, and research papers. And the semester has seemingly dormant periods, during which students may be lulled into a false sense of security about how easy classes can be.

For example, a full-time student carrying a 12-credit hour course load probably takes four three-credit classes. By the end of the second week, it is likely that each professor will have asked students to complete an assignment. That is four graded assignments. Then professors tend to settle into teaching and may assign a paper or project that is due in two or three weeks. These two or three weeks may seem like a dormant period during which there is not much to do. But if one procrastinates, there may be moments of high anxiety when this chunk of assignments is due, especially if other assignments have been made in other classes in the meantime.

There is almost always a busy time near the middle of the semester, just before the final date, to withdraw from a course. Professors should provide enough graded feedback to help a student know whether or not to continue.

And, of course, there is a frenzy of assignments, tests, and major projects at the end of the semester.

By being aware of the rhythm of the semester, a student should find it easier to plan ahead, work incrementally toward due dates, and adjust to unexpected situations (such as the student—or the professor—getting sick and deadlines needing to be modified). See Figure 7-1.

Exercise 7-1: Rhythm of *My* Semester at the end of this chapter is designed to provide students a visual representation of their busiest weeks of the semester. There is one recommendation for satisfying all those deadlines: work steadily throughout the semester. Students may have two days to complete some assignments. And students may have two or three or four weeks to complete other assignments. If a student's effort matches the graph of deadlines shown in Figure 7-1, there will be plenty of time to relax some weeks. But students will put incredible stresses on mind and body to keep up with deadlines during busy weeks. So, you think ahead to avoid all-nighters and cramming. Simply make consistent, incremental progress. See Figure 7-2.

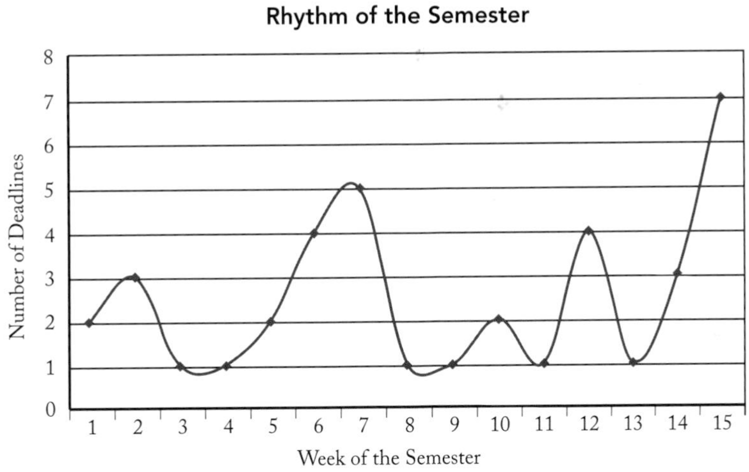

Rhythm of the Semester

Figure 7-1. Rhythm of the Semester

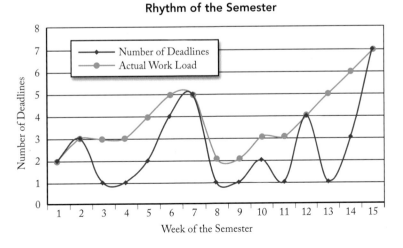

Rhythm of the Semester

Figure 7-2. Actual Work Load Compared to Number of Deadlines

Some students may decide to relax in week 3—an apparent low point. And that is fine. This is college, a place to practice responsible decision-making. But remember that decisions have consequences. And time management is an exercise in decision-making.

If a student slacks off in week 3, then week 7 will probably be a nightmare—without any sleep.

However, if a student adopts the strategy depicted by the "actual work load" line in Figure 7-2, in week 3 when there may be only one deadline, the student makes progress on the deadlines for weeks 4 and 5, as well as beginning to work on the assignments that are due during one of the busiest weeks of the semester, week 7.

Consistent effort results in better work, completed under less stressful conditions. As reported by van der Meer, Jansen, and Torenbeek (2010), first-year students surveyed in this study seem to have realistic expectations about the need to plan for completing work independently and about spending time during the week to study (p. 777). However, students had some difficulty in keeping up with their work. The first-year students in this study said future students should be advised "to start working from day one, and to work consistently throughout the semester" (p. 782). So when an assignment is made, get started!

Rhythm of Assignments

Some new college students tend to think of class-related workload as block assignments. An assignment is made; a deadline arrives. Another assignment is made; another deadline arrives. In other words, it is tempting to think of having only one active assignment at a time in each class. See Figure 7-3.

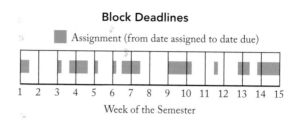

Figure 7-3. Block Deadlines

In the case of block deadlines, it may be easy to think of projects with short deadlines, such as "due tomorrow" or "due next Friday." Almost all students figure out how to satisfy teachers by completing assignments on time. But this is college. And this is a different league. Life as a student may become a little more complicated.

In college, it is quite common to have overlapping assignments. There may be multiple active assignments in one class: a paper may be due in three weeks, a homework assignment may be due the day after tomorrow, a 100-point test may be coming up in four weeks (from reading the syllabus, students know the test covers chapters 6, 9, and 11–15 of the textbook), and a major project may be due at the end of the semester—ten or twelve weeks from the day the assignment was made. See Figure 7-4 for a depiction of these overlapping assignments.

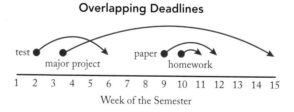

Figure 7-4. Overlapping Deadlines

This is a simple example that may demonstrate some of the deadlines for one class. If a student were to create an illustration of all the deadlines for all classes taken this semester, the depiction may look like the scene in the 1983 film *War Games* when the W.O.P.R. computer simulates all-out global thermonuclear war! Or it could look like an airline route map, like those found near the back of in-flight magazines.

Here is the point: To handle multiple active assignments with varying deadlines (from two days to fourteen weeks), students need to think ahead, make decisions about what to do and when to do it.

The Myth of Multitasking

At a college that was a laptop campus—meaning every student had a laptop computer and every classroom was wireless—many students used class time to check email, IM (instant message), update Facebook, and work on assignments for their next class. Every once in a while someone took notes related to the class in progress. When the professor asked a question, someone would quickly IM the response to the person to whom the question was directed. (By the way, this is a true story about one of the author's classes.) When challenged about whether a student was paying attention, the response usually sounded like this, "Yes. I was paying attention. And, yes. I was checking email. But that's okay because I grew up multitasking. I can do a lot of things at once."

So, one day, the professor decided to test the multitasking skills of his students by asking them to open the live chat feature of Blackboard, a course management system. He played a DVD of a film that was current and somewhat controversial and asked students to chat about their reactions to the film as they watched. He asked them to multitask.

For the first three minutes of the film, the chat room was pretty lively but not focused on the film. Mostly, students wanted to know if the professor would buy pizza or make popcorn for his students so they could enjoy the movie.

After about seven minutes, the chat room got very quiet. There was almost no activity. The professor sent a few questions and comments to the chat room to prompt responses. Nothing.

About 15 minutes into the film, the professor stopped the film and asked his students (the self-described multitasking experts) why they were not participating in the live chat. Students said, "We can't concentrate on the film and chat at the same time!"

In her *Los Angeles Times* article "We're all multitasking, but what's the cost?," Healy (2004, p. F1) says, "The term multi-tasking comes from the world of computers, where single-minded computers could devise systems flexible enough to perform several tasks at once." As digital technologies have become more pervasive, more miniaturized, and more portable, humans have tried to adapt to multitasking. Unfortunately, Healy says, "multi-tasking, which many have embraced as the key to success, is instead a formula for shoddy work, mismanaged time, rote solutions, stress, and forgetfulness."

When people try to do too much, mistakes are made. There is some pressure on college students to do well. The first semester, in particular, is an opportunity to establish oneself as a capable college student on the path to graduation and to a successful career. Effective time management—good decisions about what to do and when—involves discipline, effort, and focused thought. Yet this may be counterintuitive for students of the Millennial generation (those born after

1982) because "academic life is not the focus for Millennial students," according to Hanson, Drumheller, Mallard, McKee, and Schlegel (2011, p. 23). "Students focus more on updating their Facebook status than downloading their homework assignments, which profoundly impacts their collegiate experience" (p. 24).

Millennials multitask. According to Dr. Cora Dzubak's (2007) research article, "Multitasking: The good, the bad, and the unknown," people commonly define multitasking as "doing two or more things at the same time" (p. 1). However, researchers distinguish between "simultaneous" and "sequential" tasks. Sequential task engagement is "more characteristic of multitasking. It is the performance of multiple tasks sequentially and in quick succession," all of which requires cognitive processing and competes for limited attention.

Focused thought involves engaging a certain part of the brain. Here is a brief lesson in cognitive psychology and brain function (Dzubak, 2007, p. 4):

> It is known that the hippocampus is activated when declarative memory is used for processing context, such as information obtained from textbooks during reading or study. In contrast, a different part of the brain, the striatum, is used in the processing of procedural memory, which is used for habitual tasks and activities such as bike riding or dialing a familiar number on the telephone. The types of processing that occur in these two regions are significantly different and impact storage and retrieval. The hippocampus will sort, process, and recall information involving declarative memory. Memories in the hippocampus are easier to recall in situations different from where they were learned, whereas those stored in the striatum are closely tied to the specific situations in which they were learned. It has been found that learning with the striatum

while performing habitual or repetitive tasks leads to knowledge that cannot be generalized as well in new situations. (Poldrack as cited in Aratani, 2007) Having difficulty transferring knowledge from one situation to another is not consistent with the type of learning that we hope takes place in a college classroom and can be applied elsewhere in the future.

This means that "when learning with distractions associated with multitasking, students' brains are trying to 'wing it' by using a region, the striatum, that is not best suited for long-term memory and understanding" (Dzubak, 2007, p. 4).

According to Brazeau and Brazeau (2009), "Although multitasking has become a perceived skill in today's environment, with many data streams continually vying for our attention, a recent study published in the *Proceedings of the National Academy of Sciences* suggested that individuals who pride themselves at being proficient multitaskers in fact perform worse cognitively at the main task at hand when switching back and forth between various tasks compared with individual who multitask much less frequently" (Article 125). A similar finding has been reported by Ophir, Nass, and Wagner (2009) in their study that compared two levels of multitasking—"light" (not much) and "heavy" (very much). Their results indicated that "heavy media multitaskers are more susceptible to interference from irrelevant environmental stimuli and from irrelevant representations in memory. This led to the surprising result that heavy media multitaskers performed worse [than light media multitaskers] on a test of task-switching ability, likely due to reduced ability to filter out interference from the irrelevant task set" (Abstract).

So, if a student "studies" by reading a textbook with the television on while talking and responding to text messages on the phone while using a computer to update a Facebook account and chewing gum and checking progress on a music download while trimming fingernails, the student may be able to recall some things from the textbook, but the student probably cannot use that information to engage in critical thinking or apply that information in ways that demonstrate "higher learning."

In her article published in the *Wall Street Journal*, Shellenbarger (2004) reports on a study published in the journal *NeuroImage* that found evidence that "managing two mental tasks at once reduces the brainpower available for either task" (p. D1). Juggling tasks, such as reading this chapter while watching (or "keeping up with") a television show, takes cognitive capacity. Attention is divided. So when an individual multitasks, he or she cannot concentrate fully on one thing.

The bottom line of this research, as Shellenbarger puts it, is "a growing body of research shows one of jugglers' favorite time-saving techniques, multitasking, can actually make you less efficient and, well, stupider."

Another study, conducted by David Meyer, a psychology professor at the University of Michigan, and published in the *Journal of Experimental Psychology*, provides evidence that "people who multitask are actually less efficient than those who focus on one project at a time" (as quoted in Shellenbarger, 2004, p. D1).

In other words, a student may want to believe that multitasking enables one to work quickly, but, in reality, the work is half-fast.

Shellenbarger (2004, p. D1) states:

> Managing two mental tasks at once reduces the brainpower available for either task, according to a study published in the journal *NeuroImage*. Marcel Just of Carnegie Mellon University asked subjects to listen to sentences while comparing two rotating objects. Even though these activities engage two different parts of the brain, the resources available for processing visual input dropped 29% if the subject was trying to listen at the same time. The brain activation for listening dropped 53% if the person was trying to process visual inputs at the same time.

> "It doesn't mean you can't do several things at the same time," says Dr. Just, codirector of the university's Center for Cognitive Brain Imaging. "But we're kidding ourselves if we think we can do it without cost."

"Successful people do one thing at a time," Ziegler (2005) says. "The ability to work on one thing at a time takes *discipline*" (p. 65). And Davidson (1999) advises: "The single best way to cope with a number of different projects is to begin working on one thing until its completion, and then go on to the next project, and then the next, until you are finished" (p. 201).

Think of time management as a form of self-control or self-discipline—the deliberate process of discretionary use of time. Focus and finish.

Dzubak (2007, p. 9–10) summarizes her research findings about multitasking like this:

> Do we get better at multitasking the more we do it? The answer appears to be that we do. Many of the college freshmen of today have practiced multitasking behaviors for years and are very skilled at it. But, does this mean that they are learning more? No, it does not. Does skill in multitasking mean that we will become better thinkers or problem solvers? No, it does not. Research has shown that although some learning was occurring while multitasking, it was less flexible, more specialized, and harder to retrieve when needed. It was also difficult to transfer, generalize or extrapolate the information to a different setting. [When] information cannot be transferred or applied, it would appear to have very limited utility.

Being a successful university student, to be "higher educated," requires an ability to use what has been learned. So here is the connection between cognitive psychology and time management: When it is time to study, be determined to learn. Use the hippocampus during scheduled study sessions.

Miller (2007) reports research findings of UCLA associate professor of psychology Russ Poldrack and his colleagues. Their research involved asking research subjects in their 20s to "learn a simple classification task under two sets of circumstances: once with no distractions, and then while simultaneously counting the number of high-pitched beeps they heard through headphones" (para. 3). Their findings, according to Miller, show that the hippocampus "oversees the development of 'declarative memory'" while the "striatum governs behavioral tendencies and habits."

"Learning something new while doing stuff that requires an active response—say, updating MySpace bulletin boards—is exactly like trying to study while counting high-pitched beeps," Miller (2007, para. 7) says. "That kind of learning might enable a kid to memorize the names and dates of major Civil War battles—but be flummoxed when asked almost the same thing a different way, such as 'name the important events of 1863.' In other words, if [you] want to learn something permanently and usefully, do something very old school: Shut up, sit still, and pay attention" (para. 8).

Recall the story at the beginning of this section about the Myth of Multitasking. Students who claimed to be experts at multitasking were able to send meaningless messages about pizza and popcorn as another stimulus (the film they were to discuss) bombarded their senses. But when it came to making serious, thoughtful comments about the film in a multitasking setting, these intelligent young people came across as striatum-dominant and intellectually paralyzed.

As soon as the students watching that film said, "We can't concentrate on the film and chat at the same time!" the professor turned off the chat room, asked students to close their laptop computers, and restarted the film. After viewing the film, students engaged in a very productive, high-level discussion. They had engaged their hippocampuses, and they behaved as young scholars.

Dealing with Procrastination

Procrastination is defined as "unnecessarily delaying activities that one ultimately intends to complete, especially when done to the point of creating emotional discomfort," according to Lay and Schouwenburg (as cited in Seo, 2009, p. 911). It is easy to say, "Do not procrastinate. Do not waste time. Start working on a project as soon as an assignment is made." But it is not easy to follow that advice.

Procrastination happens. Everyone waits to begin working from time to time. It is normal and natural. But remember Alexander's (1992) words: "Once you waste time, it's gone—and it cannot be replaced" (p. 5).

During the first year in college, students may learn that procrastination cannot always be overcome with all-nighters, cramming, and emails to professors (an hour after assignment was due) begging for an extension. Some professors are unforgiving when it comes to missed deadlines. College students are accountable for meeting deadlines. Part of growing into adulthood is accepting responsibility. Some professors say it is easier to learn the hard way in college by taking a zero on a late assignment, than to learn by losing a job after graduation for failing to fulfill a client's needs in a timely manner. Life lessons are sometimes disguised as academic requirements.

Individuals may choose to learn, however, that there are ways to recognize counterproductive behaviors and to modify those behaviors to remain, or to become, successful college students.

As presented in this chapter, the "actual work load" approach (from Figure 7-2) is one method for overcoming procrastination. It enables one to maintain a reasonable lifestyle by beginning assignments early and making incremental progress as due dates approach.

Tullier (1999) wrote *The complete idiot's guide to overcoming procrastination*, which spells out 10 possible causes of procrastination (p. 44):

Fear: Fear of failure, success, or how you'll be judged.

Perfectionism: Making things more difficult and critical than they need to be.

Being overwhelmed: Finding a task so difficult or cumbersome that you don't know where or how to begin or end it.

Feeling frustrated: Having a low tolerance for the ambiguity or delayed gratification that comes with some projects.

Adrenaline rush addiction: Relying on the thrill that comes from getting something done at the last minute.

Negativity toward the task: Disliking or being uninterested in the task itself.

Rebellion: Having negative feelings toward the person who assigned the task or who will benefit from it and resenting that you have to do it.

Unrealistic view of time: Having a faulty sense of time and how much you can get done within it.

Psychological issues: Disorders such as depression or Attention Deficit Disorder, among others, make it difficult to get things done.

Physical problem: Having a physical ailment that drains your energy and makes you less likely to get things done.

This list may be used as a tool for overcoming procrastination. In moments of resistance to make progress, come back to this list of 10 possible causes of procrastination. Try to identify the cause of this particular instance of procrastination. Then ask: What are some options for finding a productive way to overcome this delay?

For example, if overwhelmed in one of those weeks when five assignments are due, ask questions such as:

- Are there any assignments that are easy, that can be completed quickly and turned in to get them off the to-do list?

- Which assignment is worth the most points? How badly are those points needed? Is this the top priority right now?

- Is there an assignment for which there is no time to focus this week, but could be completed over the weekend? If so, what are the professor's office hours? Visit the professor in person to explain the situation and ask for an extension.

According to Tullier, there are seven typical stages to overcoming procrastination (1999, p. 74):

- Acknowledge the need to change your behavior.

- Declare to yourself and to others that you're ready to change.

- Mentally prepare yourself to commit to making a change.

- Figure out how to change.

- Implement your change strategy.

- Get frustrated and accept setbacks.

- Work through the frustration and past the setbacks until a new behavior gradually replaces the old habits.

Whenever possible, try to discover systematic ways to approach challenges. Time management is a process. Once stored in the hippocampus for easy retrieval in a variety of situations, knowledge of time management strategies and methods may be applied to overcoming procrastination, dealing with multiple overlapping deadlines, and living a relatively balanced life.

Time Management Techniques

Time management experts seem to agree on three broad techniques: set goals, work with to-do lists, and apply time management strategies. The combination and interaction of elements of these broad techniques powers one's use of time. It takes practice to become a good time manager. There are only 24 hours in a day. Decisions regarding behaviors determine how well one invests efforts. Make the most of life as a university student by deliberately practicing the process of discretionary use of time.

Goal-Setting

Goal-setting is one key to successful time management. Olson (1997) says, goals "can help you decide among the dozens of alternative actions you face each week if not each day" (p. 14). Decision-making is a critical element of time management.

"The purpose of goals is to define a specific end result (desired outcome) and/or solve a problem (or problems), then set a course or path for achieving that end result or solving that problem," according to Ziegler (2005). "Goals provide clear focal points for action" (p. 17). In other words, once the destination is known, map out a strategy for reaching it.

Think about a plan for completing an assignment that asks for a 3–5 page paper about strategies for effective time management. What are the first questions a student might ask? Perhaps, "What is the deadline? And how many points is this paper worth?"

The assignment itself probably answers questions about deadline and point value. And the assignment should include a definition of the task, the purpose of the paper, and guidelines for research and writing.

For instance, the paper is due in two weeks. Assuming that "turn in a completed paper on the deadline" is one's destination, what path will be mapped out for satisfying this goal? Some students will read the assignment for the first time at 10:00 p.m. the night before the paper is due. Others will choose to break down the assignment into smaller tasks, such as focusing the topic, gathering research material, selecting and organizing source material, writing a draft of the paper, editing the paper (maybe more than once), and proofreading the paper. This example is designed to make it easy to identify a solution that best applies strategic time management for the purpose of improving academic performance. Avoid the breakdown, break it down.

A key to working with goals, according to Douglass (1998), is to "set SMART goals: Specific, Measureable, Achievable [or Actionable], Relevant, and Timed [or Time-Bound]" (p. 60). Davidson (1999) says something similar: "You want to attach goals—specific, action-oriented steps with timelines—to your priorities to reinforce them. Write them down" (p. 49). A little different approach is taken by Alexander (1992) who refers to goals as specific objectives, defined as: "written; measurable; expressed in results, not activities; realistic, challenging, yet attainable; and keyed to date of accomplishment" (p. 33).

Notice the words "timed," "timeline," and "keyed to date of accomplishment." Goals are met and new goals are set. Life is progressive. One thing leads to another. Meet a goal and move on. Time management helps that happen.

According to Ziegler (2005), the "benefits of setting and achieving challenging and specific goals…include: becoming more efficient; being more focused; being more productive; having more confidence; finding it easier to prioritize; and receiving recognition" (p. 18).

For students, recognition may be a good grade and a handwritten "nice work!" on an assignment. Or recognition may take other forms, such as a reputation among faculty and fellow students for being an outstanding student, inclusion of one's name on the Dean's List, induction into an academic honor society, or even acceptance of one's work for presentation at an academic conference.

In school and in careers after college, one challenge is to adjust personal goals to the goals others have set. Professors will make assignments that include certain criteria for successful completion. Those assignments will include a due date. One's intellectual development, the grade for the assignment, a final grade for the class, and graduation all depend on one's ability to complete assignments on time. Bosses will assign projects with specific deadlines. Continued employment depends on one's ability to satisfy those assignments at or before deadline. The goal-setting process will help one succeed.

When it comes to setting goals, get SMART: Specific, Measureable, Actionable, Relevant, and Time-Bound.

Working with To-Do Lists

"Planning is one of the most important elements of efficient time management," Cemaloglu and Filiz (2010) say. "Planning the use of time must be considered a basic skill of the individual who wants to be efficient in every phase and activity of life. Thus, students should determine their purposes and methods and plan their time for the short-, mid-, and long-term" (p. 6).

In his book *101 Ways to Make Every Second Count*, Bly (1999) identifies three lists he maintains to help him manage time: daily to-do list, projects to-do list, and long-term to-do list (pp. 17–18).

Daily to-do list. By making a list of items to be done each day, Bly creates an hour-by-hour schedule. He says he avoids taking on more than he can handle so he can meet every deadline. For a first-year student, an hour-by-hour schedule for the day may include classes, meals, study time, relaxation and time to socialize, work, and sleep.

Projects to-do list. For a first-year student, a projects list may include a list of assignments and projects due this semester (with deadlines noted).

Long-term to-do list. This list may include personal goals for which a specific deadline has not yet been set.

A similar technique is used by the author to try to keep his life somewhat organized. He creates a weekly to-do list that shows each day of the week. For each day, he maps out scheduled appointments (including teaching times, office hours, and personal fitness), and he lists other things that need to be done. He carries his weekly/daily list with him in his backpack.

His projects to-do list is kept on a dry-erase whiteboard on his office wall. This list shows deadlines for things like research papers, applications for faculty development opportunities, and committee work.

The author's long-term list is his "five-year plan," which he keeps at home. It is written on a big piece of grid paper. He divides the grid paper into rows that show the year and columns that show spring, summer, and fall semesters. The long-term plan shows more general goals, like "in Fall 2012: teach two classes; participate in two academic conferences; submit one research article for publication in an academic journal; begin to schedule learning communities for Fall 2013; and maintain a four-day fitness routine each week."

Specific goals do not necessarily appear on to-do lists. But things that appear on a to-do list often relate to a personal or academic goal.

A daily/weekly to-do list is used to remind one to get things done. The daily list shows how tasks are broken down into manageable parts and shows appointments, classes, and other scheduled events or tasks.

Time Management Strategies

The time management strategies presented in this chapter may be thought of as a "system." This system is simply a loose structure—a set of general principles—that may be applied to various time management challenges.

Exercise self-control and self-discipline. Effective use of time will result from following a system of discretionary use of time.

Try these ten strategies for designing a workable plan for time use:

Prioritize tasks. Once tasks have been listed, sort them into three groups. Choose a labeling system to indicate the relative importance of each task, such as: "1, 2, 3" or "A, B, C" or "!!!, **, ?" The 1s, As, or !!!s are top priority; completion of these tasks clearly relate to achieving or making substantial progress toward satisfying a goal.

Douglass (1998) defines "important activities" as those that "help you achieve your goals" (p. 124). Davidson (1999) says it this way: "Deciding what's important to you is a key to efficiently winning back your time. Once you have identified your priorities, you're far more likely to make incremental progress toward them" (p. 58).

Incremental progress is "the inchworm effect"—little by little adds up over time.

And Bly (1999) quotes Henry Ford: "Nothing is particularly hard if you divide it into small jobs" (p. 21).

Ask: What needs to be done first? Why?

- **Budget one's time.** Decide how long the task will take to complete, then work to complete the task in the allotted time. For example, if one thinks it should take 90 minutes to type today's lecture notes for all four of classes and study time has been planned between 3:30–5:00 p.m., then all one needs to do is type fast enough to complete the task at or before 5:00 p.m. If it is 4:30 and notes for only two classes are complete, type faster!

  This sounds easy, but "shifting gears" to complete tasks within a given time period takes practice.

  Also, it is helpful to identify one's "best times" for studying (Principles, n.d.; Bly, 1999, p. 25). For students, this means: Study when the mind is sharpest. Play video games or shop for groceries during the low-energy parts of the day.

- **Create an environment conducive to concentration.** Alexander (1992) says, "You accomplish more in one quiet hour what would normally take three" (p. 30).

  In the library, find a quiet corner for studying, rather than sit by the main entrance to greet friends. In a residence hall, consider using a designated study room. Get away from the noise and activity of residence hall living. Stereos, cheers from video game players, arguments among roommates, belching contests, and soccer games in the hallway are part of campus living. But even passively processing these distractions can prevent a productive study session.

  Bly (1999) recommends physically blocking out disturbances "as much as possible, whether by shutting your door, turning your desk away from passersby, letting your voice mail take your calls, posting a 'do not disturb' sign, or asking people to be quiet. Your mind can successfully tune out a great many signals if you tell it to" (p. 23).

- **Plan time to relax.** Give the brain a break. Stand up and move around. Take a few deep breaths. Maybe take a short nap. Working nonstop is not a good idea.

  Practice productive procrastination every once in awhile. But know when to get back to work!

  Also, set aside time for entertainment. Playing video games, going to a movie, hiking, visiting a museum, or making an entry in a journal, diary, or on Facebook can be time well spent. Sometimes one needs to slow down for awhile before performing again at full speed.

- **Exercise regularly.** "Exercise is essential for superior academic performance" (Strategies, n.d.). Clear the mind by moving the body. Nurture one's "self" with fitness and good nutrition.

- **Sleep.** "College students may need an average of nine to nine-and-a-half hours" of sleep each day, Davidson (1999, p. 82) says. In addition to scheduling regular hours for sleeping (and actually sleeping then), Davidson (1999) recommends the following: avoid watching television or reading after going to bed, avoid caffeine for six hours before going to bed, avoid consuming alcohol in the evening, exercise moderately several hours before sleeping, and take in a little protein, such as a protein shake or milk, before sleeping (p. 84).

- **Be flexible.** "Allow extra time for UnForeseen Obstacles (UFOs)" (Strategies, n.d.). Leave a few holes in the daily to-do list. That time may be needed for unexpected events or distractions. Ziegler (2005) says, "The number one reason why people don't achieve their goals or meet deadlines on time is because they didn't leave room for anything to go wrong" (p. 18).

- **Identify "floating tasks"** that can be done anywhere at any time. Be prepared to work on these with just a few minutes of dedicated effort, such as waiting to see a professor or while the washing machine goes through the spin cycle.

This is related to the "twofer" concept (Principles, n.d.): Study class notes while waiting for a haircut, or practice foreign language vocabulary using flash cards as the tank fills at a gas station, for example.

- **Survive crunch times.** "Self-sacrifice and denial are necessary during midterms and finals weeks. Scrap everything that's not absolutely essential for survival" (Strategies, n.d.).

- **Reward oneself for success.** Celebrate accomplishments. Davidson (1999) advises people to "set up a series of small rewards so that you're naturally reinforcing the behavior in which you've chosen to engage" (p. 60).

Crossing things off a to-do list is one small reward for accomplishing the task and for making progress toward a goal. Besides, according to Alexander (1992), crossing items off a to-do list is "mentally nourishing" (p. 28).

For a student, rewards can be things like saying "Good job!" to oneself upon completion of a three-page paper; attending a women's soccer game because a project was

turned in a day before deadline; buying a new pair of shoes to celebrate earning an "A" on a performance exam in dance class; or joining friends, tonight, to see a movie because this self-disciplined student said, last night, "No, thanks. I can't go with you now because I need to study for a big psych test. Maybe tomorrow night, okay?"

Time Management Tips and Tricks

A general search online for "time management" will retrieve links to career-related websites designed for sales professionals, business executives, and other employees. However, by Googling "time management" and restricting the search to retrieve only sites from an ".edu" domain, one finds many lists of time management tips written for college students.

For convenience, this chapter lists a few tips and tricks to help students think about ways to focus on good decision-making related to time use.

- **Continually improve time management techniques.** McGee-Cooper (1994) says, "By being curious about the times when I don't stick to my plan and exploring the reasons, I am improving my ability to stay on track" (p. 138).

- *Mobil sein ist alles.* That is German for "flexibility is everything."

- **Be proactive about instant priority changes (IPCs).** At some point in life, something will happen that causes one to put everything aside to respond to an instant priority change, a personal emergency that demands immediate, undivided attention. Examples of IPCs include: illness, accident, arrest, death in the family or the death of someone close, domestic violence, unplanned pregnancy, roommate or landlord matters, and involvement in intervention for substance abuse.

Such IPCs may involve students, or they may involve professors. Sometimes a student may need to adjust because a professor is unable to work for a while.

Everyone knows life is tough. How one adjusts to difficult moments is very important. Be proactive when something happens. Let someone know what is going on—professors, a counselor in the Counseling and Psychological Services (CPS) department, an advisor. Negotiate for adjustments to deadlines and attendance policies. But be prepared to provide evidence of involvement in a personal emergency—and not spending an extra week in Cancún. Try to let people know in advance of an absence or missed deadline.

- **Be selective.** According to Douglass (1998), "Be careful what you do, where you go, and who you're with. Some activities, places, and people help you fill your emotional fuel tank; others drain it" (p. 11).

- **Define "task" broadly.** A task may be class attendance, an appointment with a professor, a study group session, sleep, a meal, relaxation and recovery time, a date, a phone call to family members, work, shopping for groceries, individual study time, "playful exploration" (informal research) in the library or online, or designated time for updating a Facebook account. Write tasks onto your to-do list because "things that are scheduled are more likely to happen" (Douglass, p. 147).

- **Apply personality type to effective time management.** In some first-year seminars, instructors ask students to complete a personality type indicator exercise. Such an exercise will help one discover "what energizes you, how you collect information, how you make decisions, and how you project your 'self' to the people around you," according to Birgit Wassmuth, certified MBTI administrator (Personal communication, March 1, 2008).

In her book *Time Management for Unmanageable People*, McGee-Cooper (1994) says, "Most traditional time management systems include four basic steps: 1) plan, 2) prioritize, 3) schedule, and 4) follow your plan" (p. 82). But she says, "Traditional time management rules work wonderfully for some people.... Yet millions of us are divergent in nature. And for us, the traditional time management approach is frustrating, confusing, and counterproductive. The divergent person relies on intuitive knowledge, on spatial and complex relationships, and on creative approaches that can wreak havoc on an orderly, step-by-step plan" (p. 50–51).

Another perspective on personality and time management relates to flow and the autotelic personality. As reported in 2009 by Ishimura and Kodama (p. 48), "perceived lack of time is often related to reluctance to engage in life activities (Jackson, 1993)." Such reluctance may be described as non-flow, given the definition of flow "as a positive and gratifying state of consciousness with the perception of high challenges in the task at hand and sufficient personal skills to face those challenges (Csikszentmihalyi, 1990)" (p. 48).... Ishimura and Kodama (2009) continue by saying "Nakamura and Csikszentmihalyi (2002) defined the autotelic personality as spending more time in the flow state.

Autotelic people may use time management skills to allow for more flow activities and avoid nonflow [sic] activities. Also the goal directedness of autotelic people leads them to concentrate on what is happening around them and to integrate complicated information toward achieving the goal" (p. 48).

In other words, given that "time management is a self-regulatory skill that involves discerning the most efficient ways to use time," according to Macan (1994) as cited in Ishimura and Kodama (2009), it may be said that an individual with an autotelic personality would be expected to be sufficiently motivated to complete tasks in a manner that involves a high level of integrative thinking or critical thinking. Upon completion of a task, the autotelic individual would then move on to the next thing, thereby engaging in further personal growth and self-advancement (p. 48).

- **Seek simplicity.** Smallin's (2000) book, *7 Simple Steps to Unclutter Your Life*, takes a holistic approach to personal well-being. Putting oneself first does not necessarily mean one is selfish. Taking control of one's life is healthy. As Mr. Miyagi, in the film 1984 *Karate Kid* says, "Seek balance."

- **Eliminate distractions.** "Eliminate any distractions you can, and learn to ignore the rest," Douglass (1998, p. 44) says.

For example, try using the kind of hearing protection used by people who shoot at a gun range. This sound suppression device looks like headsets worn by broadcasters in the pits at NASCAR races. It does not silence the room, but it does a good job of reducing noise.

Putting on these "ear plugs" also reminds one of a Japanese custom. There is a headband called a hachimaki that workers put on when it is time to get serious and focus on the task at hand. The Japanese believe that "putting pressure on the forehead helps concentration. Japanese children wear the hachimaki… to help them study."

Psychologically, the hachimaki tells the wearer to get to work and do not think about anything else. Visually, it tells others "leave me alone; I'm working." And, it can mean "join me; we have work to do."

Summary

There are two rules for achieving anything. Rule No. 1: Get started. Rule No. 2: Keep going.

—Howard Hunt

This chapter has presented time management as an exercise in decision-making. Time ticks away no matter what. Decisions about time use are critical to accomplishing goals and being able to cross things off to-do lists. By employing a system, a strategy, for time management, you take control. By deliberately applying a process of discretionary use of time, one's efforts are more productive and efficient.

By entering college, students enter a new league. New students may be surprised by how busy the first semester or two can be. Demands on time increase because college offers a remarkable number of opportunities to grow academically and personally. It can be overwhelming. Just keep in mind—first on the list of predictors of GPA is time management; second on the list of predictors of personal success is time management, right after clearly defined goals (George, Dixon, Stansal, Gelb, & Pheri, 2008, p. 706).

As Douglass (1998, p. 129) says, "The very thought of having more to get done than you appear to have time to do can paralyze your will. Stop thinking about it and do something."

Time management comes down to this:

If it is to be, it is up to me.

—Alan Cimberg

References

Aratani, L. (2007, February 26). "Teens can multitask, but what are the costs?" *The Washington Post*, p. A01.

Balduf, M. (2009, Winter). Underachievement among college students. *Journal of Advanced Academics, 29*(2), 274–294.

Bly, R. (1999). *101 ways to make every second count: Time management tips and techniques for more success with less stress.* Franklin Lakes, New Jersey: The Career Press.

Brazeau, G. A., & Brazeau, D. A. (2009). The challenge of educating in a highly-connected and multitasking world. *American Journal of Pharmaceutical Education, 73*(7), Article 125.

Cemaloglu, N., & Filiz, S. (2010, June). The relation between time management skills and academic achievement of potential teachers. *Educational Research Quarterly, 33*(4), 3–23.

Csikszentmihalyi, M. (1990). *Flow: The psychology of optimal experience.* New York: Harper & Row.

Davidson, J. (1999). *The complete idiot's guide to managing your time.* New York: Alpha Books.

Demarest, L. (2001). *Out of time: How the sixteen types manage their time and work.* Gainesville, Florida: Center for Applications of Psychological Type, Inc.

Douglass, M. (1998). *ABC time tips.* New York: McGraw-Hill.

Dzubak, C. (2007, June 22). "Multitasking: The good, the bad, and the unknown." Synergy, Vol. 1, No. 2. Retrieved from http://atp.jsu.edu/Synergy_1/Syn_6.pdf

George, D., Dixon, S., Stansal, E., Gelb, S. L., & Pheri, T. (2008, May/June). Time diary and questionnaire assessment of factors associated with academic and personal success among university undergraduates. *Journal of American College Health, 56*(6), 706–715.

Hanson, T. L., Drumheller, K., Mallard, J., McKee, C., & Schlegel, P. (2011). Cell phones, text messaging, and Facebook: Competing time demands of today's college students. *College Teaching, 59*(1), 23–30.

Healy, M. (2004, July 19). "We're all multitasking, but what's the cost?" *Los Angeles Times*, p. F1.

Hembrooke, H., & Gay, G. (2003, October). "The laptop and the lecture: The effects of multitasking in learning environments," *Journal of Computing in Higher Education, 15*(1), 46–64.

Ishimura, I., & Kodama, M. (2009). Flow experience in everyday activities of Japanese college students: Autotelic people and time management. *Japanese Psychological Research, 51*(1), 47–54.

Jackson, E. L. (1993). Recognizing patterns of leisure constraints. *Journal of Leisure Research, 25*(2), 129–149.

Macan, T. H. (1994). Time management: Test of a process model. *Journal of Applied Psychology, 79*(3), 381–391.

McGee-Cooper, A., with Trammell, D. (1994). *Time management for unmanageable people*. New York: Bantam Books.

Meltzer, B. (1982). *Guidance for Living*. New York: The Dial Press.

Miller, K. (2007, Jan. 1). "The multitasking mess," *UCLA Magazine Online*. Retrieved from http://www.magazine.ucla.edu/depts/quicktakes/multitasking/

Nakamura, J., & Csikszentmihalyi, M. (2002). The concept of flow. In C.R. Snyder & S. J. Lopez (Eds.), *Handbook of positive psychology*. New York: Oxford University Press, pp. 89–105.

Olson, J. (1997). *The agile manager's guide to getting organized*. Bristol, Vermont: Velocity Business Publishing.

Ophir, E., Nass, C., & Wagner, A. D. (2009). Cognitive control in media multitaskers. *Proceedings of the National Academy of Sciences in the United States of America, 106*(37), 15583–15587.

Principles (n.d.). "Time management principles." *Student Handbook* (online). University of Minnesota—Duluth. Retrieved from http://www.d.umn.edu/kmc/student/loon/acad/strat/time_man_princ.html

Roy, A. (1992). *Commonsense time management*. New York: AMACOM Books.

Seo, E. H. (2009). The relationship of procrastination with a mastery goal versus an avoidance goal. *Social Behavior and Personality, 37*(7), 911–920.

Shellenbarger, S. (2004, July 19). "Multitasking makes you stupid: Studies show pitfalls of doing too much at once." *Wall Street Journal*, p. D1.

Smallin, D. (2000). *7 simple steps to unclutter your life*. Pownal, Vermont: Storey Publishing.

Strategies (n.d.). "Use time management strategies," Student Academic Services: Academic Skills Center, California Polytechnic State University. Retrieved from http://sas.calpoly.edu/asc/ssl/time.mgt.strategies.html

Tullier, L. M. (1999). *The complete idiot's guide to overcoming procrastination*. Indianapolis, Indiana: Alpha Books.

van der Meer, J., Jansen, E., & Torenbeek, M. (2010, November). 'It's almost a mindset that teachers need to change': First-year students need to be inducted into time management. *Studies in Higher Education, 35*(7), 777–791.

Ziegler, K. (2005). *Organizing for success: More than 100 tips, tools, ideas, and strategies for organizing and prioritizing work*. New York: McGraw-Hill.

EXERCISE 7-1
Rhythm of *My* Semester

Name _____ Date _____

The purpose of this exercise is to map your work load, by week, for the whole semester based on deadlines stated in the syllabi, or course plans, for *all* of your classes. There are two parts to the exercise. First, tally the number of deadlines for each class. Use the work area on this page to count deadlines. The second part of the exercise is to indicate the total number of deadlines for each week of the semester on the chart provided.

Create a system that makes sense to you to indicate the type of assignment. For example: P = paper; Q = quiz; T = test; E = exercise; L = lab; G = group project; H = homework.

Go through one syllabus at a time until you have noted all deadlines for all classes.

For example, let's say you are enrolled in five courses (English, Math, First-Year Seminar, Psychology, and Fitness for Living). In the first week, there are two deadlines: one paper in English and one exercise in the First-Year Seminar. The second week has three deadlines: one each in Math (quiz), First-Year Seminar (quiz), and Psychology (paper).

WEEK	NUMBER OF DEADLINES					TOTAL
	ENGL	MATH	KSU1101	PSYCH	HPS	
1	P		E			2
2		Q	Q	P		3

Here is your work space. List your classes on the second line. Indicate the deadlines for each class. Then indicate the total number of deadlines for each week.

WEEK	NUMBER OF DEADLINES	TOTAL
1		
2		
3		
4		
5		
6		
7		
8		
9		
10		
11		
12		
13		
14		
15		

Now make a line graph of your deadlines for this semester by placing one dot to indicate the total number of deadlines for Week 1. Do the same for weeks 2 through 15. Connect the dots to show the rhythm of your semester.

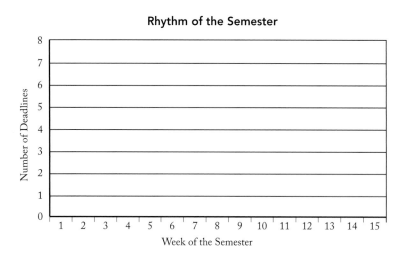

Analysis

- What are your *busiest* weeks based on total number of deadlines?

- What are your *most challenging* weeks based on the relative importance of the assignment? For example, a test is probably worth more points than a quiz. A paper that you have had three weeks to write is probably more important than a short reflection paper you wrote in class or with a two-day deadline.

- Look at your personal calendar. Are there any weeks that look like they will be packed with school work that coincide with important events in your personal life? For example, do you have a major paper due and a 100-point test on the Monday after you plan to return from Colorado after skiing with a group of classmates? Are you planning to leave town to attend your sister's wedding the weekend before final exams?

- Does it seem, now, like you will be busy this semester?

Before considering ways to accomplish everything on time, without interfering too much with your personal life, return to the chapter and continue reading.

EXERCISE 7-2
Goals, Action Steps, and To-Do Lists

Name _____ Date _____

The purpose of this exercise is to apply the goal-identification exercise you completed by answering the "Critical Thinking Questions" in the chapter titled Motivation For Student Success. Think about your short-term goals, academic goals, personal goals, and long-term goals. For now, do not worry about your professional goals.

What action will you take this semester to help you complete, or make progress toward, your goals? And how will you use your to-do lists (daily, project, and long-term) to monitor progress and achievement?

For example:

GOAL	ACTION STEP	TO-DO LIST
Academic: Take good notes in classes	Attend every class this semester	**Daily:** "Schedule" myself to attend classes
	Use a proven note-taking system	**Daily:** Read the part of this book that talks about note-taking strategies
Personal: Develop friend-ships using Facebook	Spend (scheduled) time building my Facebook profile	**Project:** Update Facebook
		Daily: Schedule two hours on Tuesday to update Facebook site

Use this table to help you get started with your own plan for reaching your goals this semester…and beyond. If you need more room, feel free to use a separate sheet of paper and set up three columns: Goal, Action Step, and To-Do List.

GOAL	ACTION STEP	TO-DO LIST

EXERCISE 7-3
Time Use Analysis

Name _____ Date _____

The purpose of this exercise is to make you aware of how you spend time throughout the week and to adjust your use of time, as appropriate.

There are three parts to this exercise:

- First, you will be asked to track time use on a daily basis for an entire week.

- Then you will be asked to total the number of hours you spent doing certain tasks, such as studying, working (for money), eating, socializing, and sleeping.

- Finally, you will be asked to evaluate your use of time and to plan adjustments, if needed.

For this exercise to work, track your time use every day. Fill in the time-tracking grid several different times each day. Avoid filling in the blanks during the opening remarks of the class period in which you discuss time management.

You may want to photocopy the exercise pages before you begin filling in the blanks. Make several sets of exercises. A key to this exercise is planning adjustments to your use of time. You may want to re-do the exercise a few weeks after making those adjustments to discover whether they have been effective for you.

Part 1. Tracking Time

This is not a to-do list. Fill in a word that indicates how you used each hour of the day. To make it easier to use this information in Part 2. Tallying Time Use by Task, use these key words:

Class	Personal Hygiene (bathing, dressing, etc.)	Studying
Commute/Travel		Work (for money)
Fitness	Recreation/Entertainment	Other 1:
Meal	Sleep	Other 2:
Meeting/Appointment	Socializing	Other 3:

Example: Tracking Time

Day

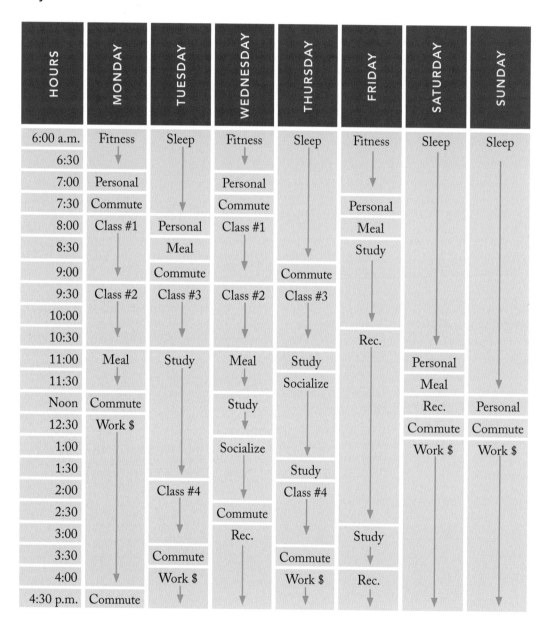

HOURS	MONDAY	TUESDAY	WEDNESDAY	THURSDAY	FRIDAY	SATURDAY	SUNDAY
6:00 a.m.	Fitness	Sleep	Fitness	Sleep	Fitness	Sleep	Sleep
6:30	↓		↓		↓		
7:00	Personal		Personal				
7:30	Commute	↓	Commute		Personal		
8:00	Class #1	Personal	Class #1		Meal		
8:30		Meal			Study		
9:00	↓	Commute	↓	Commute			
9:30	Class #2	Class #3	Class #2	Class #3			
10:00							
10:30	↓		↓	↓	Rec.	↓	
11:00	Meal	Study	Meal	Study		Personal	
11:30	↓		↓	Socialize		Meal	↓
Noon	Commute		Study			Rec.	Personal
12:30	Work $	↓	↓			Commute	Commute
1:00			Socialize	↓		Work $	Work $
1:30				Study			
2:00		Class #4	↓	Class #4			
2:30			Commute				
3:00		↓	Rec.	↓	Study		
3:30		Commute		Commute	↓		
4:00	↓	Work $	↓	Work $	Rec.	↓	↓
4:30 p.m.	Commute	↓	↓	↓	↓		

Evening and Night

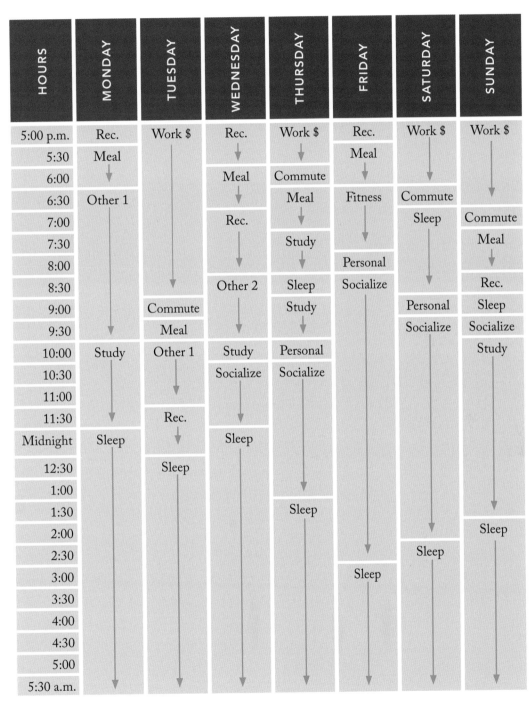

HOURS	MONDAY	TUESDAY	WEDNESDAY	THURSDAY	FRIDAY	SATURDAY	SUNDAY
5:00 p.m.	Rec.	Work $	Rec.	Work $	Rec.	Work $	Work $
5:30	Meal				Meal		
6:00			Meal	Commute		Commute	
6:30	Other 1			Meal	Fitness		Commute
7:00			Rec.			Sleep	Meal
7:30				Study			
8:00					Personal		Rec.
8:30			Other 2	Sleep	Socialize		Sleep
9:00		Commute		Study		Personal	Socialize
9:30		Meal				Socialize	
10:00	Study	Other 1	Study	Personal			Study
10:30			Socialize	Socialize			
11:00							
11:30		Rec.					
Midnight	Sleep		Sleep				
12:30		Sleep					
1:00							
1:30				Sleep			
2:00							Sleep
2:30						Sleep	
3:00					Sleep		
3:30							
4:00							
4:30							
5:00							
5:30 a.m.							

This is not a to-do list. Fill in a word that indicates how you used each hour of the day *after* you have completed the task or activity. To make it easier to use this information in Part 2. Tallying Time Use by Task, use these key words:

Class	Personal Hygiene (bathing, dressing, etc.)	Studying
Commute/Travel		Work (for money)
Fitness	Recreation/Entertainment	Other 1:
Meal	Sleep	Other 2:
Meeting/Appointment	Socializing	Other 3:

Day

HOURS	MONDAY	TUESDAY	WEDNESDAY	THURSDAY	FRIDAY	SATURDAY	SUNDAY
6:00 a.m.							
6:30							
7:00							
7:30							
8:00							
8:30							
9:00							
9:30							
10:00							
10:30							
11:00							
11:30							
Noon							
12:30							
1:00							
1:30							
2:00							
2:30							
3:00							
3:30							
4:00							
4:30 p.m.							

Evening and Night

HOURS	MONDAY	TUESDAY	WEDNESDAY	THURSDAY	FRIDAY	SATURDAY	SUNDAY
5:00 p.m.							
5:30							
6:00							
6:30							
7:00							
7:30							
8:00							
8:30							
9:00							
9:30							
10:00							
10:30							
11:00							
11:30							
Midnight							
12:30							
1:00							
1:30							
2:00							
2:30							
3:00							
3:30							
4:00							
4:30							
5:00							
5:30 a.m.							

Part 2. Tallying Time Use by Task

Total the number of hours you spent doing each task.

For example, how many hours did you spend in class each day last week? Refer to your Time Tracking sheets. How many hours did you spend commuting each day last week? Etc.

Once each day's totals have been entered, add across each task (key word) to find the total number of hours spent for each task last week. Enter that number in the "Total" column. The total for each day for all the tasks should equal 24. The grand total of hours for the week should add up to 168.

HOURS	MONDAY	TUESDAY	WEDNESDAY	THURSDAY	FRIDAY	SATURDAY	SUNDAY
Class							
Commute/Travel							
Fitness							
Meal							
Meeting/ Appointment							
Personal Hygiene							
Recreation/ Entertainment							
Sleep							
Socialize							
Study							
Work $							
Other 1							
Other 2							
Other 3							
Total	24	24	24	24	24	24	168

Part 3. Evaluating and Adjusting Time Use

Ziegler (2005) recommends keeping a timekeeping journal and analyzing your entries to determine, for each task (p. 145):

- Is this the best use of my time?

- Am I doing the right task at the right time?

- Are there any tasks that could be eliminated or put off?

- Could I cut down on the amount of time I spend on certain tasks?

Now that you have tracked your use of time for an entire week, it is time to evaluate your use of time.

Take a close look at the Tallying Time Use by Task worksheet and respond to these questions:

Are there any surprises? Did you spend more or less time than you expected doing certain tasks? If so, name them and write a few comments about why you were surprised.

How would you rate your time management last week? (Check One)

Excellent ☐   Good ☐   Okay ☐   Poor ☐   Very Poor ☐

In general, did you do the right task at the right time?

Are there any tasks that could have been eliminated or put off? If so, which ones? Why?

Do you think you should reduce—or increase—the amount of time you spend on certain tasks? If so, which ones? Why?

What other adjustments do you think you should make to use your time more effectively?

In what ways do the adjustments you plan to make contribute to helping you reach your goals?

Overall, what did you discover by completing this exercise?

CHAPTER 8

Becoming a Prepared Citizen: A Personal Responsibility

KATHY A. LYNN, M.A.

Chapter Goals

* Gain an appreciation of the civic duty for individuals to become prepared citizens

* Take responsibility for your personal safety at home, in the car, and in public

* Have increased awareness of public safety and emergency notification resources on campus

* Know how to better prepare for emergencies and disasters

* Begin to develop the mental attitude of an immediate responder and a survivor

Chapter Overview

In 95% of all emergencies, bystanders or victims themselves are the first to provide emergency assistance or to perform a rescue.

—Los Angeles Fire Department
(Bonno, 2010; Citizen Corps, n.d.a.)

Whether faced with a minor medical emergency, a potentially violent situation, or a large-scale disaster, it is your personal responsibility to be prepared and willing to respond. An individual who is prepared will take action during an emergency, while an unprepared person is likely to enter a state of denial, become very anxious, and do nothing.

For example, according to an Atlanta Business Chronicle article, "Mystery Man Pulls Man Off MARTA Tracks," by Carla Caldwell (2011), an unidentified Good Samaritan saved a man who lost consciousness as a result of heat stroke and fell onto the subway tracks. The man who witnessed the fall jumped down onto the tracks and managed to lift the disoriented man to the platform.

This Good Samaritan saw a fellow human in need, reacted quickly, and saved a life. He had the mindset of a prepared citizen.

Another example from Thames Valley, Great Britain, provides us with a "do" and "don't" comparison. *BBC News* (Teenage Samaritan, 2005) reported a 16-year-old boy's efforts to assist a 23-year-old woman who had been assaulted on a dark road. The boy used "light from his mobile phone to find the injured woman then helped her to a nearby house where he asked for an ambulance to be called…. [The woman] was walking alone on an unlit road when…three men attacked her."

Do come to the aid of a fellow human. *Don't* walk alone at night on an unlit road.

This chapter will help you see ways to behave as a Good Samaritan and to avoid behaving as a victim.

Becoming a prepared citizen is more than programming emergency responder numbers into a cell phone or learning to administer first aid. To be capable of responding to and perhaps surviving any emergency, you must develop a proper mental attitude, and that begins with acknowledging that you are ultimately responsible for your own personal safety, and, at times, the safety of others.

This chapter provides an overview of ways to anticipate and react to emergencies, threats, and disasters. The purpose of this chapter is not to stir up fear or anxiety. Rather, this chapter is designed to help you explore ways to prepare yourself and others for potentially threatening situations that may occur on campus, in your community, or when traveling outside of your community.

As you read this chapter, keep in mind that when you choose to help others, you *must* consider your own safety first. Do not take unnecessary risks as an immediate responder. Know your limitations. If you feel uncomfortable or unsafe in a response, wait for professional first responders to arrive.

Introduction

Suppose you wake up to the startling realization that there is a fire in your home, apartment, or residence hall. How will you respond? The easy answer is, "Yes, I know what to do. I learned that in elementary school: Call 9-1-1 and stop, drop, and roll." However, there is a big difference between knowing what to do and acting on that knowledge. As a first-year student on campus, how would you respond during the chaos of an emergency or disaster? For example, if the campus alert siren begins to sound while you are walking to class, would you:

- Run inside the nearest building to seek shelter?

- Rush to your car and drive away?

- Stay where you are and wait for instructions?

- Ignore the siren?

It is very easy to believe, "It will never happen to me." Psychologists refer to this as the "illusion of invulnerability" (Blass, 1991; Norris, Nurius & Dimeff, 1996; Hall, Kramer, Neal & Schlabach, 1998; Sagarin, Cialdini, Rice & Serna, 200). Statistically speaking, it may not be likely that one of your fellow students will be victimized or that a family member will be affected by a natural disaster. However, individuals who are prepared citizens anticipate less-likely possibilities and prepare to respond appropriately.

If you, a family member, or friend has ever been involved in an emergency or dangerous situation, you likely appreciate how crucial it is to have police, fire, and emergency medical technicians (EMTs) to render aid. These specially trained individuals are known as "first responders." When an emergency occurs, they are trusted to provide expert care. However, it could be several minutes before first responders can reach the scene. And in the event of a tornado, flood, mass casualty event, or other disaster, it may be impossible for them to reach you for several hours or even days. As a prepared citizen, you can equip yourself with the skills and mindset to be an "immediate responder"—a Good Samaritan—on any scene, taking care of yourself and others until trained professionals or volunteers arrive.

Laws are in place to protect from civil liability an individual who volunteers to render aid. In general, as long as you do not seek compensation for your efforts and behave in a responsible way, you are a Good Samaritan. Here is how Georgia State Legislature defines a Good Samaitan's immunity from liability of persons rendering emergency care:

> Georgia Code 51-1-29: Liability of persons rendering emergency care
>
> Any person…who in good faith renders emergency care at the scene of an accident or emergency to the victim or victims thereof without making any charge therefor shall not be liable for any civil damages as a result of any act or omission by such person in rendering emergency care or as a result of any act or failure to act to provide or arrange for further medical treatment or care for the injured person. (Georgia State Legislature, 2011a)

In Georgia, a bill was introduced to the state legislature in January 2010 that would assure emergency relief volunteers from outside the state the same immunity from civil liability as Good Samaritans from within the state (Rich & Richards, 2010, p. 2).

Emergencies and Disasters

During this post-9/11 and Hurricane Katrina era, there has been more emphasis placed on government/FEMA preparedness, but the vast majority of Americans have not grabbed onto the need to be prepared at home and at work for potential disasters. One of the harshest lessons learned from recent disasters, especially Katrina, is that you are your own first responder.

—Lt. General Russel L. Honoré (2010)

Tune in to a television news program, pick up your local newspaper, or visit your favorite online news site, and it becomes evident that emergencies and disasters occur all around you—an apartment fire, a multi-car pile-up on the interstate, a home invasion. And there are the catastrophic events such as the 9/11 terrorist attacks in 2001 (Rosen, 2001), Hurricane Katrina in 2005 (Vanden Brook & Copeland, 2005), and shootings on school campuses such as the one at Virginia Tech in 2007 (Horwitz & Craig, 2007). In September 2009, the Atlanta metropolitan area and Kennesaw State University campus were affected by unprecedented flooding that destroyed roads, homes, businesses, and schools and forced many families to evacuate to emergency shelters (Jonsson, 2009).

It is difficult to think anything like this could happen to you or those who are close to you, but it is important to understand that you can and should learn what to do during an emergency or disaster and how to prevent the events from having a traumatic impact on you, your family, and your community.

Table 8-1 lists many types of emergencies and disasters. The Internet and satellite television enable us to watch catastrophic events unfold. There is always an outpouring of emotion and people ask, "How can I help?" Consider the response to the earthquakes in Port-au-Prince, Haiti, in January of 2010. Nations around the world responded with monetry, medical, military, and volunteer assistance (Romero & Lacey, 2010). And perhaps never before on American soil has such a spirit of volunteerism emerged as it did following the 9/11 terrorist attacks (Community, 2003). The message was clear: Citizens must be trained to help; citizens want to help. As a result, Citizen Corps was created in January 2002 to make it easier for citizens to learn prevention, response, and recovery skills necessary to respond to threats of crime, terrorism, and disasters (Citizen Corps, n.d.a.; Sander & Putnam, 2002).

Citizen Corps asks that all individuals "embrace the personal responsibility to be prepared; to get training in first aid and emergency skills; and to volunteer to support local emergency responders, disaster relief, and community safety." Citizen Corps (n.d.b.) maintains that every individual may participate in making families and communities safer through:

- **Personal Responsibility**: Developing a household preparedness plan and disaster supplies kits, observing home health and safety practices, implementing disaster mitigation measures, and participating in crime prevention and reporting.

Table 8-1. Disasters and Emergencies

NATURAL/ WEATHER	HUMAN-GENERATED	MEDICAL	OTHER
Flood	**ACTS OF VIOLENCE**	Heart attack	Fire
Flash flood		Stroke	Automobile accidents/ breakdowns
Thunderstorm	Assault	Seizure	Hazardous materials
Winter storm	Rape	Loss of consciousness	Power failure or blackout
Extreme heat	Robbery	Sprain/bone injury	Water main break
Hurricane	Stalking	Bleeding	Public health (pandemic)
Tornado	Hate crime	Shock	MRSA infection
Earthquake	Abduction	Allergic reaction	Dam or levee break
Tsunami	Homicide	Heat-related conditions	
Volcano	Carjacking	Hypothermia	
Wildfire	Home invasion	Frost bite	
Mudslide	Active shooter	Alcohol poisoning	
Landslide	**TERRORISTIC THREATS**	Drug overdose	
	Bomb		
	Biological		
	Chemical		
	Radiological		
	Nuclear		
	PSYCHOLOGICAL		
	Suicide threat/attempt		
	Irrational behavior		

- **Training:** Taking classes in emergency preparedness, response capabilities, first aid, CPR, fire suppression, and search and rescue procedures.

- **Volunteer Service:** Engaging individuals in volunteer activities that support first responders, disaster relief groups, and community safety organizations. Everyone can do something to support local law enforcement, fire, emergency medical services, community public health efforts, and the four stages of emergency management: prevention, mitigation, response, and recovery efforts.

Taking personal responsibility, not only for yourself but for your community, builds self-confidence and creates a sense of belonging. There are several opportunities on the Kennesaw State campus and in Metro Atlanta to obtain the skills to become an immediate responder. As you think ahead toward a career, consider the fact that job candidates with emergency preparedness skills and experience would be sought after by employers across many job markets such as education, business, criminal justice, nursing—and more.

Personal Safety on Campus and Beyond

Most students probably feel quite safe on the Kennesaw State University campus—and so they should. Fortunately, Kennesaw State has one of the lowest crime rates among colleges and universities in the University System of Georgia (Safe and Sound, 2012). A university campus operates much like a small town, with neighborhoods, businesses, services, and recreation. There are governing bodies in the Student Government Association, the President's Cabinet, and the Faculty/Staff Senates. There is a newspaper, a magazine, and a radio station. As in any community, accidents happen, crime is committed, and risks are present. Kennesaw State has a Department of Public Safety and other security measures in place to provide protection and offer assistance. However, it is realistic to think that first responders cannot be on the crime or emergency scene in those first few critical moments. So it is essential for you to commit to taking responsibility for your own personal safety, whether you are in your home, in your car, or in public.

For more than 10 years, the author of this chapter has taught personal safety to a wide range of individuals, from middle school students to employees of major corporations. Much of this section of the chapter comes from her extensive experience and deep concern for this subject.

Personal Safety at Home

Whether you live in the residence halls or dormitories on campus or rent an apartment or house off campus, there are some simple, basic steps you should take to ensure your personal safety and protect your belongings. If you can find housing in a gated complex or neighborhood, you have the security of knowing unauthorized visitors cannot drive onto the property. The gated parking lots and decks on campus provide more than just protection from visitors occupying precious limited parking spaces. However, it is very easy for anyone to walk onto most properties, including a university campus. Below are just a few tips to consider about personal safety and the role of the prepared citizen at home:

- Prevent crime in your neighborhood and avoid being victimized yourself by simply raising your sense of awareness. Pay attention to what is going around you (Marietta Police Department, 2007).

  - Know your neighbors, even if just enough to recognize them and what vehicles they drive. Immediately report suspicious persons or vehicles to police.

  - In residence halls and apartment complexes, report lights that are out or controlled-access doors that are not functioning properly.

- Attend crime awareness and prevention seminars on campus or in your community.

- When you move into a new place, ask for proof that the locks have been re-keyed and find out who has copies of your keys—the landlord, property manager, resident assistant, maintenance staff, or others. You should receive advance notice for any access to your home. Make sure you read and understand any policies regarding this before moving into a new place. If you live on campus, this information can be found in your Residence Life Handbook.

- Avoid talking to solicitors. Solicitors may run scams and commit fraudulent acts. Always be cautious when providing your personal information (name, address, schedule, etc.) to anyone you do not know you can trust. Solicitation is also an opportunity for predators to approach potential victims. Solicitation is not allowed on campus and should be reported immediately. Cobb County requires solicitors to carry photo identification and does not allow solicitation after dark (Cobb County Police Department, n.d.).

- Take steps to deter theft, burglary, and home invasion. Fifty-four percent of burglaries in the United States in 2006 took place without forced entry, according to the Bureau of Justice Statistics (Robinson, 2010). Burglary is one of the most reported crimes, yet it is also one of the most preventable.

  - Keep your doors and windows locked when you are sleeping and when you are away. In residence halls and campus apartments, do not prop your doors open or leave your doors unlocked, even when you are leaving for just a few minutes.

  - Think like a burglar and "case" your own home: What would be the easiest access into your home? Where could you enter without being seen? Your property should be well-lit with porch lights, walkway lights, and motion-sensor flood lights. Your shrubs should be trimmed below three feet to eliminate hiding places and your trees trimmed up six feet to maintain a clear view from the house to the street. Where permitted, install wide-angle peephole door viewers and quality, heavy-duty deadbolts. Lock your doors while you are home.

  - Always know who is at the door before opening it, and do not rely on chain locks. Be aware that anyone can purchase uniforms and business cards. Home invaders may present themselves as law enforcement, utility service or maintenance workers, even charity volunteers. Do not open your door to anyone you do not know without first verifying their identity.

  - Be responsible with your keys. Never loan your keys or access cards to others. If your keys are lost or stolen, report this immediately. And do not "hide" keys outside of your door.

The reality is, accidents happen and crimes are committed. Your landlord's insurance covers the structure, not the contents (MSN Money, 2010). Therefore, it is a good idea to purchase renter's insurance for your belongings. Do your research and understand what you are purchasing. For example, your policy will likely cover a car crashing into your living room but not water damage caused by a flood. If your roommate runs a bath then falls asleep, resulting in flooding the unit below, are you protected from liability? With a little research you will find an affordable policy that provides protection and peace of mind.

Personal Safety in the Car

Many of you have received your driver's license in the last two to three years and are, therefore, very familiar with the rules of the road and the operation of your vehicle. You know you can avoid unnecessary breakdowns and problems by maintaining your vehicle: tire pressure and balance, periodic inspection of brakes, wiper blades and all lights, and keeping your gas tank filled above a quarter of a tank. The focus here is preparedness for emergencies and accidents that may occur or that you may witness while in your vehicle.

Breakdowns

For safety purposes and to receive assistance in the event of a breakdown, it is worthwhile to carry roadside assistance coverage on your auto insurance policy or purchase it from an independent automobile club. If you experience car trouble it is best, when possible, to move your car clear of traffic. Safely drive to a parking lot, an emergency lane, or off-ramp.

If you are on the road in metro Atlanta, you can dial 5-1-1 from any phone for assistance. The Georgia Department of Transportation (GDOT) Incident Management Program maintains a fleet of HERO (Highway Emergency Response Operators) trucks on the interstates and some highways. The operators assist first responders and law enforcement in clearing accidents and stalls. They are also available to help stranded motorists with minor mechanical problems such as a flat tire, coolant, or fuel. Many large cities have similar emergency services. When travelling, watch for roadside signs indicating highway emergency assistance.

Automobile Accidents

There are a few items you may want to keep in your car emergency kit that might be useful if you are involved in an accident. Reflective triangles are important to alert other drivers of your presence. You should also keep a flashlight, disposable camera (or, if available, use a cell phone camera), and a note pad and pen to document

the accident. And you should always have your (charged) cell phone with you.

For safety, Georgia Code 40-6-275 (Georgia State Legislature, 2011b) requires that if possible, all vehicles be moved to the side of the road. If there are no serious injuries and the vehicles can be safely moved, do so immediately. You are also required to report the accident to the police if there are injuries or if there are property damages exceeding $500.

As a responsible driver, if you witness an accident, you should render assistance to those involved. Never assume someone else has called for help. If there are injuries, call 9-1-1 or instruct someone else to call while you tend to the injured. Prepared citizens make a commitment to learn and maintain first aid and cardiopulmonary resuscitation (CPR) training.

Other Safety Tips

Always drive defensively and be courteous on the road. According to the National Highway Traffic Safety Administration (2009), an average of 102 people died each day in 2008 as a result of motor vehicle crashes. That is one every 14 minutes. Speeding and alcohol-impaired driving are major contributors.

If you see someone driving aggressively or erratically, stay clear. Pull over when it is safe and report the driver, providing as much information as possible (car make and model, color, tag, and specific location). Do not initiate or participate in road rage. Slow down, relax, and avoid a potentially dangerous situation. If you feel threatened, call the police or drive to a police station. Do not get out of your car, and do not drive home.

Personal Safety in Public

Whether walking to class, running errands in the city of Kennesaw, or attending a concert in downtown Atlanta, you should train yourself to be aware of what is going on around you at all times. With practice, awareness becomes a daily habit, much like brushing your teeth or having your morning cup of coffee. Accidents often occur when people are careless. Criminals look for vulnerability; they are not looking for a challenge. Develop a proper mental attitude, practice awareness, and learn to recognize potentially dangerous situations, and you may never be targeted as a victim.

Developing a Proper Mental Attitude

A proper mental attitude begins with the acknowledgement that accidents, emergencies, and violent crime can happen to anyone, and you are ultimately responsible for your own personal safety and at times, the safety of others. Practice walking with good posture, alert, with your head up. Be confident and trust your intuition—if something feels wrong, it probably is. In a life-threatening situation, you must allow yourself to become aggressive, even combative. Remember, criminals want a victim, not a challenge.

Practicing Awareness

Some people seem to go about their business oblivious to what is going on around them. Observe those around you. Notice people with ear buds stuffed in their ears, heads down, walking, and texting. Even those who make a deliberate effort to pay attention can easily get distracted. Students may be very busy and have much or their minds. "How am I going to finish my English essay, get by the Bursar's to pay fees, and show up for my student organization meeting, all before my 2:00 p.m. calculus class?"

It requires practice to take control of your mental state and always focus on your surroundings and belongings. But these efforts lessen the odds of being involved in an emergency or violent crime. Often, crime and accident victims say, "I never saw it coming." Prepared citizens practice their observation skills.

Protect yourself and look out for others by making awareness a daily habit. An excellent way to practice awareness and to develop a proper mental attitude is to play the "What if?" game.

Playing the "What if?" game requires mentally rehearsing what to do in the event of an emergency or potentially dangerous situation. The time to decide what to do when you or someone else needs help is not in the midst of the chaos and confusion that occurs during an emergency. Even if you have not yet received first aid, disaster response, personal safety, or self-defense training, it is still better to have an action plan rather than risk freezing on the scene and becoming a victim or helpless bystander. While it is impossible to imagine every possible event, by visualizing scenes, mentally rehearsing what you can and should do, and playing the scene through to a victorious outcome, you are developing the mind of a responder and survivor. For example:

- **What if** you are in the east parking deck walking to your car and you believe someone is following you?

- **What if** you are playing Frisbee on the campus green and the emergency alert siren begins to wail?

- **What if** you are sitting in a lecture when a classmate loses consciousness?

- **What if** you are enjoying a family gathering and someone you love suffers a heart attack?

Potentially Dangerous Situations

While it is important to be aware or your surroundings during most waking hours, there are potentially dangerous areas and situations in which it is necessary to heighten your sense of awareness. One of these is a "transition area." By definition, a transition area is any place where you are moving from one area of safety to another. For example, parking lots and garages, stairwells and elevators, even your driveway, are all transition areas. Crimes often occur in transition areas. Condition yourself to be particularly alert in these areas. It is a great idea to periodically attend personal safety, crime prevention, and self-defense seminars to learn more. The list below provides a few basic tips:

- If possible, do not walk alone; stay in public, open, well-lit areas.

- Always park in well-lit areas and avoid parking near hiding places, such as stairwells, shrubs, or pillars.

- Have your keys out and in your hand when walking to your car or home.

- Check around your home as you drive up, and around your car as you walk toward it. Be aware of anyone or anything that looks out of place. If your home has been entered, drive to a safe place and call the police.

- When you enter your car, immediately lock your doors.

- Pay particular attention to activities and people as you approach the ATM, convenience store, or bank.

- Be cautious in areas around your complex, such as the laundry room, mail area, or Dumpster.

Criminals are often clever, methodical planners. In fact, plotting crimes and finding victims is a full-time job for many criminals. They are good at it. If a stranger approaches, condition yourself to question, "Could this be a potentially dangerous encounter?" Be aware that the most common method of attack is the "con approach," according to Robert Lowrey, founder and master instructor of Dynamic Self Defense International (personal communication, September 9, 2002). Someone may ask for money, directions, or help in an effort to lower your defenses and get near you. If someone approaches you, it is best to keep a safe distance. If you feel uncomfortable, simply keep moving and calmly but firmly tell the person in a clear, confident voice you are unable to help him or her. If the person persists, it is a safe bet there are criminal intentions. Tell the person—in a *loud* voice—to stay away, or you can run away. Do not worry about making a scene! Use your voice to make other people in the area notice and witness your situation. Criminals look for an easy target. Your resistance and commanding voice are often deterrent enough. This is not a suggestion to become paranoid and frightened of strangers. Fortunately, the "good guys" still outnumber the bad. This is simply a reminder of the importance of developing personal safety habits.

The Crime of Rape

Based on the findings of the 2000 National College Women Sexual Victimization (NCWSV) study, Fisher, Collen, and Turner (2000) estimate that for every 10,000 female students, more than 350 rapes may occur each year. An estimated 20% to 25% of college women in the United States experience attempted or completed rape during their college career. The study also indicated that less than 5% of rapes were reported to police for such reasons as 1) it was not clear a crime was committed (acquaintance rape), 2) fear of family members finding out, or 3) lack of proof (p. iii).

Kennesaw State University holds the highest expectations for respectful and ethical behavior for all members of our university community. We are particularly mindful of victims' rights, and strive to provide services and resources that allow victims to take control of their own healing process. I encourage every student to visit the website site for KSU's Taskforce on Interpersonal Violence (TIV) at http://www.kennesaw.edu/tiv/ and get involved with the student organization (STIV) to help prevent crimes of violence on our campus.

—Michael L. Sanseviro, Ph.D., Dean of Student Success, Kennesaw State University

---

Rape is a violent crime. That must be acknowledged, and measures should be taken to prevent this crime.

Students—males and females alike—should take responsibility to learn and understand the laws regarding rape and the rights of victims. Unless consent is given, the sex act is rape, even when you know the offender and even if you are on a date. Take these precautions to protect yourself from rape in social settings (Rape, Abuse, & Incest National Network, 2009):

- Go out with friends you trust and look out for one another.

- Plan dates carefully and always meet in a public place until you know and trust the person.

- If someone is making you uncomfortable, find an excuse (even if you have to make one up) to get away.

- Limit your alcohol consumption; stay in control of your senses.

- Do not accept drinks from someone you do not know or trust, to avoid possible ingestion of "date rape" drugs.

- Do not feel obligated to do anything you do not want to do.

- If you share a residence with roommates, sleep with your bedroom door locked.

- Do not send mixed signals; communicate desires and boundaries clearly.

- Take a rape prevention course.

Become as knowledgeable as possible about the issues of acquaintance rape, date rape, and rape on college campuses. Commit to share your knowledge, and help others to create a culture of respect and intimacy, rather than a culture of silent acceptance of a violent, invasive act.

Medical Emergencies

Prepared citizens learn and maintain skills for medical emergencies. You may decide to learn advanced first aid skills to treat a variety of injuries, or you may learn triage skills for managing mass casualty events. At a minimum, you should be trained to respond to life-threatening emergecies including heart attacks, loss of consciousness, and severe bleeding. While it is beyond the scope of the chapter to teach these skills, a short list of resources is provided at the end of this chapter to direct you to opportunities to receive training. And, once again, being aware of what's going on around you, having the proper mental attitude, and playing through "What if?" scenarios will better enable you to recognize and respond to a life-threatening medical emergency.

Alcohol and Other Drug (AOD) Risk Assessment

Because alcohol is a part of the college culture for many, developing awareness and understanding the risk associated with Alcohol and Drug use is another skill of the prepared citizen. Injuries, accidents, impairment, and even death may occur as a result of alcohol and/or drug use. In fact, 1,825 college students die each year in an alcohol related death, more than 2.8 million students drove under the influence, and 25% of college students suffered academically (NIAAA, 2012).

To help college students understand where they stand in assessing their own risk as it relates to alcohol and other drugs, Kennesaw State University provides several sources of education and prevention. The "eCHECKUP TO GO" program is an evidence-based, online prevention intervention for alcohol and marijuana. It is designed to motivate individuals to reduce their consumption based on personalized information about their own drinking and risk factors. By participating in this self-assessment through your first-year program you will not only learn more about yourself, you will help to contribute to on-going research and data collection. Information on participation in this program is available on the online textbook website under chapter 8 resources.

Teresa Johnston, Director of the Center for Young Adult Addiction and Recovery at KSU, encourages every student to understand alcohol and drug use from a risk assessment perspective. "Participating in both the online educational tool and attending an AOD presentation will

provide students with the type of information they need to make wise choices, assess risks, and impact their community," Johnston says.

As a prepared citizen in the collegiate community it is critical to recognize alcohol poisoning. Left untreated alcohol poising can lead to brain damage or even death. If you suspect someone has alcohol poisoning, immediately call for help. See Table 8-2 for a list of alcohol poisoning symptoms.

Table 8-2.

SIGNS AND SYMPTOMS OF ALCOHOL POISONING
Confusion, stupor
Vomiting
Seizures
Slow breathing (less than eight breaths a minute)
Irregular breathing
Blue-tinged skin or pale skin
Low body temperature (hypothermia)
Unconsciousness ("passing out")
It is not necessary for all of these symptoms to be present before you seek help. A person who is unconscious or can't be roused is at risk of dying.

Data Source: Mayo Clinic (2008)

Getting Help on Campus

The KSU campus Department of Public Safety includes both state-certified police officers and a team of security officers. The police officers receive annual training for firearms qualification, criminal law procedures, maintaining first responder skills for medical emergencies, and more. They patrol campus 24 hours a day, seven days a week to provide security, prevent crimes, enforce laws, respond to emergencies, conduct

Table 8-3. Contact Information for KSU's Department of Public Safety (campus police)

	EMERGENCY	NON-EMERGENCY
Phone	770-423-6666 or ext. 6666 on campus	770-423-6206 or ext. 6206 on campus
Email	n/a	safensound@kennesaw.edu
Tipster (Anonymous)	n/a	770-423-6305 or ext. 6305 on campus

investigations, and promote safety awareness. The security officers on campus patrol parking lots and buildings, assist motorists, and provide safety escorts.

The KSU Department of Public Safety sends "Timely Warning" messages through the campus email system. For example, you may receive a "watch your belongings" message to remind you to be aware of possible theft of laptop computers or backpacks. Check your KSU email account frequently.

Someone is always available to respond to criminal and life-threatening emergencies. If you are on campus, call the KSU Department of Public Safety, rather than 9-1-1, because campus police are likely to arrive on scene before Cobb County or Kennesaw police. If, in the chaos of an emergency, you call 9-1-1 instead, be certain to immediately inform the dispatcher that you are on the Kennesaw State University campus.

The KSU Department of Public Safety also sponsors seminars for students, faculty and staff, including personal safety, rape prevention, campus safety, and alcohol awareness. For more information, see www.kennesaw.edu/police.

Your cell phone is an important tool for personal safety. You should always keep your cell phone charged and accessible (not buried deep in your backpack or purse). Program emergency and non-emergency numbers for the campus police as well as your hometown city and county first responders. The phone numbers and other contact information for our Department of Public Safety are listed in Table 8-3.

Emergency phones are available on campus. As part of your awareness practice, look for these in parking lots and decks, building hallways, elevators, and across campus to learn where they are located. These provide direct contact with the KSU police department. However, if you feel unsafe remaining next to a phone, walk or run toward safety and access each phone along the way. The police will be able to track this as well.

General Preparation for All Disasters

Many internationally recognized emergency preparedness organizations, such as the Federal Emergency Management Agency (FEMA), American Red Cross (ARC), and Centers for Disease Control and Prevention (CDC) provide similar guidance for disaster and emergency preparation: Build an emergency kit, have a plan, and be informed.

Build Emergency Kits

When you think of building your prepared citizen's emergency kit, perhaps the first thing to come to mind is gathering first aid supplies to tend to injuries until first responders arrive. But suppose you need to immediately evacuate your home. There may be little to no time to gather personal belongings such as a change of clothes, personal care items, or even a few creature comforts that will make your evacuation less traumatic. For this you will need an evacuation kit packed and readily accessible. In extreme cases, you may need to survive on your own for several days, so you will need water, food, and perhaps even shelter. Consider what the citizens of New Orleans experienced in 2005, when Hurricane Katrina hit. Flooded and debris-blocked roads prevented first responders from reaching the scene for days. A similar story unfolded in January 2010, when earthquakes destroyed the city of Port-au-Prince in Haiti, where almost all shelter was destroyed. And in October of 2012 Superstorm Sandy left more than 8.6 million people along the east coast of the United States without power, many for as long as two weeks (Costs from Sandy, 2012). Hopefully you will never be the victim of a massive, devastating disaster, but even a winter storm or tornado could force you to "shelter-in-place" at your home or workplace for several days. You need to have appropriate supplies.

Water and food are essential. The American Red Cross suggests a three-day supply for evacuation, and a two-week supply for sheltering-in-place at home. The general rule for water is at least one gallon per person per day (National Crime Prevention Center, 2010). This would provide two quarts for consumption and two quarts for sanitation and food preparation. Visit the FEMA (www.fema.gov) or CDC (www.cdc.gov) website for suggestions on how and where to store large supplies of water. The foods you choose must have a long shelf-life and be ready-to-eat canned meats, vegetables, fruits, and fruit juices. You may not have the means to cook meals. Peanut butter, granola bars, and other high-energy foods are good choices. Store your food in sealable plastic bags and covered storage bins. Water and food supplies should be rotated every three to six months. Consume what is stored and replace with new items.

As you develop your own personal lists for emergency kits, plan specifically for the needs of you and your family. Always consider the special needs of elderly persons, small children, anyone with a disability or medical condition, and pets. First aid kits should be kept in your home, car, and place of business. Evacuation and shelter-in-place kits may be purchased for individuals, couples, families, and pets. You may decide to build and maintain your emergency kits specific to your needs. Remember to include items such as prescriptions, spare keys, cash or traveler's checks, important documents, an inventory of valuable household items, and contact information for family, friends, doctors, and others you may need to contact. Keep all supplies in easy-carry containers. Visit the FEMA and ARC websites for detailed lists of recommended items. Customizable checklists are available on the textbook website under chapter 8 resources.

First Aid Kit (for home and cars)

You may choose to build your own first aid kit or purchase it from ARC or other suppliers. Your kit should be stocked with items similar to those recommended by FEMA (Federal Emergency Management Agency, 2009).

Evacuation and Shelter-in-Place Kit

Evacuation and shelter-in-place kits may be purchased for individuals, couples, families, and pets. Again, customize a kit for your family needs. Keep these supplies in an easy-carry container.

The personal safety section of this chapter listed some supplies to carry that may be helpful if you are involved in a traffic accident. It is also a good idea to equip your car with a portable emergency preparedness kit. If you are stranded in your vehicle, or if a disaster occurs while you are away from home and you are unable to return for supplies, you will want to have some of these essential items.

Because students are often out "on foot" for several hours at a time when on campus, consider stocking some basic preparedness items in a book bag or backpack. Of course, you will have your cell phone charged and accessible. Always carry your car keys, driver's license, and medical and contact information in case you need to evacuate and are unable to return to your home or office. Even if you keep it simple by including limited first aid supplies, flashlight, multipurpose tools, snack bars, and water, you will be very glad you did if an emergency does occur.

Develop a Plan and Be Informed

Natural or human-generated disasters can cause tremendous disruption to your daily life. Essential planning may help to alleviate some of the hardships and risks that can result. For example, do you know how to shut off the water, gas, and electricity in your home if instructed to do so? It is a simple task that can feel stressful during the chaos of an emergency. Everyone should know how and when to use a fire extinguisher. Plan evacuation routes from every room in your home, from your workplace, and from any other place you frequent. And if you do need to evacuate your home for a period of time, where will you go? Your plan may be to go to a friend's house or a local church or public shelter. Have the phone number for your destination and multiple routes for reaching it in your evacuation kit. Some cities, particularly those in hurricane-prone areas, will have marked evacuation routes. Be aware of these and alternate routes in the event roads should become blocked.

Decide who will be included in your plan—family, friends, roommates, pets, etc. Everyone in your plan should be involved in discussions about what disasters could occur in your area and how to prepare for them. Common disaster risks in Georgia include fires, floods, severe storms, winter weather, and tornados. If your volunteerism, vacation, study abroad, or job takes you to another area of the United States or to another country, research what types of emergencies could occur there. Consider potential dangers other than fire and weather disasters, such as terrorist attacks or accidents at nuclear power plants or hazardous material manufacturing facilities.

Perhaps the most important component to your plan is to ensure you can connect with family and friends in the event that you are not together when disaster strikes. Determine how you will reconnect with family members and loved ones after a disaster. If there is a sudden emergency, such as a fire, identify a meeting place outside your home. If you are not home when an emergency occurs, select somewhere to meet outside of your neighborhood. But plan for the worst-case scenario—streets are blocked and power, phone lines, and cell phone towers are down. Arrange for an out-of-town family member or friend to serve as the contact for everyone in your plan. If local phone lines are down or jammed, you may be able to place a long-distance call, get a text message through, or perhaps find access to the Internet. Every member in your plan will need to know the contact person's phone number and have coins or calling cards for placing long-distance calls. FEMA and ARC both have sample emergency contact and information cards on their websites. Another option is to select an online or telephone-based service for finding loved ones after a disaster. ARC and other organizations have developed such services.

In the previous section, you were given some guidance for building emergency preparedness kits for your home. You need to determine who will update the kits and when. This is particularly important for water, food, batteries, prescription medications, and any documents that may change. You also must decide where kits will be stored so that you can pick up your supplies and leave in a hurry. Perhaps you will use duffle bags, suitcases, or backpacks. Perhaps it makes sense to store these in a shelter-in room you have identified for certain emergencies such as tornados or chemical spills. Or you may choose to store these in your bedroom or somewhere along your home evacuation route.

In Case of Emergency (ICE): Identity and Life-Saving Information

Imagine you are an Emergency Medical Technician (EMT). You arrive on the scene of an accident and find two unresponsive victims. You need to contact someone to ask about your patients' medical histories. Neither wallet includes any medical information. Neither victim is wearing a medical alert bracelet. You examine the victims' cell phones. You open the contact list in patient #1's cell phone and find five names (that is not many, but this is just an example): Cathy, Helen, Keisha, Ralph, and Stephen. Whom do you call? Time is ticking away as your patient's hold on life becomes tenuous. Patient #2 has 12 entries in her phone's contact list: Carlton, Carolee, Deborah, ICE 1, ICE 2, ICE 3, Jim, Ken, Kim, Natasha, Rick, and Ruth. Three emergency contacts have been provided, so you have three chances to obtain information that may save your patient's life.

Bob Brotchie, a British paramedic, saw the need for a uniform method of programming emergency contact information into a cell phone (Dakss, 2005). In May of 2005, he launched a radio campaign in the United Kingdom to encourage people to program In Case of Emergency (ICE) contacts into their cell phones so police, fire, and EMT responders could call for critical medical information that would help them provide rapid and appropriate medical attention to victims. News of bombings by terrorists in London in July 2005 reported more than 700 injured and 50 killed—many of whom were unidentified (BBC News, 2005). An email campaign was launched to encourage people to carry In Case of Emergency information with them at all times. ICE spread around the world like wildfire.

A life-threatening condition means minutes count. If your cell phone is lost or damaged and if you are injured or ill and are unable to communicate with first responders, how will they know your blood type, medications, allergies, or even your name? Have a back-up plan. Make this information available and easy to find by carrying a card that identifies you, your emergency contacts, and medical information. It is a good idea to have the card laminated. See Figure 8-1 for a sample template.

Name _____ DOB _____

Medical Conditions _____

_____

Medications _____

_____

Allergies _____

_____ Blood Type _____

----------------------FOLD----------------------

Emergency Contact Names and Numbers

_____

_____

Insurance # _____

Additional Information

Figure 8-1. **Sample Template for an In Case of Emergency (ICE) Card**

Emergency Alert Systems and Crisis Management Teams

Knowing how to prepare to shelter in your home or how to evacuate is great, but how will you know what to do and when to do it? Emergency Alert Systems (EAS) are provided at federal, state, and local levels (Public Safety and Homeland Security Bureau, n.d.). The alerts you see on your television are a collaborative effort by the Federal Communications Commission (FCC), Federal Emergency Management Agency (FEMA), and the National Weather Service (NWS). Weather radios and apps for smartphones and other portable devices are readily available. The wailing sirens you hear during a severe thunderstorm or threat of tornado are systems maintained by your county and/or state emergency management agency. It is necessary to learn the terminology to warn of weather emergencies (advisory vs. warning vs. watch) and for actions to take (evacuate vs. shelter-in-place vs. lockdown). These terms are defined in the glossary at the end of this chapter. Kennesaw State University notifies the campus community of emergencies and disasters through three campus alert systems that have been implemented and are maintained by our Department of Strategic Security and Safety (SSS). The three systems are: Kennesaw Alert System, Kennesaw Siren System, and Kennesaw Pop-Up Alert System (KSU Alert Systems, 2009). Figure 8-2 is the Emergency Quick Reference Guide for responding to KSU alerts.

The **Kennesaw Alert System** uses email, text messages, phones, and voicemail to deliver critical information to the campus community during and following emergencies. This system will be used for evacuation notifications. To be sure alerts reach students, contact information should be kept updated by accessing Owl Express and selecting the "personal information" link.

Kennesaw State University is committed to providing a safe and secure environment for our Students, Faculty, and Staff through a layered approach to notifications and response, provided by the Strategic Security and Safety Department. Our ability to contact anyone in our system through their cell phones using voice and texts, along with emails and alert desktop "Pop-Ups" with emergency messages, ensures you will receive the emergency notification when required. Response mechanisms which result from the early notification system include a dedicated crisis management program with more than 150 crisis coordinators individually trained in CPR, AED and First Aid to assist our Public Safety Department in any crisis situation.

—Robert Lang, Assistant Vice President
of Strategic Security and Safety,
Kennesaw State University

The **Kennesaw Siren System** alerts the campus and surrounding community of events such as tornados, hazardous chemical spills, or an active shooter event. If you hear the siren you are to remain inside, or seek shelter, and await further instructions. The siren is not activated for evacuation notification. [Note: The siren is tested on the first Wednesday of each month at noon.]

The **Kennesaw Pop-Up Alert System** was implemented to address the concern that cell phone service may not be available inside some buildings. When activated, this system pushes alert messages to all computer connected to the KSU network, including those in labs and those installed in classrooms for instructional use.

EMERGENCY
QUICK REFERENCE GUIDE
CALL: x6666 or 770-423-6666

Fire

- When a fire alarm sounds, evacuate.
- Gather your personal belongings, if time permits (coats, keys, purse, etc.), and exit the building.
- Do not use elevators.
- Use stairs to reach ground level.
- Follow all instructions given by Crisis Managers wearing orange vests and/or black and gold KSU I.D. badges.

Tornado Warning

- Shelter-in-place.
- Select an interior room.
- Stay away from windows.
- If in dorms/residence halls, move to the lowest level interior hallway, and avoid rooms with windows.
- Remain sheltered-in-place until Campus Administrators issue the "ALL CLEAR" message.

Active Shooter

- Lockdown and shelter-in-place.
- DO NOT activate fire alarms.
- Help direct people with special needs to a safe place.
- Go to the nearest room or office.
- Close, lock/barricade doors, and cover windows.
- Keep quiet, and silence cell phones.
- DO NOT answer the door.
- Remain calm, be safe, and be patient.
- Remain under lockdown until Campus Administrators issue the "ALL CLEAR" message.

Crisis Managers

CMs are identified by orange vests and/or black and gold KSU I.D. badges.

Each CM has been granted full administrative decision making authority for Critical Incident Response.

Fire Extinguisher

Use Fire Extinguishers on small fires only!

P.A.S.S.

- **Pull** the clip
- **Aim** at base of fire
- **Squeeze** handle
- **Sweep** side to side

KSU Sirens

If siren activates, follow shelter-in procedures.

Evacuation

When evacuation is ordered, fully cooperate with Crisis Managers, Public Safety, and Campus Administrators.

- Take personal belongings, if time permits (coats, keys, purse, etc.).
- Evacuate in a safe, orderly manner via the closest exit.
- Help direct people with special needs to a safe place.
- Do not use elevators to transport people.
- Do not re-enter the building until Campus Administrators issue the "ALL CLEAR" message.

Shelter-In-Place

- If outside, seek shelter indoors.
- Remain inside for your own safety.
- Select interior rooms.
- Stay away from exterior windows and doors.
- Do not exit the building until Campus Administrators issue the "ALL CLEAR" message.

Lockdown

- Remain indoors for your own personal safety.
- Lock all exterior doors.
- DO NOT exit the building.
- Remain under lockdown until Campus Administrators issue the "ALL CLEAR" message.

If outside:
- Seek shelter inside the building closest to you.
- Stay indoors. DO NOT exit the building.
- Go directly to an enclosed, windowless area.
- Help direct people with special needs to a safe place.

Kennesaw State UNIVERSITY
Department of Strategic Security & Safety

Created by: Department of Strategic Security & Safety
Phone: 770-423-6985 or x6985
Internet: https://web.kennesaw.edu/sss/

Figure 8-2.

Crisis Management Teams

There are volunteer **Crisis Coordinators** in every building on campus. These faculty and staff members are trained in emergency preparedness, emergency response, crisis mitigation, first aid, cardiopulmonary resuscitation (CPR), use of an automated external defibrillator (AED), and security awareness.

It has been shown that many of the current crises: Virginia Tech, Northern Illinois and other man-made situations, are over in the first three minutes. Our Crisis Coordinators act as "Immediate Responders" while the KSU Police and Cobb Fire are the "First Responders." Our Crisis Coordinators mitigate the immediate situation while awaiting the arrival of trained first responders. In this way, immediate help is rendered along with trained support for sustained assistance.

—Crisis Coordinator (2009)

In the event of an emergency, you will see crisis coordinators in buildings and on campus wearing orange vests. They have radio contact with SSS and can provide instructions and updates for you until first responders (police, fire, EMTs) can arrive on the scene. Once first responders arrive, crisis coordinators take direction from and assist these professionals.

A registered student organization, **Emergency Student Response Team** (ESRT), was established in the fall semester of 2009. Students in this organization are first trained to be disaster aware. Those desiring advanced training may become certified in first aid, CPR and AED, emergency preparedness and response, crisis mitigation, relief shelter protocol, and more. Students completing classroom and hands-on training through our Department of Strategic Security and Safety, the American Red Cross, and other state and community organizations are invited to join the faculty and staff crisis coordinators in campus drills and exercises simulating emergencies such as fire, tornado, active shooter, or relief sheltering.

All Kennesaw State students are encouraged to join ESRT. For more information, please contact Kathy Lynn (klynn1@kennesaw.edu), faculty advisor to ESRT.

Through training in emergency preparedness, Kennesaw State students in ESRT are prepared to respond in the event of a campus or community emergency. In addition, regardless of career goals, these students possess skills that enhance their marketability in any job sector.

Natural and Weather Emergencies in North Georgia

A tsunami or volcano eruption is not likely to occur here in Georgia. However, if you are interested in learning more about natural and weather emergencies or terroristic threats, a great place to start is the Federal Emergency Management Association website (www.fema.gov). This chapter is limited to natural disasters that can and do occur in the KSU area and how to prepare for them. Many of you may move to other regions of the United States or perhaps to other countries during your life. It is a good idea to research what natural disasters are possible in your community. In North Georgia, the concerns are primarily with fires, floods, winter storms, tornados, thunderstorms, and heavy storms that result from hurricanes. The prevention and preparation information that follows has been adapted from the FEMA website.

Fire

Each year, more than 4,000 Americans die and more than 25,000 are injured in fires, many of which could have been prevented (Centers for Disease Control and Prevention, 2009). Direct property loss due to fires is estimated at $8.6 billion annually (Karter, 2009).

To protect yourself, it is important to understand the basic characteristics of fire. Fire spreads quickly; there is no time to gather valuables or make a phone call. In just two minutes, a fire can become life-threatening. In five minutes, a residence can be engulfed in flames.

Heat and smoke from fire can be more dangerous than flames. Inhaling super-hot air can sear lung tissue. Fire produces poisonous gases that can make a person disoriented and drowsy. Instead of being awakened by a fire, a person may fall into a deeper sleep. Asphyxiation is the leading cause of fire deaths, exceeding burns by a three-to-one ratio.

Prevention

- Place smoke alarms on every level of your residence. Place them outside bedrooms on the ceiling or high on the wall (4 to 12 inches from ceiling), at the top of open stairways, or at the bottom of enclosed stairs and near (but not in) the kitchen.

- Test and clean smoke alarms once a month and replace batteries at least once a year. Replace smoke alarms once every 10 years.

- Install A-B-C-type fire extinguishers in your residence and teach family members how to use them.

- Be careful when using alternative heating sources.

- Store flammable liquids in approved containers in well-ventilated storage areas.

Be Prepared

- Review escape routes with your family. Practice escaping from each room.

- Make sure windows are not nailed or painted shut.

- Consider escape ladders if your residence has more than one level.

- Stay low to the floor (where the air is safer in a fire).

- If your clothes catch on fire, stop, drop, and roll. Running only makes the fire burn faster.

- If you are escaping through a closed door, use the back of your hand to feel for heat.

  - HOT = Do not open; escape through a window or signal for help.

  - COLD = Open slowly; if clear of fire and smoke, leave immediately. Always close doors behind you to slow the spread of the fire.

Flood

Very small streams, gullies, creeks, culverts, dry streambeds, or low-lying grounds that appear harmless in dry weather can flood. Some floods develop slowly, sometimes over a period of days. But flash floods can develop quickly, sometimes in just a few minutes and without any visible signs of rain. Flooding can also occur when a dam or levee breaks, producing effects similar to flash floods.

Flood effects may be local (impacting a community) or very large (affecting entire river basins and multiple states). Flash floods often have a dangerous wall of roaring water that carries rocks, mud, and other debris and can sweep away most things in its path. Every state is at risk from this hazard.

Be Prepared

- Listen to weather radio or television newscasts for the latest information.

- Be aware of streams, creeks, drainage channels, and other areas known to flood suddenly. Flash floods can occur in these areas quickly.

- If there is any possibility of a flash flood, move immediately to higher ground. Do not wait for instructions to move.

If You Must Prepare to Evacuate

- If you have time, bring in outdoor furniture. Move essential items to an upper floor.

- Turn off utilities at the main switches if instructed to do so. Disconnect electrical appliances.

- Do not touch electrical equipment if you are wet or standing in water.

If You Have to Evacuate Your Home

- Secure your home.

- Do not walk through moving water. Six inches of moving water can make you fall. If you have to walk in water, walk where the water is not moving. Use a stick to check the firmness of the ground in front of you.

If You Are in Your Car
(drive only if it is absolutely necessary)

- If floodwaters rise around your car, abandon the car and move to higher ground if you can do so safely.

- Do not drive into flooded areas. You and the vehicle can be quickly swept away.

  - Six inches of water will reach the bottom of most passenger cars, causing loss of control and possible stalling.

  - A foot of water will float many vehicles.

  - Two feet of rushing water can carry away most vehicles including sport utility vehicles (SUVs) and pickups.

Winter Storm and Extreme Cold

Heavy snowfall and extreme cold can immobilize an entire region. Even areas that normally experience mild winters can be hit with a major snowstorm or extreme cold.

Winter storms can result in closed and blocked roads, downed power lines, and hypothermia.

Be Prepared
Your Home and Family

- Have sufficient, appropriate heating units and fuel; regular fuel sources and/or electricity may be cut off. Take precautions to avoid risks of carbon monoxide poisoning and fire.

- Keep fire extinguishers on hand, and make sure everyone knows how to use them. House fires pose an additional risk as some people turn to alternate heating sources without taking necessary safety precautions.

- Allow faucets to drip a little during cold weather to avoid freezing.

- Learn how to shut off water valves (in case a pipe bursts).

- Purchase rock salt to melt ice on walkways and sand to improve traction.

- Know ahead of time what you should do to help elderly or disabled friends and neighbors.

Your Car
(drive only if it is absolutely necessary)

- Check or have a mechanic check the following items on your car:

  - Antifreeze levels

  - Battery and ignition system

  - Replace fuel and air filters (keep water out of fuel lines by using additives)

  - Heater, defroster, and thermostat

  - Lights and flashing hazard lights

  - Oil (level and weight)—heavier oils congeal more at low temperatures

  - Windshield wipers (fluid and wiper blades)

- Maintain at least a half tank of gas during the winter season.

- Place an appropriately stocked winter emergency kit in each car.

Dress for the Weather
- Wear several layers of loose fitting, lightweight, warm clothing rather than one layer of heavy clothing. Outer garments should be water repellent. Wear sturdy, waterproof boots. Avoid cotton clothing; wear materials that wick moisture away from the skin, such as wool or microfiber, to maintain warmth.
- Wear mittens (warmer than gloves), a hat, and a scarf (cover your mouth).

Tornado
Tornados are spawned from powerful thunderstorms. Generally occurring near the trailing edge of a thunderstorm, they appear as a rotating, funnel-shaped cloud that extends from a storm to the ground. Whirling winds can reach 300 miles per hour, creating damage paths in excess of one mile wide and 50 miles long. Every state is at some risk from this hazard. Tornados can cause fatalities and devastate a neighborhood in seconds.

- Occasionally, tornados develop so rapidly that little, if any, advance warning is possible.
- Peak tornado season in southern states is March through May.
- Tornados are most likely to occur between 3 p.m. and 9 p.m., but can occur at any time.
- Before a tornado hits, wind may die down and the air may become very still.
- Some tornados are clearly visible, while rain or nearby low-hanging clouds obscure others.
- It is not uncommon to see clear, sunlit skies behind a tornado.
- They may be nearly transparent until dust and debris are picked up or a cloud forms in the funnel.

- The average tornado moves southwest to northeast, but tornados can move in any direction.
- The average forward speed of a tornado is 30 mph, but may vary from stationary to 70 mph.

Be Prepared
- Listen to weather radio or television newscasts for the latest information.
- Look and listen for the danger signs of approaching storms:
  - Dark, often greenish sky
  - Large hail
  - A large, dark, low-lying cloud (particularly if rotating)
  - Loud roar, similar to a freight train
- If you see a storm approaching or any of the danger signs, take shelter immediately.

Inside a Building
- Go to a predesignated shelter area (basement, storm cellar, or the lowest level of a building).
- If there is no basement, go to the center of an interior room on the lowest level (closet, interior hallway) away from corners, windows, doors, and outside walls. Put as many walls as possible between you and the outside.
- Get under a sturdy table and use your arms to protect your head and neck.
- Do not open windows.

Outside or in a Vehicle
- If a sturdy building is nearby, get inside and go to the lowest floor.
- If no building is nearby:

- Lie flat in a nearby ditch or depression and cover your head with your hands. Be aware of the potential for flooding.

- Do not get under an overpass or bridge. You are safer in a low, flat location.

- Never try to outrun a tornado in urban or congested areas in a car or truck. Instead, leave the vehicle immediately for safe shelter.

- Watch out for flying debris. Flying debris from tornados causes most fatalities and injuries.

Thunderstorms and Lightning

All thunderstorms are dangerous. Every thunderstorm produces lightning. Although most lightning victims survive, people struck by lightning often report a variety of long-term, debilitating symptoms. Other associated dangers of thunderstorms include tornados, strong winds, hail, and flash flooding.

- Thunderstorms may occur singly, in clusters, or in lines.

- Warm, humid conditions are highly favorable for thunderstorm development.

- About 10 percent of thunderstorms are classified as severe—one that produces hail at least three-quarters of an inch in diameter, has winds of 58 miles per hour or higher, or produces a tornado.

- Lightning's unpredictability increases the risk to individuals and property.

- Lightning often strikes outside of heavy rain; it may occur as far as 10 miles away from rainfall.

- "Heat lightning" is actually lightning from a thunderstorm too far away for thunder to be heard.

- Most lightning deaths and injuries occur when people are caught outdoors in the summer months during the afternoon and evening.

- Lightning strike victims carry no electrical charge and should be attended to immediately.

Be Prepared

- Listen to weather radio or television newscasts for the latest information.

- Stay indoors until 30 minutes have passed after hearing the last clap of thunder. No place outside is safe when lightning is in the area.

Inside a Building

- Avoid contact with corded phones.

- Avoid contact with electrical equipment or cords. If you plan to unplug any electronic equipment, do so well before the storm arrives.

- Unplug appliances and other electrical items such as computers and turn off air conditioners.

- Power surges from lightning can cause serious damage.

- Avoid contact with plumbing. Do not take a shower, wash dishes, or do laundry.

- Stay away from windows and doors, and stay off porches.

- Do not lie on concrete floors and do not lean against concrete walls.

Outside

If possible, get inside a home, building, or hard-top automobile. Although you may be injured if lightning strikes your car, you are much safer inside a vehicle than outside. (Remember, rubber-soled shoes and rubber tires provide no protection from lightning. However, the steel frame of a hard-topped vehicle provides increased protection if you are not touching metal.)

If unable to reach shelter:

- Avoid natural lightning rods such as a tall, isolated tree in an open area.

- In wooded areas, seek shelter in a low area under a thick growth of small trees.

- Avoid hilltops, open fields, the beach, or a boat on the water.

- In an open area, go to a low place such as a ravine or valley. Be alert for flash floods.

- Avoid isolated sheds or other small structures in open areas.

- Avoid anything metal; e.g., motorcycles, golf carts, golf clubs, and bicycles.

If you feel your hair stand on end, lightning is about to strike. Squat low to the ground on the balls of your feet. Place your hands over your ears and your head between your knees. Make yourself a small target and minimize contact to the ground. Do not lie flat on the ground.

Summary

The decision to take responsibility for your own personal safety and well-being as well as that of your loved ones and community is yours. Becoming a prepared citizen does not happen overnight. It is a lifelong commitment that you can begin today. Start with a few of the simplest tasks, such as programming the ICE contacts in your cell phone and creating and carrying emergency cards in your car and wallet. Begin developing awareness as a daily habit by being present in every moment, people watching, and taking in all that is going on around you. Condition yourself to identify potential dangers (an aggressive or impaired driver, a fire hazard, suspicious behaviors, etc.) and to become increasingly aware of the presence of those things that may be needed in the event of an emergency (fire extinguishers and alarm pulls, AEDs, and exits).

Continue the process by carrying your checklist of supplies for your home, car, and pesonal emergency kits with you. Each time you are out running errands, pick up one or two items on the list. Soon you will have your kits assembled and in place. Invite a friend or family member to attend a class with you—perhaps a course in first aid, CPR, disaster awareness, neighborhood watch, fire suppression, or personal safety and self-defense. Develop your new skills by volunteering with disaster relief groups, first responders' activities, or community response teams. Share what you learn with those in your community and encourage others to practice awareness and preparedness.

Finally, remember that getting trained, building kits, making plans, and getting informed is just part of the preparation. Where there is an emergency or disaster, you can expect chaos and confusion. Unprepared victims and witnesses will likely become paralyzed with fear, disbelief, and/or indecision, rendering themselves incapable of or perhaps even unwilling to help themselves or others. As a prepared citizen, you must know that you should, that you can, and that you will respond without hesitation to any violent attack, medical emergency, or devastating disaster. You do this by developing the mental attitude of an immediate responder and a survivor. As you accomplish preparation tasks and begin to learn awareness and response skills, continue to ask yourself the "What if?" question habitually—in a restaurant, at the grocery checkout line, or even while watching the evening news or your favorite television program. Include a variety of scenarios that end in victorious responses. You may be surprised how quickly you gain the confidence and determination to respond appropriately to any situation.

Glossary

American Red Cross (ARC): a non-profit, emergency response organization that offers neutral humanitarian care to the victims of war, and aids victims of devastating natural disasters in an effort to prevent and relieve suffering.

Automated External Defibrillator (AED): a computerized medical device for detecting heart rhythm, recognizing and advising when shock is required, and delivering shock.

Cardiopulmonary Resuscitation (CPR): a technique used in life-threatening emergencies including heart attack, near drowning, or when breathing or heartbeat has stopped.

Center for Disease Control (CDC): a government agency that provides expertise, information, and tools that people and communities need to protect their health: through health promotion, prevention of disease, injury and disability, and preparedness for new health threats.

Crisis Coordinator: Kennesaw State University faculty and staff volunteers trained in Emergency Preparedness, Emergency Response, Crisis Mitigation, First Aid, CPR, AED, and Security Awareness. Crisis Coordinators serve as "Immediate Responders" in each building on campus and mitigate immediate emergency situations while awaiting the arrival of trained first responders.

Emergency Student Response Team (ESRT): a registered student organization that offers Kennesaw State University students disaster awareness and emergency response training, preparing them to respond in the event of a campus or community crisis.

Emergency Medical Technician (EMT): first responder trained to provide emergency medical procedures and transport patient(s) to a hospital.

Emergency Alert Systems (EAS): a national public warning system that requires broadcasters, cable television systems, wireless cable systems, satellite digital audio radio service (SDARS) providers, and direct broadcast satellite (DBS) providers to provide the communcations capability to the President to address the American public during a national emergency. The system also may be used by state and local authorities to deliver important emergency information, such as AMBER alerts and weather information targeted to specific areas.

Evacuate: walk quickly to the nearest exit and move clear of the building. Follow the instructions provided by crisis coordinators and first responders.

Federal Emergency Management Agency (FEMA): a government agency providing support to citizens and first responders to ensure that as a nation we work together to build, sustain, and improve our capability to prepare for, protect against, respond to, recover from, and mitigate all hazards.

Federal Communications Commission (FCC): an independent United States government agency charged with regulating interstate and international communications by radio, television, wire, satellite, and cable.

First Responder: a public safety official such as a law enforcement officer, firefighter, or emergency medical technician (EMT).

Good Samaritan: an individual who volunteers to render aid, protected from civil liability by Good Samaritan laws.

Immediate Responder: an individual who is among the first to respond to an emergency as a result of being on the scene when the event occurred or on the scene prior to professional first responders.

Lock Down: remain indoors, close windows, and lock doors. If outside, enter the nearest building. Remain indoors until an "All Clear" message is received.

Public Safety, Department of: campus police, responsible for ensuring "a safe and secure community conducive to the free exchange of ideas in an academic setting."

Shelter In: remain inside and move to an interior room away from windows. If outside, enter the nearest building. Remain indoors until an "All Clear" message is received.

Strategic Security and Safety, Department of (SSS): the department responsible for providing a comprehensive security and emergency management program for Kennesaw State University.

Weather

Flash Flood Warning: a flash flood is occurring; seek higher ground on foot immediately.

Flash Flood Watch: flash flooding is possible. Be prepared to move to higher ground; listen to NOAA Weather Radio, commercial radio, or television for information.

Flood Warning: flooding is occurring or will occur soon. If advised to evacuate, do so immediately.

Flood Watch: flooding is possible. Tune in to NOAA Weather Radio, commercial radio, or television for information.

Freezing Rain: rain that freezes when it hits the ground, creating a coating of ice on roads, walkways, trees, and power lines.

Frost/Freeze Warning: below freezing temperatures are expected.

National Oceanic and Atmospheric Administration (NOAA) and National Weather Service (NWS): U.S. Department of Commerce official weather, marine, fire, and aviation forecasts, warnings, and climate forecasts.

Sleet: rain that turns to ice pellets before reaching the ground. Sleet also causes moisture on roads to freeze and become slippery.

Severe Thunderstorm Watch: severe thunderstorms are likely to occur. Watch the sky and stay tuned to NOAA Weather Radio, commercial radio, or television for information.

Severe Thunderstorm Warning: severe weather has been reported by spotters or indicated by radar. Warnings indicate imminent danger to life and property to those in the path of the storm.

Tornado Watch: tornados are possible. Remain alert for approaching storms. Watch the sky and stay tuned to NOAA Weather Radio, commercial radio, or television for information.

Tornado Warning: a tornado has been sighted or indicated by weather radar. Take shelter immediately.

Winter Storm Watch: a winter storm is possible in your area. Tune in to NOAA Weather Radio, commercial radio, or television for more information.

Winter Storm Warning: a winter storm is occurring or will soon occur in your area.

For Further Training

Visit these sites for additional information and to sign up for online and classroom training.

American Heart Association	www.americanheart.org
American Red Cross	www.redcross.org
Be Ready Campaign	www.ready.gov
Centers for Disease Control	www.cdc.gov
Citizen Corps	www.citizenscorps.gov
Cobb County Emergency First Response (CERT)	ema.cobbcountyga.gov/cert.htm
Department of Homeland Security	www.dhs.gov
Federal Emergency Management Agency	www.fema.gov
National Weather Service	www.nws.noaa.gov
National Crime Prevention Center	www.ncpc.org

References

ACTS World Relief (2010). Citizen Corps and CERT organizations. Slide 9. Retrieved February 6, 2010, from http://www.actswr.org/c/.../01-CITIZEN-CORPS-CERT-ORGANIZATIONS.ppt

BBC News (2005, July 7). Bombings: Overview. Retrieved from http://news.bbc.co.uk/2/shared/spl/hi/uk/05/london_blasts/what_happened/html

Blass, T. (1991). Understanding behavior in the Milgram obedience experiment. *Journal of Personality and Social Psychology, 60,* 398–413.

Bonno, T. (2010). When professional responders can't respond: Why you need a well-trained corporate CERT. Retrieved from http://www.disaster-resource.com/articles/07p_152.shtml

Caldwell, R. (2011, August 3). Mystery man pulls man off MARTA tracks. *Atlanta Business Chronicle.* Retrieved from http://www.bizjournals.com/atlanta/morning_call/2011/08/mystery-man-pulls-man-off-marta-tracks.html

Centers for Disease Control and Prevention (2009, September 29). Home and recreational safety: Fire prevention. Retrieved January 20, 2010, from http://www.cdc.gov/HomeandRecreationalSafety/Fire-Prevention/index.html

Citizen Corps (n.d.a). About Citizen Corps. Retrieved February 6, 2010, from http://www.citizencorps.gov/about.shtm

Citizen Corps (n.d.b). Citizen Corps Councils. Retrieved February 6, 2010, from http://www.citizencorps.gov/councils/

Cobb County Police Department (n.d.). Cobb County Education Unit. Retrieved January 26, 2010, from http://police.cobbcountyga.gov/crime-prevention.htm

Community (2003, September 11). 9/11 brought sense of community. *USA Today,* p. 12A.

Costs from Sandy (2012, November 13). Costs from Sandy into the billions as thousands struggle, still, without power. CNN. Retrieved from http://www.cnn.com/2012/11/12/us/northeast-weather

Crisis Coordinator (2009). KSU crisis coordinator program. Kennesaw State University Department of Strategic Security and Safety. Retrieved February 10, 2010, from www.kennesaw.edu/sss/CrisisManagers

Dakss, B. (2005, July 26). ICE your cell phone for safety: Contact info saved in devices could help owners in distress. Retrieved from http://www.cbsnews.com/stories/2005/07/26/earlyshow/main711715.shtml?tag=currentVideoInfo;videoMetaInfo

Fisher, B. S., Cullen F. T., & Turner, M. G. (2000, December). *The sexual victimization of college women.* (NIJ Publication No. NCJ 182369). Washington, DC: U.S. Government Printing Office.

Georgia Code. (2011a). O.C.G.A. § 51-1-29. TITLE 51. TORTS, CHAPTER 1. GENERAL PROVISIONS, § 51-1-29. Liability of persons rendering emergency care. O.C.G.A. § 51-1-29. Retrieved from http://www.lexisnexis.com/hottopics/gacode/Default.asp

Georgia Code. (2011b). O.C.G.A. § 40-6-275 (2011), TITLE 40. MOTOR VEHICLES AND TRAFFIC, CHAPTER 6. UNIFORM RULES OF THE ROAD, ARTICLE 12. ACCIDENTS , § 40-6-275. Duty to remove vehicle from public roads; removal of incapacitated vehicle from state highway. Retrieved from http://www.lexisnexis.com/hottopics/gacode/Default.asp

Hall, S., Kramer, W., Neal, J., & Schlabach, J. (1998). Health and society: Big government versus big tobacco industry. Retrieved from http://www.units.muohio.edu/psybersite/News/p324s98na4.shtml

Honoré, R. L. (2010). General Russel Honoré, LLC. Retrieved from http://www.generalhonore.com

Horwitz, S. & Craig, T. (2007, August 30). Va. Tech criticized in massacre probe; Lack of earlycampus alert cited by panel. *The Washington Post*, p. A01.

Jonsson, P. (2009, September 23). Atlanta flood: After drought, residents caught by surprise. *The Christian Science Monitor*, Section: USA, p. 1.

Karter, M. J. (2009). *Fire loss in the United States during 2008*. Quincy, MA: National Fire Protection Association, Fire Analysis and Research Division.

KSU Alert Systems (2009). KSU alert systems. Kennesaw State University Department of Strategic Security and Safety. Retrieved February 5, 2010, from www.kennesaw.edu/sss

Marietta Police Department (2007). Public service announcements: Don't be a victim. Retrieved January 25, 2010, from http://www.mariettaga.gov/departments/emergency/police/psa.aspx

Mayo Clinic (2008). Alcohol poisoning. Retrieved from http://www.mayoclinic.com/health/alcohol-poisoning/DS00861

MSN Money (2010). The basics: The basics of renter's insurance. Retrieved from http://moneycentral.msn.com/content/CollegeandFamily/Moneyinyour20s/P36957.asp

National Crime Prevention Center (2010). Disaster preparedness. Retrieved from http://www.ncpc.org/topics/preparedness

National Highway Traffic Safety Administration (2009, June). *Traffic safety facts: Crash stats: 2008 traffic safety annual assessment—Highlights.* (NHTSA Publication No. DOT HS 811 172). Washington, DC: NHTSA National Center for Statistics and Analysis.

NIAAA (2012). College Drinking. Retrieved from http://www.niaaa.nih.gov/alcohol-health/special-populations-co-occurring-disorders/college-drinking

Norris, J., Nurius, P. S., & Dimeff, L. A. (1996). Through her eyes: Factors affecting women's perception of and resistance to acquaintance sexual aggression threat. *Psychology of Women Quarterly, 20,* 123–145.

Public Safety and Homeland Security Bureau (n.d.). Emergency alert system. Retrieved from http://www.fcc.gov/pshs/services/eas/

Rape, Abuse & Incest National Network (2009). Ways to reduce your risk of sexual assault. Retrieved from http://www.rainn.org/get-information/sexual-assault-prevention

Rich, M. & Richards, K. (2010, January 13). "Senator Preston Smith introduces Volunteer Emergency Assistance Bill," *Upper Chamber Report,* Day-3, p. 2. Retrieved from http://www.legis.ga.gov/legis/2009_10/senate/UpperChamber/2010/issue%20three%201_13_10.pdf

Robinson, J. E. U. S. Department of Justice, Bureau of Justice Statistics. (2010). *National crime victimization survey* (NCJ 231173). Retrieved from http://bjs.ojp.usdoj.gov/content/pub/pdf/cvus08.pdf

Romero, S. & Lacey, M. (2010, January 29). Grudges put on hold, mostly, in Haiti: On the ground, aid teams from rival countries overlook their differences. *The International Herald Tribune,* p. 4.

Rosen, M. (2001, September 12). Shaken survivors tell tales of luck and bravery. *St. Petersburg Times* (Florida), p. 7A.

Safe and Sound (2012). *Safe and Sound: Safety information for the Kennesaw State University Community.* Kennesaw, GA: Kennesaw State University Department of Public Safety.

Sagarin, B. J., Cialdini, R. B., Rice, W. E., & Serna, S. B. (2002). Dispelling the illusion of invulnerability: The motivations and mechanisms of resistance to persuasion. *Journal of Personality and Social Psychology, 83,* 526–541.

Sander, T. H. & Putnam, R. D. (2002, February 19). Walking the civic talk after Sept. 11. *Christian Science Monitor,* Opinion, p. 11.

Teenage Samaritan (2005, November 7). Teenage Samaritan hailed a hero. BBC News. Retrieved from http://news.bbc.co.uk/2/hi/uk_news/england/beds/bucks/herts/ 4415342.stm

Vanden Brook, T. & Copeland, L. (2005, August 29). Hurricane Katrina: 160-mph "monster." *USA Today,* p. 1A.

Washington State Legislature (2009, December 9). *Immunity from liability for certain types of medical care* (Publication No. RCW 4.24.300). Retrieved from http://apps.leg.wa.gov/RCW/default.aspx?cite=4.24.300

The author would like to acknowledge Dr. David R. Thompson for his assistance with this chapter and to offer gratitude for his direction, guidance, editing, encouragement, and patience.

Critical Thinking Questions

1. As you begin to think about becoming a prepared citizen, list your assets. What do you "bring to the table" already? For example, you might say, "I already have a cell phone, my doctor's phone number, a fire extinguisher in my car, a predetermined place to meet family in case of a natural disaster, etc."

2. How could being prepared for emergencies or disasters be beneficial to you? your family? your community?

3. Now that you have read this chapter, what concerns do you have about becoming a "prepared citizen"? How might you address or resolve those concerns?

4. What steps are you willing to take to become a prepared citizen? What is your personal plan to become a prepared citizen?

EXERCISE 8-1

Name _____ Date _____

While reading this chapter, you may have remembered an event or experience in which you might have acted as an immediate responder. What was the situation? How did you react? What was the outcome of your actions?

Learn your way around campus by mapping all emergency phones from the East Parking Deck to the West Deck and from KSU Place to University Place. Look in parking lots, along sidewalks, and inside buildings. Use an existing campus map as a starting point. To provide more detail, create your own map. Feel free to take pictures of emergency phones; include something in the background to show context (in other words, do not just take a close-up photo of an emergency phone).

How many emergency phones did you find?

Did you notice any locations that seem as though emergency phones should be placed there? Where, exactly? Why do you think an emergency phone should be installed at that location?

EXERCISE 8-3
The "What If?" Game

Name _____ Date _____

Consider the following "What If?" scenarios. Visualize yourself responding appropriately. Remember to play all the way through to the finish. See yourself "doing the right thing." Where personal safety is involved, see yourself victorious.

What if you pull up to the drive-through window at your bank just as the teller is being robbed?

What if you are walking from the parking deck to class and the Kennesaw Siren System begins to sound?

What if your roommate comes home from a party and passes out in the living room?

What if you are staying at a hotel on the beach during Spring Break and the fire alarm sounds in the middle of the night?

What if you are playing ping-pong in the Student Center game room and you hear gunshots?

What if you live off campus and you are studying for a mid-term exam in the library when you receive a KSU Alert System text message that campus is closing because of flooding? On your way to your car in the East Parking Deck, another text message arrives that says the lower level of the East Parking Deck is flooded. Your car is sitting in water up to its door handles.

EXERCISE 8-4
ICE

Name _____ Date _____

Visit the textbook website chapter 8 resources. There is an interactive tool for developing ICE cards. Create an In Case of Emergency (ICE) card for yourself. Repeat this process for at least two other people about whom you care, and give them their cards.

EXERCISE 8-5
Make a Plan

Name _____ Date _____

Pretend a train derails five miles northwest of your residence. Police call for evacuation of your neighborhood because there is a credible risk that toxic vapors may enter the area within 30 minutes.

In what ways have you prepared for such an occasion? (Hint: Show your maps of at least two emergency evacuation routes from your home to safety. Mention where your home emergency kit for evacuation would be kept. List the contents of that emergency kit.)

CHAPTER 9

Discover Yourself...Discover Your Career
LYNN BOETTLER, M.A.

Chapter Goals

- Develop a better understanding of the career decision-making process

- Understand that career planning is a process that develops over time

- Be able to effectively evaluate yourself using different instruments to help determine a career "fit"

- Understand the importance of the three steps of career planning

- Know the career planning resources available at KSU

Chapter Overview

What Does Career Have to Do with It?

Those in higher education like to believe students come to college to broaden their horizons and to engage in learning at a higher level. Students want to learn about art, music, history, cultures, and literature. Right? Well, that may be part of the reason you are here in college, but realistically speaking, one of the main reasons most students come to college is to gain the knowledge and skills necessary for a good career. Another reality check is that many college students are uncertain about their career choices, and even those coming into school thinking they know what they want to do often change their minds.

Here are three important facts:

- Fact 1: Research shows that students who do not know their majors or career choices are less likely to stay in school.

- Fact 2: People change their careers several times in their lives.

- Fact 3: Most college students change their majors once or twice before graduating.

Since it is KSU's business (and yours, too) to ensure your success in school and give you skills and knowledge for your future success, it is advisable that you explore some career resources and learn some career-discovery strategies that will be useful to you now and down the road.

Career Discovery: Not Just Once in a Lifetime

To understand the career discovery process, it is helpful to consider this analogy. Suppose you are a personal shopper, and your new client tells you she needs some clothes. The first thing you would have to do is find out a little bit about your client and her likes and dislikes. You would need to know things such as her size, the colors she likes, the style of clothes she prefers, and the brands that appeal to her. Another thing you would need to know something about is the occasion or the type of environment for which she needed the clothes, not to mention her budget. Are the clothes for work or for leisure? Does she need them for a special event? Are they for outdoors or indoors? Once you have gathered this information, you will have a good start at figuring out what clothes will work for your client.

Career planning is very similar. If you want to figure out what career best suits you, you will need to have ample information about yourself.

What are your interests and skills? What is important to you? What is your personality? You will also need to know something about the career and the working environment. How much education does the career require? What is the job demand for that career? What is the salary? Is the job outdoors or indoors? Once you have gathered this information, you will have a good start at figuring out what career will work for you.

Returning to the personal shopper analogy—you have all the information you need, and you have made your decisions and bought the clothes for your client. You give them to her, and what happens? She tries them on, and they do not fit. Or, maybe they do fit, and she loves them and keeps them for a while, but then she gets tired of them. Maybe they go out of style. Maybe the clothes just wear out. Maybe she loses or gains weight so the clothes no longer fit. Then, you go back to the beginning to learn about your client and her changing needs.

Well, the same holds true when thinking about or selecting careers. You go through this process of exploring yourself and researching the work world, you integrate the information, and you settle on a career. You follow the corresponding major, finish your education, and find a job in your desired career field. Then you start working that job, and what happens? You find out it does not fit after all? Perhaps after a couple of years, you master the job skills and outgrow it; maybe technology you are unfamiliar with infiltrates your job, so in a sense the job outgrows you. Perhaps life experiences and personal development cause you to think differently or to value different things so that you are no longer fulfilled or interested in that career. A number of things could happen. The idea here is that you think about career discovery as a lifetime process. If you change and the work world changes (and both will), you will go back to the beginning of the process and reevaluate your interests, values, and abilities, as well as the work world, and make new decisions.

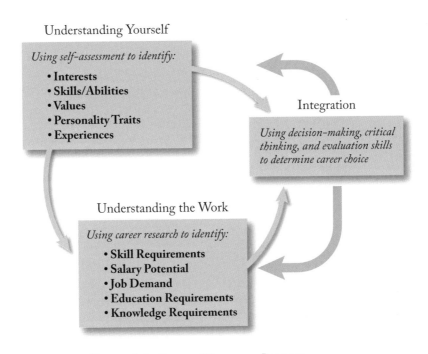

Figure 9-1. **Career Discovery Process**

Figure 9-1 portrays the career discovery process. As you go through the exercises in this chapter, it is essential to remember that the career discovery process is something you may use not only now but throughout your life.

Understanding Yourself: How Do You Do It?

The first stage in the career discovery process is understanding yourself. While most people have an idea of their interests and preferences with regard to potential careers, one of the ways to explore these things systematically and at a deeper level is to complete some self-assessments. Typically in the career discovery process, assessments are designed to help you more fully identify your interests, skills, values, and personality characteristics. Exercises 9-1–9-5 at the end of this chapter provide several assessments to help you in systematically identifying these aspects of yourself.

Career Resources

Georgia Career Information Center http://www.gcic.edu/

The *Georgia Career Information Center* (GCIC) is comprehensive resource offering a variety of career assessments, occupational information, financial aid resources, and information on colleges in the United States. One of the most valuable features of the GCIC is that its many databases are searchable. If you want to find out what colleges offer a bachelor's degree in nursing in Alaska, you can find them with a quick search. If you want to learn what careers match your interests, your skills, and your values, you can answer some questions about yourself, and you'll receive a long list of occupations that fit you. This is a resource you do not want to miss!

Occupational Outlook Handbook http://www.bls.gov/ooh/

The *Occupational Outlook Handbook*, developed through the Department of Labor and the Bureau of Labor Statistics, is an excellent reference for anyone seeking information on a particular career field or job. The OOH provides descriptions of various careers, the working conditions, the type of work, potential earnings, training and educational requirements, job outlook, and other relevant information.

O*NET http://www.onetonline.org/

The *Occupational Information Network*, or O*NET, is essentially a one-stop shop for potential employees. O*NET provides a wide range of information about any given occupation from characteristics of employees in the position to job descriptions and requirements.

America's Career InfoNet http://www.acinet.org/

The *Career InfoNet* is a clearinghouse for students in finding job and career-related information. This site is divided into three sections: (1) Career Information, (2) Industry Information, and (3) State Information. The Career Information option allows students to search for specific information as it relates to a chosen or preferred career. Information such as education needed, prospect for growth, and salary information are all found with this option. The Industry Information option allows you to sort for jobs in specific industries. You have the ability to see the wage trends for any given industry, which industry has the highest employment rate, as well as which industries are projected to grow the fastest. The State Information option looks at the labor markets in specific states. This option gives a state-by-state breakdown on labor statistics, markets, and resources including education, cultural, and recreational resources applicable to the state chosen.

The Dictionary of Occupational Titles http://www.occupationalinfo.org/

The *Dictionary of Occupational Titles* (DOT) is provided through the federal government and the Department of Labor. The DOT is exactly what it sounds like, a listing of thousands of common occupations such as accountant or lawyer but also lists some unusual occupations such as *cake inspector* or *mammalogist*. Although the DOT doesn't give extensive information about careers, it does give a short dictionary definition of that occupation for just about every job title in existence in the U.S.

Figure 9-2. Career Resources

Understanding the Work World: How and Where Do You Look for Information?

After completing Exercise 9-1–9-6, you should have a pretty good understanding of yourself and a list of careers that may suit you. The next step of the career discovery process involves gaining a better understanding of the actual careers in order to keep moving you toward making decisions. For example, what kind of work environment could you expect in that career? What is the job demand for that career? What kind of salary would you make with that career? What type of education/training is required? How/where can you get that education/training? To gain that understanding, you will need to do a little research. There are many available resources to help you to research information on specific occupations (see Figure 9-2, Career Resources). Exercise 9-7 uses the Georgia Career Information System to help you research one of the careers on your list.

Integration: I Have This Information; What Do I Do with It?

The final aspect of the career discovery process is integrating the information you have about yourself and the work and then making some decisions. Making decisions is probably the most difficult part of the process in determining a career you would like to pursue. The following examples offer a systematic process that can be useful in making career or other life decisions.

The toughest thing to do is clearly define the decision in terms of the **possible alternatives.** Here are some examples.

Decision to be made: I want to decide what my career will be.

Alternatives: I want to decide whether I should be a social worker or an accountant.

Decision to be made: I want to decide what to do next summer.

Alternatives: I want to decide whether I should:

- Stay with parents and work at home.
- Stay in my own apartment and work a full-time job.
- Go to summer school.

The next step is identifying what kind of result you want, or your **desired outcomes**, and ranking them in order of importance. This might be a good time to look at your values generated from the values inventory (Exercise 9-5) and your career research (Exercise 9-7) to help determine and evaluate your desired outcomes.

Table 9-1.

DECISION REGARDING CAREER	
DESIRED OUTCOME	**RANK**
Make between $50,000–$60,000 per year	1
Allows me to use creativity	4
Job security (will there be jobs out there)	2
Plenty of interaction with others	3

Table 9-2.

DECISION REGARDING WHAT TO DO IN THE SUMMER	
DESIRED OUTCOME	**RANK**
Become more independent	1
Earn about $500	4
Spend time with boy/girlfriend	2
Have a good time	3

After you have established your desired outcomes, you can use a decision-making table to help you make decisions. The idea here is that you determine how well each **alternative** will help achieve your **desired outcomes**.

After filling in the outcomes and alternatives, evaluate which alternatives will allow you to achieve the greatest number of outcomes. In the following example, the person used information from his or her career research to identify that only the accountant alternative met the desired outcome of a salary between $50,000 and $60,000. Then he or she went through each of the outcomes and alternatives marking where appropriate. Based on this process, this person would most likely choose to be a social worker because social worker met more of the desired outcomes than accountant. Granted, the decision-making chart is not an exact science. It may be a good idea to weight certain outcomes higher than others. For example, if it is extremely important for you to have a job with plenty of interaction with others, you might want to give two marks to that outcome. You may also list several more desired outcomes.

Table 9-3.

DECISION REGARDING CAREER	ALTERNATIVES	
	Accountant	Social Worker
OUTCOME Make between $50,000–$60,000 per year		
Allows me to use creativity		
Job security (will there be jobs out there)		
Plenty of interaction with others		
TOTAL		

Table 9-4.

DECISION REGARDING CAREER	ALTERNATIVES	
	Accountant	Social Worker
OUTCOME Make between $50,000–$60,000 per year	×	
Allows me to use creativity		×
Job security (will there be jobs out there)	×	×
Plenty of interaction with others		×
TOTAL	2	3

Here is another example using the decision about what to do for the summer.

Table 9-5.

DECISION REGARDING WHAT TO DO FOR THE SUMMER		ALTERNATIVES		
		Stay with parents and work at home	Stay in apartment and work full-time job	Go to summer school, live in apartment, work part-time
OUTCOME	Become more independent		×	×
	Earn about $500	×	×	
	Spend time with boy/girlfriend		×	×
	Have a good time		×	×
	TOTAL	1	4	3

Now it is your turn. Use the decision-making chart for a decision you want to make.

Table 9-6.

DECISION		ALTERNATIVES		
OUTCOME	1.			
	2.			
	3.			
	4.			
	TOTAL			

What Is in a Major?

After narrowing down your alternatives and making some decisions, you might ask yourself what college major will lead you to the career of your choice. As common sense will tell you, some careers, such as nursing, require specific college majors, while other careers, such as employee training specialists, might be available to multiple majors like business, psychology, or education. As you go through the career discovery process and utilize many of the resources mentioned in this chapter, such as the link to "What Can I Do with a Major In…?" (Exercise 9-4) the occupational information available through the Georgia Career Information System (GCIS), or informational interviews you may conduct with people in your desired career, you will find that there are many majors that lead to the same career. The inverse also holds true. Your college major will often give you multiple career options. The thing to remember is that while your choice of major is not an insignificant factor in getting the career you want, many other factors such as experience, recommendations, networking, and skills are also important in employers' hiring decisions.

Digging Deeper

While the assessments and the resources you have utilized thus far are invaluable, you may wish to explore potential careers more extensively. There are many resources and experiences out there to help you dig deeper, get more information, or gain some real-world experiences that will help you in your decision-making and may even prepare you for that career.

So how do you go about getting this information or hands-on experience? There are a variety of ways.

Informational Interview

A great way to get information about a particular job or career is to talk with someone who is in that career. This does a couple of things: It not only gives you great first-hand experience from someone who is currently in the field, but it also gives you the opportunity to begin making contacts that could be useful in your job search. These conversations can be very casual, such as talking with family or friends who are in the desired field, or they can be formal, in which you contact the person you are interested in talking with and schedule an appointment. No matter which approach you decide to take, be sure it is the one that is most comfortable for you.

Professional Assistance

Kennesaw State University has many great resources that are available to students to aid in the career decision-making process.

Counseling and Psychological Services Center (CPS) offers opportunities for guided career exploration:

- **Career 101:** This counselor-led, hour-long workshop focuses on helping students make academic major and career decisions. The focus of the workshop is on teaching students about how their particular interests, personality, values, and skills relate to their academic major and career choices. Prior to the workshop, students complete two assessments, and they receive their individual test results in the form of a profile report at the workshop. There is a $25 cost to cover the test administration, scoring, and interpretation fees. For more information, visit the KSU Counseling and Psychological Services Center.

- **Individual Career Counseling:** CPS also provides one-on-one individual career counseling for any student not able to attend a workshop due to a class or work conflict. Call CPS at 770-423-6600 for more information.

Career Services Center: This center offers many different resources to help you find the job that is right for you. Here you can meet with a career services professional, evaluate and build your résumé, participate in career fairs, practice your interviewing skills, and get information about co-ops and internships. Career Services is located in Kennesaw Hall, Room 2617.

Experience

There are several ways in which you can go about getting the hands-on experience that will really help you determine whether a specific career is right for you, and the Career Services Center is the best place to get more information.

Job Shadow: Job shadowing is a great way to get short-term information about a particular job. In the job-shadow process you simply identify the job you are interested in and, through the Career Services Center, you will work to get in touch with an individual in the local community in that position. You will then arrange either a half day or a full day, during which you will go on site and shadow the professional for the day. This is an excellent way to get a feel for the day-to-day activities that are involved in a certain position, as well as to get more experience and to collect information on whether that position is right for you.

Internship: An internship is a great opportunity for on-the-job experience. As an intern you will be asked to continue your studies but also put in hours working in the particular position you have chosen. In the internship process you will identify a company or position, and, through the Career Services Center, you will establish some guidelines for your intern position. In many cases, these guidelines will require you to work a minimum number of hours for the company or establish whether you will be paid for your work. Most internships are non-paying

positions; however, there are some that do pay. One of the best things about an internship, besides the real-life experience, is that many students may receive job offers after graduation from the companies where they interned. For an internship to be initiated through the Career Services Center, there are some basic qualifications that need to be met. These include being a junior, senior, or graduate student; being in an eligible declared major; and meeting the GPA requirement/accumulated semester hour requirement for your major.

Co-Op: A co-op is another great way to get on-the-job experience. In a co-operative position, you will split time between your studies and your position. The typical co-op experience at KSU has a student go to school for the fall semester and then co-op for the spring semester. For more information about co-ops, contact Career Services or visit the website.

Volunteering and Service: Most campuses have a "volunteer services" office. KSU has Volunteer KSU (VKSU) located in the Carmichael Student Center. This is an office that maintains a database of local volunteer opportunities as well as tracks the number of hours that a student volunteers. Volunteering is a great way to network with potential employers as well as to get hands-on experience of what a job might possibly be like. (And you might just make a difference in your community!)

So What Can I Do NOW to Get That Dream Job?

In addition to acquiring hands-on experience, there are several things you can start doing now that will help get you ready for that dream job down the road.

Start Your Career Portfolio: A career portfolio is a collection of materials that provides evidence of your experiences and skills that might be useful in your future careers. As a student, this could mean evidence of service projects, papers you have written, copies of recommendation letters, examples of your coursework, and more. Many students are using KSU's Online Career Portfolio (OLCP) available through Career Services to keep a record of their experiences and work.

Network: Make connections with people now! Other students, professors, staff, current employers, and your parents' friends might very well be the people to help you get your foot in the door for your dream job.

Develop a Résumé: Even though you may not be applying for a job, if you start developing a résumé now, you can easily update it as you gain more experience.

Practice Interviewing: Many people have excellent résumés, but they get nervous and do not perform well when they get to the interview. Do not let this happen to you. Instead, get some coaching, videotape yourself, go to a workshop, and use KSU Career Services so you can learn how to interview well.

Go to Career Fairs: KSU has job fairs for which employers come to campus and recruit employees. Even if you are not looking for your dream job this year, go to the career fair anyway. You may meet someone who will still be recruiting when you are looking for a job. They will be more likely to remember you if they have seen you several times at career fairs.

Get Skills: Book learning is great, but most employers are looking for people who have skills. If you do not want to work or do an internship, at least volunteer for something that will help you develop or hone your skills.

Summary

Career development is a process. This means that there are specific things that need to be accomplished in order to make a successful career-related decision. If you do not take the time to get to know your interests and skills and choose a career based solely on salary, location, or growth, you will be disregarding something that is a large part of who you are and what paths you will take in life. Conversely, if you do not plan well for your career, you may end up with the wrong skill set, or worse, no skill set at all. It is important to take each of these steps in the career discovery process individually, being sure to give yourself ample time to determine your skills, abilities, and interests, as well as to determine which potential career interests you.

Despite all of the pressure you may be under to choose a major or plan your career, do not worry! Statistics have shown that many people do not remain in their first careers for their entire working lives. It is normal and natural for you to change careers, not just jobs. Your interests may change; your skills and abilities may change as well. You have probably already noticed that your personality has changed over the past few years as you have come into more responsibility. So it is only natural that as your skills, interests, and personality change, the job you do reflects those changes.

The career discovery process is made up of three steps: understanding yourself, understanding the work, and the integration of the two—that is, combining knowledge of yourself with the knowledge you have gained about your potential career in order to help make the best decisions. In order to help facilitate this process, you have been given activities to help you learn more about yourself as well as resources and materials in order to learn more about potential careers. Now it is up to you to bring these two together and make the final decision.

References

Department of Labor. (1991–present). *Dictionary of Occupational Titles*. Retrieved from http://www.occupationalinfo.org/

Department of Labor. (2012–present). *Occupational Outlook Handbook*. Retrieved from http://www.bls.gov/oco/

Georgia Career Information Center. (2012). Retrieved from http://www.gcic.edu/

Holland, J. L. (1997). *Making vocational choices: A theory of vocational personalities and work environments* (3rd ed.). PAR, Inc.

Kansas State University. (n.d.). Academic and Career Information Center. *What can I do with a major in…* Retrieved February 8, 2011, from http://www.k-state.edu/acic/majorin/

Kennesaw State University. (n.d.) Career Services. What can I do with this major? Retrieved February 7, 2013 from http://careerctr2.kennesaw.edu/whatcanido/whatcanido.html

Northern Illinois University. (n.d.). Career Services. *NIU Majors*. Retrieved February 8, 2011, from http://www.niu.edu/careerservices/weblinks/majors

O*NET Online. (2007). Retrieved from http://online.onetcenter.org/skills/

University of North Carolina–Williamton. (n.d.). The Career Center. *What can I do with a major in…* Retrieved January 18, 2012, from http://uncw.edu/career/WhatCanIDoWithaMajorIn.html

Wayne State College. (2007). Advising services. Retrieved March 20, 2007, from http://www.wsc.edu/advising_services/

Critical Thinking Questions

1. Given the ever-changing job market and technological advances, the career you choose to pursue today may not exist 10 years down the road. What kinds of things can you do to prepare for this inevitability?

2. If you had a choice between taking a job that paid a high salary but was not one that you would enjoy versus one that paid a low salary but that you know you would love, which would you choose?

3. What three things do you enjoy doing more than anything else? Could you find a career that incorporated one, two, or all three of those things?

EXERCISE 9-1
Interest Profiler

Name _____ Date _____

1. Go to http://www.gcic.edu/.

2. Click on this graphic:

3. Enter log in: **ksusss** and password: **gcis901** (Note: This login and password change from time to time. Your instructor will let you know if there have been any changes.)

4. Follow the link in the left: **Interest Profiler**

5. Complete inventory until you get to the page that gives you scores in the following six areas. **Please write in your scores here:**

Realistic = _____   Investigative = _____   Artistic = _____

Social = _____   Enterprising = _____   Conventional = _____

6. Read about the different interest areas, and then follow the links for the areas in which you scored the highest. For example, if you scored high in "artistic," click on the link for artistic.

7. You will see lists of occupations that match these interests.

8. Review the lists of occupations in your highest interest areas and list 4–8 that interest you:

CAREERS BY INTERESTS		

Name _____ Date _____

There are several personality style inventories available. These instruments ask you to answer a series of questions and provide you with a profile that offers you insight on how you prefer to operate in the world. Instruments like these present yet another resource to help guide you in finding a career that fits you well. Many personality profiles are based on trait theory, which holds that there are broad sets of personality traits (i.e., extroverted, introverted, emotional, rational, etc.) and that these traits can be assessed by asking individuals a series of questions. Instruments like these have been in existence for some time, and you can find formal versions (typically available through university counseling centers) as well as more informal versions of them (available online).

If you have not completed a personality inventory, you will find one available in the online resources that came with this textbook. The results for this inventory will provide you with a four-letter constellation, based on four dimensions.

Extrovert (E)	or	Introvert (I)
Sensing (S)	or	iNtuitive (N)
Thinking (T)	or	Feeling (F)
Judging (J)	or	Perceiving (P)

Your four-letter constellation is made up of one characteristic from each dimension. For example, you may be ENFP, ISFJ, INTP, etc. These constellations can then be used to find lists of careers that correspond to them. (See #8 of this exercise.) If you choose to take this personality inventory, please make sure to read about what the characteristics mean after you receive your results, or if you would like to have a professional interpretation, visit the Counseling Center on campus. If you have already completed a personality style assessment and know your four-letter constellation, go directly to #7.

1.   Go to the online textbook website for your course:
      KSU 1101/1200 students: http://dynamicbooks.haydenmcneil.com
      KSU 1111/1121 students: http://dynamicbooks.haydenmcneil.com

2.   Log in to the website.

3.   In the e-book, navigate to the end of Chapter 9 and locate the Personality Assessment and Knowledge Module link.

4.   Click on the link and enter your email address when prompted.

5.   Upon entering your email address, you will be sent directly to the assessment. If you've already completed the assessment, you will receive an email containing your results.

6.   After you have completed the assessment, you will receive a results page that indicates your four-letter personality style. Write your four letters here:

☐ ☐ ☐ ☐

      You can learn more about your personality style and how it relates to the way you learn, how you function in groups, or how you manage stress. To read more about your type, follow the link on the results page that says "Click here for a more detailed report and to see all 16 PLSI types." On the next page, find your four-letter type and expand the information by clicking on the  .

      You may also gain more information about your type by following the **Knowledge Module** link on the results page.

7.   With your four-letter personality style, you can search for careers that suit your style and that people with your style typically find appealing. Go to the following website:

      http://www.wsc.edu/advising_services/career_planning/exploration/personality_careers/

8. Select your personality type (the four letter code from the personality inventory).

9. Read through the description of your type.

10. Go to the bottom of the page, and review some of the careers for your type. List 4–8 that interest you.

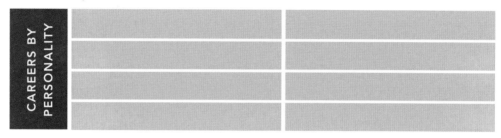

EXERCISE 9-3
Skills Assessment

Name _____ Date _____

1. Go to http://www.gcic.edu/.

2. Click on this graphic:

3. Enter log in: **ksusss** and password: **gcis901** (Note: This login and password change from time to time. Your instructor will let you know if there have been any changes.)

4. Follow the link in the left: **SKILLS**.

5. Scroll down the page to where it says "Match Your Skills to an Occupation." Read the instructions and then follow the blue link marked "Select Skills." Please note that as you rate these skills, you should be selecting those skills you would find satisfying to use in your prospective career. In other words, you may not have these skills but may acquire them through education and training.

6. After you have completed the sorting, click on the button that reads, "Rate My Skills."

7. Above **Summary of Selected Skills**, you will see several links in blue text. Follow the link for **Top 30 Occupations**.

8. Review the list and enter 4–8 occupations that appeal to you from this list.

CAREERS BY SKILLS		

EXERCISE 9-4
What Can I Do
with a Major In...?

1. You have probably thought of some possible majors for yourself. List two ideas you are considering:

   _____   _____

2. There are several websites that provide lists of occupations according to academic majors. Here are a few good ones.

   http://careerctr2.kennesaw.edu/whatcanido/whatcanido.html

   http://uncw.edu/career/WhatCanIDoWithaMajorIn.html

   http://www.k-state.edu/acic/majorin/

   http://www.niu.edu/careerservices/weblinks/majors/index.shtml

3. Follow one of the links above to find lists of occupations related to the major(s) you are exploring.

4. Review the various titles and list 3–6 titles that appeal to you.

CAREERS BY MAJOR

EXERCISE 9-5
Importance Locator/Work Values Inventory

Name _____ Date _____

1. Go to http://www.gcic.edu/.

2. Click on this graphic:

3. Enter log in: **ksusss** and password: **gcis901** (Note: This login and password change from time to time. Your instructor will let you know if there have been any changes.)

4. Follow the link in the left: **Work Importance Locator**.

5. Read and follow the instructions.

6. Once you have arranged these work values according to importance, click on the link **Get My Results**.

7. Review the list and enter 4–8 occupations that appeal to you from this list.

CAREERS BY VALUES		

EXERCISE 9-6
Putting It All Together

Name _____ Date _____

The idea behind doing all of these self-exploration inventories and exercises is for you to start working toward developing a list of careers that you might want to investigate further. In exercises 9-1–9-5 you developed lists of careers and career fields based on your interests, skills, values, and personality. You would ideally hope that a career or two would appear on all five lists, meaning that a career matches your interests, personality, values, and skills. Looking back at the exercises, which careers:

Appeared on all five lists? _____

Appeared on four lists? _____

Appeared on three lists? _____

Appeared on two lists? _____

Reflection
After doing these self-assessment exercises, do you have any immediate thoughts regarding your future career options? Which careers do you think you would like to investigate further?

EXERCISE 9-7
Career Research

Name _____ Date _____

Based on Exercise 9-6, select an occupation that you found on one or more of your lists and complete the following research project. If you had a career that was on all five or even three or four of your list, this is a great place to start.

1. Go to http://www.gcic.edu/.

2. Click on this graphic:

3. Enter log in: **ksusss** and password: **gcis901** (Note: This login and password change from time to time. Your instructor will let you know if there have been any changes.)

4. Click on the **Occupations** link under the **Careers** column on the left.

5. Find the occupation you plan to investigate.

6. Complete this worksheet.

Job Title/Occupation: _____

1. What are the work activities?

2. What is the knowledge required to do the job?

3. What skills and abilities are needed to do this job, and do you have them?

SKILLS AND ABILITIES	DO YOU POSSESS? Y/N

4. Do you have transferable skills or past work experience that can be used if you pursue this occupational interest? If so, what skills can you use?

5. If you do not have the skills, abilities, or knowledge, how can you get them? What preparation is required?

6. What are the typical interests of someone in this career? How are those interests similar or different from your own?

7. Where is the work done? What is the setting like?

8. Is special licensing needed? What kind?

9. What are some programs of study you can follow for this career?

10. What are physical demands of this career? Are you able to meet them?

11. What are the wages for this career?

Nationally _____ Regionally _____

12. What is the outlook for this job? Is it growing or declining and by how much?

13. Would there be opportunities for advancement? What are they?

14. What are some related occupations?

15. What do you really like about this career (salary, hours, benefits, etc.)?

16. What do you dislike about this career?

17. Where can you get more information about this career?

18. Is this an occupation you want to keep on your list as a possible career choice? Why or why not?

CHAPTER 10

Managing Money Through Budgeting

DEBORAH MIXSON-BROOKSHIRE, M.B.A.

Chapter Goals

- Understand the importance of a budget

- Identify the relationship between goal-setting and budgeting

- Analyze behaviors in the budgeting process

- Realize the effects of debt

- Plan for the future

Chapter Overview

A budget is a reflection of an individual's income and spending habits; it allows the opportunity to create a plan for managing money during a given period of time. This chapter teaches five steps to manage money through budgeting:

- Identify spending habits

- Understand debt

- Set financial goals and plan for the future

- Create and implement a budget

- Monitor and modify budgets as necessary

Budgets teach discipline and patience. One can enhance skills through practicing effective budget techniques. There are many opportunities throughout this chapter to assess your approach toward budgeting.

Money, Money, Money

Money, money, money: is that what makes the world the place it is today? Money is something that allows one the opportunity to dream and to plan for the future. All budgets involve bringing in and paying out money. In order to reach financial goals, spending wisely is a priority. Budgeting is a great way to organize and plan for the future. Be wise and manage money through budgeting. *Money* magazine (Poppick, 2011) lists the following U.S. annual income levels: 4% of population earns up to $16,358, 8% earns $16,359–32,188, 13% earns $32,189–$57,212, 20% earns $57,213–$97,298, and the remaining 55% have income above $97,298 (p. 24). Clearly income brackets vary, and it is important to understand income can change as one's life changes over time. Therefore, planning for fluctuations in income and expenditures is part of the budget process.

Spending Money

A budget is an indicator of spending habits. In order to have an effective budget, understanding spending habits is part of the process. According to the National Endowment of Financial Education (NEFE), most college students have one or more credit cards ("Credit Card Companies," n.d.):

- 84% of undergraduates have at least one credit card

- 50% of all college students have four or more credit cards

CARD Act Legislation went into effect February 22, 2010, and states the following: "Lenders will be prohibited from issuing credit cards to individuals under the age of 21 unless they can demonstrate the ability to make payments on their own or have a parent or guardian co-sign the application" ("Credit Card Companies," 2011).

Are more college students spending money and going into debt for their credit card purchases? The majority of college students have a credit card even with the new legislation, but can they afford the debt? Because debt results from credit card spending, it is important to consider income and expenses before getting a credit card.

Holiday shopping is an example of how purchasing can be a perilous dive into debt. According to NEFE, the following were percentages for payment methods for holiday spending ("Tis the Season," 2011).

- 2% will use a short-term loan

- 3% will get help from relatives/friends

- 5% will use a holiday/year-end bonus

- 7% will use layaway

- 17% will use savings

- 45% will pay by credit

- 13% will not pay full balance within the first statement cycle

- 32% will pay full balance within the first statement cycle

- 67% will use cash

It is a positive behavior that the majority of the individuals will be using cash to pay for holiday shopping, but many individuals will go into debt. This example illustrates the importance of budgeting and living within one's means. Even holiday shopping requires a budget and should be monitored closely so an unwanted debt does not occur. Nonetheless, NEFE indicates that "Six in 10 Americans will not use budgeting for holiday shopping" ("Tis the Season," 2011). Budgeting should be used any time money is going to be spent. Evaluating spending habits is part of the process to becoming an effective budget manager. Consider the five steps that follow to assist in this evaluation.

Step 1: Identify Spending Habits

WHERE DO YOU SPEND YOUR MONEY?	
Check the categories on which you spend your money ↓	Rank the categories that apply to you 1 = high priority to 17 = low priority ↓
College book/materials	
Tuition	
Mortgage/Rent	
Utilities	
Car payment	
Food	
Clothing	
Gifts	
Health insurance	
Car insurance	
Other insurance	
Car maintenance	
Car gas	
Credit card interest	
Recreational activities	
Vacations	
Non-food essential items	

Does your spending coincide with your current ranking of categories? If it does, you are on the right track to making a connection with your budget goals. If your ranking is not reflective of your spending habits, you need to be aware of your approach to budgeting and any habits prohibiting you from reaching your goals.

Think about spending habits and why spending is a necessary function of day-to-day living. It is important to be able to purchase the necessities of life and to pay bills to keep belongings and a home. Spending using credit cards versus cash is an ongoing debate and, as an individual, one must decide if he or she can afford the purchases made on a credit card, or if using cash is the better choice. A budget can be used to monitor spending habits in order to reach goals and allows for modifications when necessary.

Consult the Following Guidelines for Spending

Splurge within reason; moderation is key.

Prepare mentally; emotional spending can have a negative impact on a budget.

Expect the unexpected: cash flow can change suddenly.

Navigate through the budgetary process; success is only a modification away.

Decide to be positive with money and to make an impact.

Investigate finance rates and charges for loans and credit cards.

Never spend without thinking about the purchase.

Give to others; donate to a cause that is serving a purpose.

Being a smart spender can take dedication and determination to *save*; it is also a step in the successful money manager skill set. The following are some smart spending ideas to further the dollar within a budget.

Smart Spending 101

- Use coupons on items normally purchased.

- Utilize purchase incentives to your advantage.

- Evaluate cost of generic brands vs. brand names.

- Plan life goals and spend accordingly.

- Compare provider's cost, service, and rates.

- Spend money when necessary.

- Differentiate essential items vs. nonessential items before spending.

- Prioritize goals when budgeting.

- Look at money as a part of living but not the only reason for living.

Guidelines for spending and smart spending 101 are good to keep in mind when developing a budget and planning for the future.

Before creating a budget, evaluate spending behaviors. Take a moment and reflect on your mental state when you spend money. Understanding spending behavior is a component of creating a successful budget. Many young adults might see reviewing spending habits as an unnecessary component of a budget, but remember developing good budgeting and spending habits allow you to accomplish your goals in the present and future. And it is always good to have money saved for unexpected expenses. While spending is a component of the budgeting process, it sometimes results in debt.

Debt

As of 2010, total consumer debt in the U.S. was nearly $2.4 trillion. Thirty-three percent of the debt was revolving credit or credit cards, and 67% of the debt was in the form of student, car, home, and other loans. The average consumer carried four credit cards, and the average U.S. household debt was $6,500 (Zuliani, 2011).

Is debt always bad? Yes and no. Americans are a society of individuals who need items that are expensive, and many must pay for them on credit, which puts them in debt. Are there examples when debt might not be avoided? When

accumulating debt for a purchase, understanding how much the purchase will ultimately cost with interest and finance charges is a part of the process. Knowing that, you can proceed with the realization of the true cost of the purchase.

NEFE has given the following statistics regarding debt and spending:

- Studies have confirmed that consumers tend to spend more when paying with credit than when we paying with cash ("Smart Spending," 2012).

- College seniors are graduating with credit card debt averaging $4,100 ("Credit Card Companies," n.d.).

Since some consumers spend more when purchasing using a credit card, is a credit card the right choice? Suze Orman (2009) states, "If you have a credit card balance that will remain unpaid at the end of this month, you are participating in your own brand of dishonesty because you are living beyond your means" (p. 18). Carrying debt on credit cards can become very expensive and stressful. Beware of finance charges compounding while accruing on credit card balances.

Example of Credit Card Usage with 18% Interest

PURCHASES MADE ON CREDIT CARD

$125.00	Groceries and personal items
$65.00	Clothing
$280.00	Car expenses (Gas, etc.)
$30.00	Restaurant
$500.00	**Total**

You can afford only $15/month. How long will it take you to pay off this debt? Approximately four years. How much interest will you pay? $180.00.

cost of purchases with interest: $680.00
(NEFE, 2011)

Figure 10-1.

In the example above, the cost of the items was 36% more expensive than the original purchase price. Were the purchases worth the additional money paid? Using credit cards and not paying them off in the first statement cycle will cost you additional money. Make wise purchase decisions and think before you purchase.

Tip: Consumers should review their credit report on an annual basis for inaccuracies and for knowing your credit score. Currently in the state of Georgia, consumers are allowed two free copies of their credit report each year. Credit reports are obtained from one of the three credit agencies: Experian, TransUnion, and Equifax.

It is a good habit to review your credit report within the first and fourth quarters of the year. Check for any inconsistencies, incorrect information, possible credit card fraud, or identity theft. Immediately address any discrepancies. **Credit card fraud** occurs when your credit card and/or credit card number are stolen and purchases are made unbeknownst to you. **Identity theft** occurs when someone assumes your identity and opens accounts, makes purchases, and/or changes your address. Be aware that credit scores are used for a variety of purposes, such as determining interest rates on car loans, home mortgages, and credit cards; further, some employers review them for possible employment.

Step 2: Understand Debt

Be cautious of accumulating debt by buying items you must pay for over time. Oftentimes, individuals find themselves accruing debt for:

* Home
* Car
* Furniture/appliances
* Education
* Vacations
* Nonessential items
* Essential items

Which items are debt-worthy? That is, for which items are you willing to pay more than the sticker price? Why are you willing to go into debt? Do you understand the true cost of the item? Can you afford all of the expenses associated with the purchase? Did you budget for the payments for the length of time of the debt?

Paying for college can be difficult and educational loans are sometimes unavoidable. There are many pros and cons that come with both private and government educational loans, and all of these should be considered prior to signing a contract for a loan. There are many organizations that can help you evaluate various types of loans:

- NEFE.org

- finaid.org

- Students.gov

- Fafsa.ed.gov

- Private bank websites

The following examples show the estimated cost of educational loans (obtained from finaid.org loan calculator, 2011).

Student Education Loan Examples

Example 1
$40,000 borrowed at 6.8% with a repayment plan for 10 years:

Loan Balance $40,000.00
Loan Interest Rate 6.80%
Loan Term . . . . 10 years
Monthly Loan Payment $460.32
Number of Payments 120
Cumulative Payments $55,238.63
Total Interest Paid $15,238.63

Note: The monthly loan payment was calculated at 119 payments of $460.32 plus a final payment of $460.55.

Example 2
$32,000 borrowed at 8% with a repayment plan for 10 years:

Loan Balance $32,000.00
Loan Interest Rate 8.00%
Loan Term . . . . 10 years
Monthly Loan Payment $388.25
Number of Payments 120
Cumulative Payments $46,589.69
Total Interest Paid $14,589.69

Note: The monthly loan payment was calculated at 119 payments of $388.25 plus a final payment of $387.94.

Example 3
$32,000 borrowed at 8% with a repayment plan for 25 years:

Loan Balance $32,000.00
Loan Interest Rate 8.00%
Loan Term . . . . 25 years
Monthly Loan Payment $246.98
Number of Payments 301
Cumulative Payments $74,095.14
Total Interest Paid $42,095.14

Note: The monthly loan payment was calculated at 300 payments of $246.98 plus a final payment of $1.14.

Loans can vary in amount borrowed, interest rate, and repayment terms. Always review and understand the terms from your lender before signing papers. As you can see in the examples, the longer you are in repayment, the more interest you will pay. Before you borrow for educational purposes, evaluate the following:

- How much do you need to borrow for your intended education?

- Have you exhausted all other resources (e.g., scholarships, grants etc.)?

- Do you want to borrow from the government or a private company?

- What are the pros and cons of all researched lenders for your personal situation?

- What are the interest rate and repayment terms—will you be able to afford the payments in the future?

- Are you mentally prepared for the debt (true cost) you are going to incur with an educational loan?

Laws for educational loans change, thus it is important for you to stay abreast of any tax incentives, loan forgiveness, and deferment policies involving your educational loan.

Debt can bring about eustress (good stress) and distress (bad stress). Understanding debt allows an individual to take control of their finances. Deciding to go into debt should be taken very seriously. Prior to going into debt, take into account the following:

- What is the true purchase cost vs. the benefit?

- Is the cost worth the debt?

- What sacrifices will be needed if this debt is incurred?

- Is this debt in line with your goals?

- Are you ready to mentally take on the debt?

- Did you budget for this debt?

- Are you adhering to budget percentage guidelines?

Remember, if you do not have the cash or if the purchase is not in your budget, do not spend or go into debt without first thoroughly analyzing the expense. Persevere and resolve your cost vs. benefit before spending your hard-earned income. Remember the old adage: Money does not grow on trees. Goals can be attained through effective budgeting. Always think before you spend or go into debt.

Budgeting

Everyone needs a budget to ensure their needs are met and their personal, professional, and academic goals can be attained.

Budgets and Preferred Learning Styles

A visual preferred learner might want to consider using spreadsheets, graphs, and charts, adding various colors to enhance their experience with budgets. A tactile/kinesthetic preferred learner might consider making a notebook for budget information for comparisons and updates. An auditory preferred learner could keep a written or typed budget record and could repeat out loud their goals and the breakdown of the budget to ensure understanding of the process. Use the best approach for individual success, but regardless of learning style, the budget should be reviewed regularly to ensure accuracy and changes should be made as necessary. Going through life, priorities change, and budgets will need to be adjusted. Keep in mind the following:

Beware of interest rates and finance charges; they can wreak havoc on a budget.

Understand your spending habits for essential vs. nonessential items.

Develop a budget to your style—should it be rigid or flexible?

Gain knowledge about major purchases before buying.

Evaluate your budget on a regular basis and make modifications.

Think before you spend.

Why Is a Budget Important?

A budget is an essential key to being a successful money manager. Consider this example of a student graduating, seeking a career, and realizing the value of an effective budget.

Student example: Alexia has just graduated from Kennesaw State University with a Bachelor of Science in Sports Management; she is eager to begin working in her field. She is feeling immense pressure to get a job so she can have health insurance and a steady income to pay all of her credit card bills and student loans. She sends out her résumé and within two weeks hears from a prominent cruise line that is interested in interviewing her for an entry-level position. Alexia is ecstatic and goes out to celebrate with friends. She buys dinner and dessert for all of her friends on her credit card. An interview is set up, but the location is out of state. Alexia is in a quandary about how to get to the interview.

Her car is not in top shape, and she does not know if it will make the trip. She could fly, but her credit cards are maxed out. (The dinner for her friends put her over her credit limit.)

Alexia's stress level is high, and she wishes she had planned for this momentous event in her life. She has to call her parents and ask for money. They are willing to lend her the money but are concerned about her spending habits. Alexia goes to the interview and gets the job of her dreams, but she continues to splurge a little too much and is unable to make her monthly car payment. Her parents step in again to lend a hand but require Alexia to pay them back within six months. She realizes she should have been budgeting throughout her college journey in order to have financial security. Alexia sits down and organizes a budget to meet her needs and to repay her parents.

Alexia is a college graduate now and has taken control of her finances, but is it too late? She has also accumulated a great amount of debt with credit cards and student loans. (She lost her scholarship her first year because she did not have good time-management skills.)

- How could Alexia have avoided stress and the call to her parents to borrow money?

- Will you have to move to a new location for your career?

- Will you need new clothes for your career?

- Will you have to travel for your interviews?

This is an example of how poor money management can get out of hand and intensify an already difficult situation. Be an effective money manager by budgeting and planning for the future.

Step 3: Set Financial Goals and Plan for the Future

Short-term and long-term goals will change as one grows professionally, academically, and personally. Short-term goals can be defined as those occurring within one year or less, and long-term goals can be defined as goals occurring beyond a year. Short-term goals can also break down by quarters within a year (e.g., one goal every three months). Values are a vital piece in the decision-making budgetary process. Keep in mind what is important. When planning ahead with short- and long-term goals, ask: is this a *need*, or is this a *want*?

Table 10-1. Short-Term vs. Long-Term Budget Goals (goals can vary from one individual to another and can vary in the classification of the goal)

SPENDING MONEY		
Short-term or long-term goal? ↓		How much is necessary to accomplish this goal? ↓
	Pay off credit card debt	
	Get ahead one month for rent/mortgage	
	Pay off borrowed money	
	Save for a nonessential item	
	Save for an essential item	
	Save for a down payment on a car	
	Save for a down payment for a house/apartment	
	Save for a vacation	

Categorizing a budget can be difficult because some items serve a dual purpose within a budget. A budget will have variable and fixed income and expenses depending on the goals and situation of the individual. If the income or expenses are variable, they will vary from month to month or quarter to quarter. If the income or expenses are fixed, they will be the same from month to month or quarter to quarter. When planning for a budget involving variable income or expenses, take the average and use that for the planning stage and then compare it to the actual income and expenses to make modifications.

Which of the following are variable and which are fixed? The expenses can vary for different individuals depending on lifestyle. Check which categories apply to you and rank the categories fixed or variable:

☐ Income _____

☐ Mortgage/rent _____

☐ Utilities _____

☐ Car payment _____

☐ Food _____

☐ Clothing _____

☐ Gifts _____

☐ Health insurance _____

☐ Car insurance _____

☐ Other insurance _____

☐ Car maintenance _____

☐ Car gas _____

☐ Credit card interest _____

☐ Recreational activities _____

☐ Vacations _____

☐ Non-food essential items _____

Understanding interest and finance charges are components of the budget process. Interest can be a positive or a negative depending on your utilization of paying additional money for an item. According to the *Encyclopedia Dictionary of Business Terms* (DeVries, 1997), "Interest is the rate charged or paid for the use of money." Purchasing an item with credit and understanding if the interest is simple or compound and if it is fixed or variable are important to being an effective money manager.

Now apply your behavioral knowledge and see if you need all of the expenses. If they are variable expenses, can they be decreased? Do you need to decrease your variable expenses? If so, how will you go about decreasing them? What is feasible for you to live and to be content with as an individual and still continue to achieve your goals? Will you be able to meet your goals with your current income and expenses? If not, what changes can you make?

MONTHLY SPENDING GUIDELINES BASED ON NET INCOME

Housing (rent, mortgage, etc.)	30–35%
Transportation (car payment, bus, taxi, gas, maintenance, insurance)	10–15%
Other (vacation, clothing, entertainment, food)	20–25%
Debt (student loans, personal loans, credit cards)	10–15%
Savings (this is how you get *rich*)	5–10%
Goals (short-term and long-term)	1–25%

Step 4: Create and Implement a Budget

Budgetary guideline percentages for expenditures are important to consider in the budgetary process. On a monthly basis, individual or family expenses should fall within the percentages in the following table to help them to survive emergency situations, meet goals, save and plan for retirement or loss of income, and obtain financial security. Analyze and critically think about your budget: Are you effectively and efficiently accomplishing your goals within a reasonable amount of time? Are your goals realistic, measurable, and flexible? Do your habits coincide with your budget philosophy? What action steps do you need to take to make your essential goals a priority in your budget planning stage?

The exercises at the end of the chapter will help you to begin the process of developing your budget and goals for your future. Keep in mind all of the steps of the budgeting process. Implementation will occur when you make the decision to act on your budget.

Step 5: Monitor and Modify Your Budget as Necessary

Budgets should be updated any time goals change, life changes, or there is an increase or decrease in income and/or expenses. It is also a good habit to update to reflect any fluctuations in prices (e.g., gas or food). Budgets should be updated at least quarterly and should be monitored monthly in order to monitor variances in income and/or expenses. Monitoring and modification guidelines for activities on a monthly, quarterly, or annual basis involving budgets follow.

Monthly Activities for a Budget

- Balance all household checking and saving accounts.

- Review income and spending for reconciliation purposes.

- Assess actual income and expenses vs. budgeted income and expenses.

- Review any positive or negative variances.

Quarterly Activities for a Budget
* Revise goals with budgetary needs.

* Adjust budget when goal changes.

* Review and reconcile savings statement.

Yearly Activities for a Budget
* Review annual income and expenses.

* Reflect on goals and accomplishments: What changes will you make in the future? What were your habits?

Tip	Choose a bank that offers free (no fees of any kind) checking and unlimited ATM usage for college students.
Tip	Do not get a debit card for your savings account.
Tip	Create a chart showing percentages and compare to budget chart.

Planning for the Future

With a volatile and ever-changing economy, a constant assessment of spending behaviors, budgets, and debt are a necessary and vital component to successful money managing. Planning for the future needs to achieve short- and long-term goals are essential. Ensuring a plan is laid while taking into account the unreliability of the economy/markets is a steadfast way to successfully meet realistic goals.

Thinking of the future, what comes to mind? Money? Happiness? Family? Career? All of these things are important aspects of living. How will goals be reached for the future? Will you invest to make more money? For your future when you are considering investing your money in stocks, bonds, or funds, make sure you understand the risks associated with investing money. It is never too early to begin to plan for retirement. At what age would you like to retire?

Is that age going to be feasible with your budget and lifestyle? As you can see, your budget process is going to affect your life now and in the future. It is a good idea to plan ahead and to be proactive. Take into account potential repercussions and benefits from decisions regarding budgetary and debt issues. For your future, are your goals realistic, specific, and measurable? How will you be able to meet your goals? Remember, life changes and budgets need to be flexible. Keep in mind a budget is a money plan for the future and can be utilized to realize goals.

The Rule of 72 is a mathematic calculation that shows how to double money and can help with the planning stage of an individual's goals.

A mathematic calculation allowing you to see how long it will take you to double your money.

72 / potential interest rate earned on your money = amount of years your money will double

72 / amount of years you will invest your money = % of interest rate you need in order to double your money

(NEFE, 2001)

Figure 10-2. **Rule of 72**

1. Suppose you had an opportunity to invest $1000 at 8% interest. How many years will it take you to double your investment?

Rule of 72 example: Divide: 72 / 8 = 9 years to double your investment

2. Suppose you had an opportunity to invest $500 for 6 years. What interest rate would you need to double your investment?

Rule of 72 example: Divide 72 / 6 = 12% interest to double your investment

Figure 10-3. **Rule of 72 Examples**

When considering investing and planning for the future, the following example from NEFE (2011) shows the value of investing early versus investing later.

AGE	SAVING EARLY AT 7%	VS.	AGE	SAVING LATER AT 7%
18	$2,000		31	$2,000

Investing $2,000 annually through age 65, but beginning at different times life will result in different accrued savings. See the following estimated results:

SAVED EARLY BEGINNING AT AGE 18		VS.	SAVED LATER BEGINNING AT AGE 31	
AGE	SAVED EST. AMOUNT ACCRUED		AGE	SAVED EST. AMOUNT ACCRUED
65	$706,000		65	$276,474

The monetary outcome is substantial when considering your future early in life; it can have its advantages as noted in the above example.

Most individuals have fears about not having financial security, so the following guidelines can help to alleviate some fears and assist in planning for financial security. According to the article "Saving Through the Years" by Linda Jerkins (2005) with guidelines offered by Owen Malcolm, vice president and chief operating officer of Sanders Financial Management, they offer the following guidelines:

- In your 20s:

  - Pay off student loans.

  - Reduce credit card debt.

  - Create a budget and track expenses.

  - Have a written financial plan and update it as circumstances change.

  - Buy a home and start building real estate equity.

  - Invest in yourself. Consider an advanced degree or professional certification.

  - Build a cash emergency fund of three to six months once credit cards and loans are paid off.

  - Set aside 10% of your income for retirement, if possible.

- In your 30s:

  - Buy life insurance.

  - Invest in your company retirement savings plans, such as 401(k), and personal plans, such as a Roth IRA.

  - Have key estate planning documents, including a will, living will, and durable powers of attorney for health care and finances.

  - Finance education by setting up a college savings plan such as a Coverdell account or a 529 plan.

For those interested, the article also covers guidelines for those in their 40s, 50s, and 60s.

Summary

Managing money through budgeting is a stepping stone to succeeding and reaching goals. Always understand who you are and make smart, purposeful decisions. Knowing spending habits allows one to overcome obstacles and to make adjustments in order to reach goals. If your finances are in good shape, your stress level is reduced and you are able to concentrate on other important aspects of life. A well-balanced and successful student is an effective manager over his or her own finances.

References

Credit card companies dropping out of college. (2011). Denver, CO: National Endowment for Financial Education. Retrieved from http://www.nefe.org/NEFENews/PressRoom/PressRelease/CREDITCARDCOMPANIESDROPPINGOUTOFCOLLEGE/tabid/765/Default.aspx

DeVries, M. A. (1997). *The encyclopedic dictionary of business terms*. New York: Berkley Publishing.

Jerkins, L. (2005, November 12). *Savings through the years*. Atlanta Journal-Constitution, p. FE6.

NEFE high school financial planning program. (2001). Greenwood Village, CO: National Endowment for Financial Education.

Orman, S. (2009). *Suze Orman's 2009 action plan*. New York: Spiegel and Grau.

Poppick, S. (2011, December). What percent are you? *Money*. 24.

Ramsey, D. (2004). *The money answer book*. Nashville, TN: Thomas Nelson Book Group.

Smart spending: should you pay with credit or cash. (2012). Retrieved from http://money.msn.com/saving-money-tips/post.aspx?post=a15dfeb9-9c3f-4a89-927c-6bf9eb2ec442

The Smart Student Guide to Financial Aid. (2011). Loan Calculator. Retrieved from http://www.finaid.org

Tis the season for spending. (2011). Denver, CO: National Endowment for Financial Education. Retrieved from http://www.nefe.org/PressRoom/News/TistheSeasonforSpending/tabid/1085/Default.aspx

Zuliani, L. (2011). *A dozen alarming consumer debt statistics*. Retrieved from http://www.economywatch.com/economy-business-and-finance-news/a-dozen-alarming-consumer-debt-statistics.21-05.html

Critical Thinking Questions

1. How do you propose to budget your way through college?

2. Do your goals correlate with your budget?

3. What will be your strategy to ensure your goals are met?

4. Can you relate to Alexia's situation? Give your own example.

5. What are your behaviors pre- and post-spending?

6. What changes do you need to make in order to be an effective budgeter?

7. What is the difference between credit card fraud and identity theft?

8. What is the meaning of evaluating cost vs. benefit prior to a purchase?

Name _____ Date _____

List your top six goals.

1. _____

2. _____

3. _____

4. _____

5. _____

6. _____

Now list your strategies to reach those goals.

1. _____

2. _____

3. _____

4. _____

5. _____

6. _____

How can budgeting assist you in reaching these six goals?

1. _____
   _____

2. _____
   _____

3. _____
   _____

4. _____
   _____

5. _____
   _____

6. _____
   _____

Name _____ Date _____

Current income and expenses. Is there room to grow and save?

CASH IN: (MONTHLY, SEMESTER, QUARTERLY, OR YEARLY)	
Parents' contribution	$
Job/employment	$
Other	$
Student loan	$
Grant/scholarship	$
TOTAL CASH IN	$
CASH OUT: (MONTHLY, SEMESTER, QUARTERLY, OR YEARLY)	
College books/materials	$
Tuition	$
Mortgage/rent	$
Utilities	$
Car payment	$
Food	$
Clothing	$
Gifts	$
Health insurance	$
Car insurance	$
Other insurance	$
Car maintenance	$
Car gas	$
Credit card interest	$
Recreational activities	$
Vacations	$
Non-food essential items	$
TOTAL CASH OUT	$

Subtract total cash out from total cash in $ _____
If the difference is positive, you have money left over for savings. If the difference is negative, you need to reevaluate your expenditures.

EXERCISE 10-3
Planning Stage for Your Budget

Name _____ Date _____

1. Reflect on your goals from Exercise 10-1.

2. Plan for next month, semester, or year.

3. For cash out: list dollar amount, % of total cash in, fixed/variable expense.

   Example: Food $225/22.5% of total cash in of $1000/variable.

ANTICIPATED CASH IN: (MONTHLY, SEMESTER, QUARTERLY, OR YEARLY)		
INCOME		**TYPE OF EXPENSE: F/V**
Parents' contribution	$	
Job/employment	$	
Other	$	
Student loan	$	
Grant/scholarship	$	
TOTAL CASH IN	$	
ANTICIPATED CASH OUT: (MONTHLY, SEMESTER, QUARTERLY, OR YEARLY)		
EXPENSES		
College books/materials	$	
Tuition	$	
Mortgage/rent	$	
Utilities	$	
Car payment	$	
Food	$	
Clothing	$	
Gifts	$	
Health insurance	$	
Car insurance	$	
Other insurance	$	
Car maintenance	$	

Car gas	$	
Credit card interest	$	
Recreational activities	$	
Vacations	$	
Non-food essential items	$	
TOTAL CASH OUT	$	
GOALS		

Subtract total cash out from total cash in $ _____

If the difference is positive, you have money left over for savings or your specific goals. If the difference is negative, you need to reevaluate your expenditures.

- Are the percentages coinciding with the formula percentages in the chapter? If not, are you comfortable with where they are and can you make changes?

- Will you be able to meet your goals with this budget plan?

- Are you realistic with your anticipated cash in and out?

Name _____ Date _____

In your lifetime, would you like to have any of the following? Check which items you would like to have, and note what you think the annual cost of each item will be.

_____ Car   _____

_____ Home   _____

_____ Vacation home   _____

_____ International vacation   _____

_____ Domestic vacation   _____

_____ Children/family   _____

_____ Furniture/appliances   _____

_____ Pool   _____

_____ Computer   _____

_____ Boat   _____

_____ Jet ski   _____

_____ Four wheeler   _____

_____ Golf cart   _____

_____ Motorcycle   _____

_____ Plane   _____

_____ Education   _____

_____ Home gym   _____

_____ Utilities   _____

_____ Food   _____

_____ Entertainment   _____

TOTAL   _____

Now, check out websites listed in the career chapter to see what your beginning salary will be for the career of your choice.

Will you have enough income for your planned purchases?

How realistic are you in planning for your future?

FOUNDATIONS FOR
GLOBAL LEARNING

CHAPTER 11

Successful Skills for Diversity: An Open Mind

KATHY MATTHEWS, M.A. AND KIMBERLY GRIMES FRAZIER, Ph.D.

Chapter Goals

- Provide background on inclusion issues and how they affect others

- Help students gain an understanding of diversity issues of today

- Promote the value of human diversity and respect for others from a variety of backgrounds

- Broaden awareness of the ever-increasing diversity of the United States and the world

- Help students understand the skills and competencies needed for success in a global society

Chapter Overview

This chapter introduces an important skill set in interpersonal communication that is vital for success in negotiating personal and professional relationships in today's diverse world. You will work on developing the competencies that enable you to interact with others in a way that respects and values differences. Discussions on diversity are an important part of your education and career preparation. Why? Because many employers realize the importance of having a workforce that can compete in a multicultural society and global community—companies seek to hire students who have developed cultural competence. The ideas discussed in this chapter will lay the groundwork for that development.

The chapter presents the terminology to foster open and honest discussions on the issues related to diversity and helps students learn how to critically examine situational contexts when diversity has and has not been valued, honored, and/or appreciated. Students will have the opportunity to work with experiential contexts to deepen an understanding of differences and will use problem-solving skills related to diverse issues.

It seems there are more and more discussions about how the world is rapidly being transformed into a global community. And, undoubtedly, you have been exposed to myriad situations that offer evidence that this observation is true. Later in this unit you will read some of the data and reports that support the idea that you are "living in a global community."

The changes brought about by the "global community" can be viewed as challenging but also exciting. The true challenge is being prepared to meet the changes. College is an ideal place to acquire the skills needed to succeed in this diverse world. Take a minute to notice: the university community is, in many ways, a microcosm of society. It brings together many unique populations—people of all ages and backgrounds. Students who take advantage of the opportunities to learn from encounters with different people and benefit from the diversity that surrounds them will gain valuable experiences and information that will prepare them to work in a global economy and live in a multicultural society.

The primary focus of getting an education is about learning things you did not previously know—in other words, becoming open-minded in the fullest sense of the word. First, you will learn that by being open to diversity, you soon discover that people are more alike than different. You can achieve an appreciation and respect for diversity and cultural differences while continuing to take pride in your own culture.

Dimensions of Diversity

KSU has taken a leadership role in affirming the value of the human experience and the diversity it represents. Take pride in being a member of a campus community that promotes a philosophy of invitational education and commitment to cultural diversity.

Diversity Statement for KSU
The KSU population reflects differing backgrounds and experiences including but not limited to age, disability, ethnicity, family structure, gender, geographic region, giftedness, language, race, religion, sexual orientation, and socioeconomic status.

It is our goal to foster a community in which every human being is treated with dignity, respect, and justice. The KSU academic experience will provide students with the opportunity to gain knowledge and experiences necessary to thrive in a diverse, global environment.

Figure 11-1.

The Diversity Statement for KSU (Figure 11-1) contains some of the basic concepts needed to be familiar with while developing a diversity consciousness. The "differing backgrounds and experiences" listed in the Diversity Statement appear frequently in the literature of The Anti-Defamation League and other organizations that offer diversity training workshops as primary and secondary dimensions of diversity. Evaluating **primary** and **secondary dimensions of diversity** often depends on categorizations by the **immutable** or **mutable** characteristics.

Primary dimensions of diversity are those **immutable** human differences that are inborn and/or that exert an important impact on our early socialization and have an ongoing impact throughout our lives. These characteristics are those over which we have little control. People may try to disguise or to deemphasize certain aspects about themselves, but can they really change these characteristics?

The elements in the core of the diversity wheel (Figure 11-2) are regarded as **primary dimensions**. Elements in the outer layer are referred to as **secondary dimensions**. The primary (immutable) dimensions are:

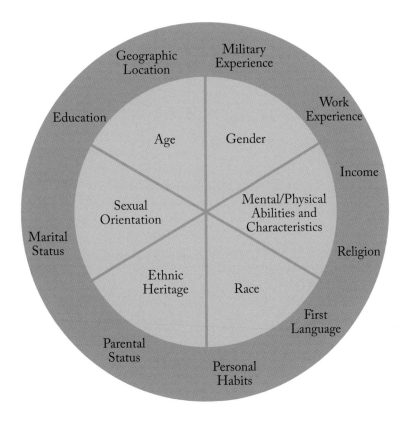

Figure 11-2. **The Diversity Wheel**

- Ethnicity

- Age

- Race

- Sexual orientation

- Gender

- Ability

Although physical abilities/disabilities may change over time, for the most part, we do not choose those physical abilities/disabilities.

Some people think of the primary dimensions of diversity as factors that can be seen, but remember to be careful about forming opinions and judgments based on physical characteristics. Sadly, society's history is full of accounts of discriminatory acts related to these primary dimensions. But people have also been discriminated against because of characteristics that are not visible at all.

Secondary dimensions of diversity are mainly the "invisible" characteristics. Unlike primary dimensions, secondary dimensions can be changed. They are **mutable** differences that are acquired, discarded, and/or modified throughout life. Some are elements that you may identify with or choose to pursue because of your own particular interests. The secondary dimensions of diversity include but are not limited to:

- Educational background

- Learning styles

- Geographical location

- Socioeconomic status

- National citizenship

- Native language

- Political philosophy

- Religious/spiritual beliefs

- Family status

- Romantic relationship status

- Parental status

- Generation

- Military experience

- Work experience

- Personality styles

Often the secondary dimensions of diversity are those with which people most strongly identify. For instance, people may speak of themselves in these terms: "I'm a student," or "I'm from up North," or "I'm a single parent," or "I'm a conservative," or "I'm a liberal." The dynamic interactions among all the dimensions influence an individual's self-image, values, opportunities, and expectations. These categories give definition to the multifaceted and unique personality and history that is *you*—the diverse person.

A key point to remember when thinking about diversity is this: Diversity is YOU. You may have been encouraged to think of all people as "the same." A nice idea philosophically, but in reality, it is false. There is only one unique you. "Diversity" means different, and you are truly different from everyone else. Use the Iceberg Activity in Figure 11-3 to examine who you really are.

Discussing Diversity Issues

It is not easy to discuss diversity issues. Why? Stereotypes, prejudice, and discrimination can form barriers to communication. A clearer understanding of what these terms mean might make it easier to discuss and analyze diversity issues. Keep in mind the dimensions of diversity while weighing these concepts. It will also be helpful to remember that diversity issues are viewed mainly as issues of social inequality. In this regard, the terms "majority" and "minority"

refer to power and to privilege, not numbers. **Majority** refers to the group with power and privilege. **Minority** refers to the group at a disadvantage with regard to power and to privilege (Bucher, 2001). In this context, it is easy to understand how some majority group members might also have minority status. Can you give an example? A more traditional use of the terms "majority" and "minority" referenced racial groups, with the term "majority" being assigned to whites and "minority" assigned to people of color. You will see how these basic terms and meanings factor in diversity issues.

Stereotypes

A stereotype is a preconceived or oversimplified generalization about an entire group of people without regard for individual differences. The characteristics of a given social stereotype may or may not have much basis in fact; many stereotypes are based on images that were created. Movies, magazines, and other media encourage and reinforce stereotyping. Stereotypes can be positive or negative; however, even when stereotypes are positive, the impact of stereotyping is negative and can feed into discrimination. Negative stereotyping is a key feature in prejudicial beliefs, sexism, racism, ageism, and crimes of hate. While reading down the list of primary and secondary dimensions, one can gauge which concepts evoke a stereotyped image of someone of that group: women (gender), disabled (ability), elderly men (age), Muslims or Jews (religious beliefs), black males (racial/gender), or Southerners (geographic location).

Prejudice

Let's face it: Everyone has been guilty of prejudicial thinking, but no one wants to say, "I'm prejudiced," mainly because of the pejorative and often hateful association with the term. Prejudice is "prejudging" a person or a group, usually on the basis of characteristics such as race, gender, sexual orientation, religion, or age.

Activity: Think of yourself as an iceberg. Download the image from the chapter 11 resources on the textbook website. Use the image of the iceberg to illustrate the primary and secondary dimensions that help define aspects of your background and identity. Remember, this is who you define yourself to be. List the characteristics that can be seen on that part of the iceberg above the waterline. Write some of your qualities or traits that might not be visible on the iceberg "beneath the surface."

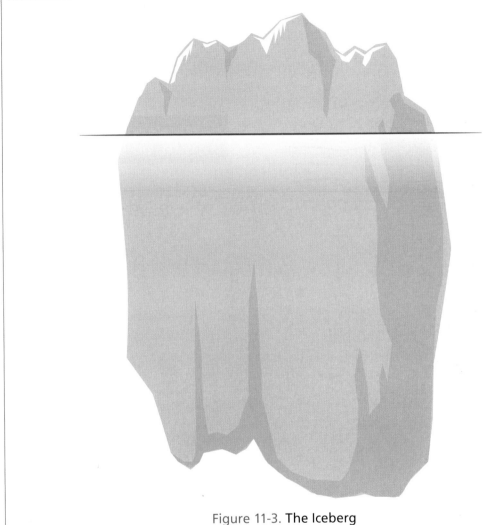

Figure 11-3. **The Iceberg**

This preconceived judgment is usually based on stereotypes, some of which have been learned from family, peers, and community. Oftentimes, prejudice is an irrational attitude of hostility directed against an individual, a group, a race, or their supposed characteristics, and can lead to discrimination.

Discrimination

Discrimination means to "distinguish between." Socially, this is to make a distinction between people on the basis of class or category without regard to individual merit. Prejudice often accompanies discrimination. How often do we hear of cases in which people expressed that they were the victims of discrimination, perhaps in being denied employment, or housing, or admission to school, or access to events? Discrimination has been a factor in cases where various dimensions of diversity were involved: race, religion, gender, age, sexual orientation, disability, ethnicity, height, and size-related characteristics.

Hate Crimes

Acts of discrimination in the extreme can lead to violence and hate crimes. Criminologist Dr. Jack McDevitt points out that hate crimes are "message crimes." They are different from other crimes in that the offender is sending a message to members of a certain group that they are unwelcome (Siasoco, 1999).

> The Anti-Defamation League (ADL) concentrates efforts to counteract hate crimes because of their widespread repercussion. The threat that hate crimes present to the security of communities is echoed in an ADL report: "Minority communities become fearful, angry, and suspicious of other groups—and of the power structure that is supposed to protect them—these incidents can damage the fabric of our society and fragment communities" (Hate Crimes, n.d., n.p.).

Do some research here and read about the tragic cases in 1998 of Matthew Shepard and James Byrd—both examples of hate crimes. These cases left communities questioning and numb. These incidents exemplify the worst in human interaction—man's inhumanity to man.

In recent years, the number of hate crimes has continued to escalate. Incidents in the hate crimes category include simple assault, aggravated assault, forcible sex offenses, and arson. Violent bigotry can also lead to manslaughter and to murder.

The Southern Poverty Law Center encourages students to join in the fight against hate. Tolerance.org extracts concepts from UNESCO's Declaration on the Principles of Tolerance that are helpful in thinking about ways students can promote tolerance (Willoughby, 2003): "Because things improve only when people like you take action. Because each student activist has the power to make a difference. And because apathy, in some ways, is as dangerous as hate. Tolerance is harmony in difference" (p. 3).

TEN WAYS TO FIGHT HATE ON CAMPUS

1. Rise Up
2. Pull Together
3. Speak Out
4. Support the Victims
5. Name It, Know It
6. Understand the Media
7. Know Your Campus
8. Teach Tolerance
9. Maintain Momentum
10. Pass the Torch

Figure 11-4.

For fuller details on how you can ensure that diversity is valued, honored, and appreciated, see the guide for college activists in the chapter 11 resources on the textbook website.

> First they came for the Jews, and I did not speak out because I was not a Jew. Then they came for the Communists, and I did not speak out because I was not a Communist. Then they came for the trade unionists, and I did not speak out because I was not a trade unionist. Then they came for me, and there was no one left to speak out for me.
>
> —Rev. Martin Niemöller

Diversity-Related Concepts and Key Terminology

To further appreciate diversity, take a look at how diversity is conceptualized in the form of "isms," define it, and analyze it for better understanding.

Concepts

"isms"

Ableism: discrimination or injustice toward people who are emotionally, mentally, or physically disabled.

Ageism: discrimination or injustice toward senior citizens, aged, or elderly.

Classism: discrimination or injustice against people of a lower socioeconomic class/status.

Ethnocentrism: the perspective that one's own ethnic group or culture is superior while another's is inferior or less important.

Racism: discrimination, injustice, and hatred based on skin color and asserting that one human race is superior to another.

Sexism: discrimination or injustice based on the inherent belief that one gender, biological make-up, or sex is more superior to another.

Institutional racism: discrimination or injustice that is culturally embedded in an organization that through policies and practices disadvantages a particular ethnic group.

Multiculturalism: a celebration of differences that preserves cultural identities within the same unified society or community.

Nationalism: excessive patriotism, devotion, and loyalty to one's own nation and asserting its interest and needs over another nation.

"phobias"

Homophobia: discrimination due to an irrational fear and/or hatred toward homosexuals or homosexuality.

Xenophobia: discrimination and irrational fear or hatred toward strangers or foreigners.

Terminology

Bias: a prejudice or unreasonable judgment, view, or outlook drawn before gathering all the facts.

Civility: a conduct of courtesy or politeness toward humanity or to act in a humane manner.

Cross-cultural: associating or comparing two different cultures or cultural regions.

Cultural competence: the knowledge and capability to interact with diverse cultures and people and with sufficiency.

Discrimination: the act or process of treating another unfairly or differently categorically or individually.

Diversity: the celebration and inclusion of different cultures and people.

Ethnic group (Ethnicity): those of the same group or shared cultural and personal characteristics and experiences.

GLBT: an acronym for people that practice gay, lesbian, bisexual, and transgender lifestyles.

Privilege: a bestowed right, advantage, or benefit given to a person, group, or position.

Redlining: a practice of discriminately withholding financial loans or investments from low socioeconomic areas or locations, historically African-American neighborhoods.

Religious bigotry: discrimination or injustice shown toward those with differing religious beliefs and practices.

Scapegoat: assigning blame to a person or group without particular justification or cause.

Segregation: the intentional, voluntary separation of a race, class, or ethnic group from another group.

Socioeconomic status (SES): the separation of people or groups into social classes based on levels of income or educational attainment.

Developing Diversity Skills

Now that you have a better grasp of some of the concepts and terms fundamental to diversity discussions, you are ready to explore some of the issues that will help you develop your diversity skills. Begin with the concept itself: diversity. Diversity is a term that has many shades of meaning and can evoke strong feelings, both positive and negative. What kind of responses and feelings do you have when you use the word diversity? Perhaps you have encountered beliefs similar to those echoed in these statements:

- "Diversity is about them—not me." Usually "them" refers to women and to minorities. But the reality is that diversity is about everyone. Each individual brings different talents and perspectives to school and to work. Remember the point of the iceberg? You are uniquely different; there is no one else like you. Diversity begins with you.

- "Diversity and multiculturalism are pulling America apart." In truth, the division stems from the inability to respect and to learn from our differences. Being exposed to diversity can help bring people together.

Metaphors for Diversity

Recent criticisms about diversity and multiculturalism are related to a fear that something very basic and fundamental to America is being threatened. These comments relate to a metaphor for America that appear in some of the first lessons on American history. The concept of America's "melting pot" is a prime example. For years, students were taught that the immigration of different people to the United States created the metaphorical melting pot. As diverse groups migrated to this land, their cultures and customs mixed into this American pot to create a new society. Truly, for many groups such as the Irish, French, and Germans, the "melting" was

easily accomplished. These immigrants changed their names, gave up their native language, and learned English. Today, members of these groups are more likely to see themselves as "just American." It is important to note, however, that many European Americans have retained strong ethnic ties.

Equally important is the recognition that not all immigrant groups could be as easily assimilated into the melting pot. In addition to the obvious physical attributes that made "blending in" difficult, if not impossible, non-European groups—such as the Africans, Japanese, and Chinese—found both laws and racial barriers impeding their integration into the culture at large.

As a result, many sociologists and educators concluded that the uniqueness of America's multicultural society is less like a melting pot and more like a vegetable stew or a "salad bowl." Like the items on the salad bar or the vegetables that are put into the vegetable stew, each group in our society has its own unique characteristics and flavor. While each item could be enjoyed alone, there is a more delectable delight when they are combined. After years of stressing commonalities, the new focus highlighted differences.

Cultural pluralism displaced the melting pot theory. Under cultural pluralism, each group is free to celebrate and to practice its customs and traditions, and in return, each group is expected to participate in general mainstream culture and to abide by its laws.

Diversity is a topic that stimulates new and creative thinking, as this discussion on cultural metaphors shows. Asserting that these two metaphors may yet be inadequate to reflect the true nature of the diversity experience, Professor Joe Cuseo suggests a different metaphor to help

THE EXPERIMENT

On the day after Martin Luther King Jr. was murdered in April 1968, Jane Elliott's third graders from the small, all-white town of Riceville, Iowa, came to class confused and upset. They recently had made King their "Hero of the Month," and they couldn't understand why someone would kill him. So Elliott decided to teach her class a daring lesson in the meaning of discrimination. She wanted to show her pupils what discrimination feels like, and what it can do to people.

Elliott divided her class by eye color—those with blue eyes and those with brown. On the first day, the blue-eyed children were told they were smarter, nicer, neater, and better than those with brown eyes. Throughout the day, Elliott praised them and allowed them privileges such as taking a longer recess and being first in the lunch line. In contrast, the brown-eyed children had to wear collars around their necks, and their behavior and performance were criticized and ridiculed by Elliott. On the second day, the roles were reversed, and the blue-eyed children were made to feel inferior while the brown-eyed were designated the dominant group.

What happened over the course of the unique two-day exercise astonished both students and teacher. On both days, children who were designated as inferior took on the look and behavior of genuinely inferior students, performing poorly on tests and other work. In contrast, the "superior" students—students who had been sweet and tolerant before the exercise—became mean-spirited and seemed to like discriminating against the "inferior" group.

"I watched what had been marvelous, cooperative, wonderful, thoughtful children turn into nasty, vicious, discriminating little third-graders in a space of fifteen minutes," says Elliott. She says she realized then that she had "created a microcosm of society in a third-grade classroom."

Elliott repeated the exercise with her new classes in the following year. The third time, in 1970, cameras were present. Fourteen years later, *FRONTLINE*'s "A Class Divided" chronicled a mini-reunion of that 1970 third-grade class. As young adults, Elliott's former students watched themselves on film and talked about the impact Elliott's lesson in bigotry has had on their lives and attitudes. It was Jane Elliott's first chance to find out how much of her lesson her students had retained.

"Nobody likes to be looked down upon. Nobody likes to be hated, teased or discriminated against," says Verla, one of the former students.

Jane Elliott expresses what she hopes people who participate in the workshops she conducts or who view the tapes of her students' experiences learn:

> I think the films of the exercise teach some really important lessons. I think they prove you can "teach an old dog new tricks." I think they demonstrate that racism is not human nature; it's a learned response. We know that anything you learn you can unlearn, and the tapes give people who watch them hope that they can unlearn and, ultimately, give up their racism.

Visit the textbook website chapter 11 resources to view the PBS program and learn more about this well-known social experiment.

readers understand and appreciate the fabric of society. In his book, *Thriving in College and Beyond*, Cuseo says that to describe American society, the image of a quilt is, figuratively, more appropriate:

> The quilt metaphor acknowledges the identity and beauty of all cultures. It differs from the old American "melting pot" metaphor—which viewed differences as something that should be melted down or eliminated, and the "salad bowl" metaphor—which suggests that America is a hodgepodge or mishmash of different cultures thrown together without any common connection. In contrast, the quilt metaphor suggests that the cultures of different ethnic groups can and should be recognized. Yet these differences may be woven together to create a unified whole—as in the Latin expression: "E pluribus Unum" ("Out of many, one"). This expression has become a motto of the United States, and you will find it printed on all its coins (Cuseo et al., 2008, p. 254).

We have become not a melting pot, but a beautiful mosaic. Different people, different beliefs, different yearnings, different hopes, different dreams.

—Jimmy Carter
Former President of the United States

Reflective Journal: Consider Carter's statement on America's cultural metaphor. Can Americans unite under a common culture while accentuating differences? Do they champion national identity over ethnic and class identity?

The "New Majority"

No matter what metaphor is used to discuss the many different elements of society, one truth can be agreed upon: our society is changing. By the time the U.S. population reaches 400 million—expected in 2043—the combined forces of immigration, aging, technological change, and globalization will have reshaped the country, experts say. According to U.S. Census Bureau data and projections by social scientists, such as Passel and Cohn (2008), the following picture can be cast:

Table 11-1.

TOTAL U.S. POPULATION	WHITES	BLACKS	HISPANICS	ASIANS	65+ AGED CITIZENS
AS OF 2005	67%	13%	14%	5%	13%
PREDICTED BY 2050	47%	13%	29%	9%	20%

Identities Outside the Box

The blurring of racial identities is evident in recent Census reports. Data on racial groups reported on the U.S. Census (American Community Survey, 2007) reflects changes in the manner in which groups are identified.

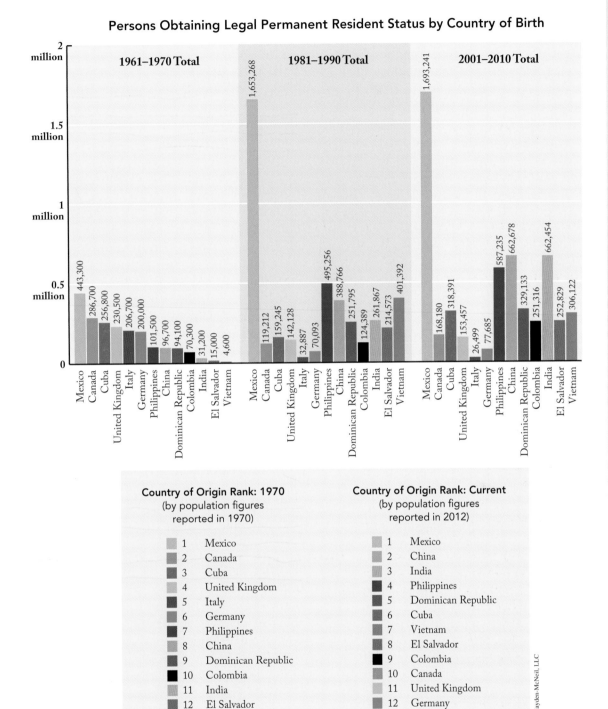

Persons Obtaining Legal Permanent Resident Status by Country of Birth

Country of Origin Rank: 1970
(by population figures reported in 1970)

1	Mexico
2	Canada
3	Cuba
4	United Kingdom
5	Italy
6	Germany
7	Philippines
8	China
9	Dominican Republic
10	Colombia
11	India
12	El Salvador
13	Vietnam

Country of Origin Rank: Current
(by population figures reported in 2012)

1	Mexico
2	China
3	India
4	Philippines
5	Dominican Republic
6	Cuba
7	Vietnam
8	El Salvador
9	Colombia
10	Canada
11	United Kingdom
12	Germany
13	Italy

Source: U.S. Census Bureau, The 2010 Statistical Abstract: The National Data Book http://www.census.gov/compendia/statab/cats/population.html

Figure 11-5.

Earlier census takers would identify people by the way they looked. Today, however, the different racial categories are listed on the form; 2000 was the first time the multiracial box appeared as an option. Important, too, is that people are allowed to identify themselves. Many people who are of multiracial backgrounds decline to identify themselves in a racial category and choose instead to mark the box "Other." The 2010 U.S. Census reports 2.9% of respondents identified themselves as being "two or more races." Asserting one's racial identity can indeed be complex, as Tiger Woods has shown. Tiger chooses to define himself with a term he made up: "Cablinasian." The word reflects his Caucasian, Black, Indian, and Asian heritage (Bucher, 2001, p. 4).

Diversity Awareness: The National Picture

The make-up of the American population is changing as a result of immigration patterns and significant increases among racially, ethnically, culturally, and linguistically diverse populations already residing in the United States. Based on newly released census data, the analysis confirms that America is an increasingly multiracial, multinational, and multilingual nation. Many reports are punctuated with the refrain of the shifting demographics.

One of the U.S. Census Bureau population charts provides data on the number of immigrants who have obtained Legal Resident status by country of birth. It is significant to note the decrease in the number of immigrants from Europe and the increase in the number of immigrants from Asia, as reflected in Figure 11-5 that captures Census data at 10-year intervals: 1961–1970; 1981–1990; 2001–2010. As you review the figures here, consider the political, economic, and social forces that might have influenced the development of America's diverse citizenship.

Developing Cultural Competence

Bridging Cultures

What is **culture**? Culture can be defined as a distinctive pattern of beliefs and values that develop among a group of people who share the same social heritage and traditions. Culture is a neutral term, neither good nor bad. It refers to the collective historical patterns, values, societal arrangements, manners, ideas, and ways of living—which includes style of speaking, fashion, food, art, and music—that people have used to order their society. It is made up of all those things people learn as part of growing up, including religion, beliefs about economic and social relations, political organization, and the thousands of "Dos and Don'ts" society deems important to know to become a functioning member of that group.

Culture plays an important role in any diversity situation. Different cultures can exist within the same nation, and are commonly called **multicultural differences**. Different cultures exist across different nations, and are often referred to as **cross-cultural differences**.

Cultural competence is the knowledge of others' backgrounds, histories, customs, and perspectives. To develop cultural competence, strive to become aware of the key patterns of the lives and peoples of the world. The appreciation of various cultures will help you to see the world as a mosaic and to challenge you to think of diversity as something to be valued. Several opportunities to interact with a different culture will present themselves mainly because of the degree to which technology is changing the world. Indeed, the advances in communication technology, computers, and satellites have brought the world closer together, enabling us to live *globally locally*.

Fear makes strangers of people who would otherwise be friends.

—Author Unknown

Follow these strategies to help increase your understanding and sensitivity to other cultures as you get global!

- Interact with people on campus from backgrounds that are different from yours. Reach out and engage someone in a conversation. Not sure what to talk about? Begin with the points you have in common: you are both students—briefly compare experiences of the semester. You can also use the Internet to chat with students from diverse backgrounds.

- Develop cultural competence through travel and/or study abroad programs. The best way to learn about people from other cultures is to see and to experience those cultures firsthand. Take a trip to Europe, Africa, South America, Asia, or Australia during a college vacation. Or take advantage of study abroad opportunities to expand your knowledge, break down stereotypes, gain experience in communicating across cultures, and earn some course credit. An overseas experience can create new interests, abilities, and linguistic and cultural skills that are not only valuable to you, but could also be very attractive to your future employers. Apply for the KSU Global Engagement Certification (GEC). For more information on this opportunity, visit the GEC website at http://www.kennesaw.edu/globalengagement/.

- Enroll in a course to study other cultures and customs. General Education programs provide course offerings that cover the culture, history, religion, or art of another group so you can expand your knowledge of other people's background. Also, some majors require courses with global perspectives. You could also enroll in a global-themed course for elective credit, if you meet the prerequisites.

- Attend cultural programs on topics of global concern. Watch for announcements of cultural activities and programming sponsored by student groups to highlight cultural as well as sociopolitical concerns of global communities. Go beyond the role of spectator at these events; join a student group for more direct involvement.

You will need to remember that your intercultural experiences are learning experiences. Expect differences and accept differences. Your cultural competence grows when you do.

Summary

This chapter has presented concepts that will help in your continual growth and development of a diversity consciousness. The goal of diversity and inclusion is one that intimately affects each of us, regardless of our race, ethnicity, gender, or other identifying features. In fact, we are all diverse individuals. Rely upon your knowledge and understanding of primary and secondary dimensions of diversity to give more insights on other people's backgrounds and the influences that shape their values, attitudes, and beliefs as well as your own. Begin to apply diversity skills in everyday interactions. Cultivate intercultural sensitivity, particularly across religious, racial, and socioeconomic lines.

One of the key lessons from this chapter is the importance of acquiring cultural competence to participate fully in the changing multicultural society and global community. Cultural norms are always evaluated in a context. Be aware of difference and how to evaluate and react to it.

This first year of college affords many opportunities to develop and hone the important and necessary diversity skills. However, the first year is just that: a beginning. Continue to seek out and to use the information sources (books, films, courses, campus organizations, cultural events, community organizations) that will help increase your cultural competence. Your intercultural communication skills comprise the value-added experiences that enhance your résumé.

Remember to take advantage of the most important resource available to assist in your growth and development: the different people around you.

We are all the same, and we are all unique.

—Georgia Dunston

References

American Community Survey. (2007). *Language Use in the United States.* Retrieved from http://www.census.gov/prod/2010pubs/acs-12.pdf

Bucher, R. (2001). *Diversity consciousness.* Upper Saddle River, NJ: Prentice-Hall.

Cuseo, J., Fecas, V. S., & Thompson, A. (2008). *Thriving in college & beyond.* Dubuque: Kendall-Hunt.

Diversity-Related Concepts and Key Terms. Retrieved February 22, 2012, from http://www.merriam-webster.com

Diversity Wheel. (n.d.). Retrieved from http://www.loden.com

Dunston, G. (2005, May 1). A human paradox. *Discover Magazine.* Retrieved from http://discovermagazine.com/2005/may/letters

Hate Crimes. (n.d.) Retrieved from http://www.adl.org/99hatecrime/intro.asp

Jimmy Carter on diversity mosaic. (n.d.) In J. J. Johnson, *Wisdom quotes: Quotations to inspire and challenge.* Retrieved from http://www.wisdomquotes.com/cat_diversity.html

Niemöller, M. (1945). Quote found on Tolerance.org. Southern Poverty Law Center. Retrieved from http://www.tolerance.org/campus/pledges.jsp

Passel, J., & Cohn, D. (2008). *U. S. Population Projections; 2005–2050.* Washington, DC: Pew Center Research. Retrieved December 2, 2011 from http://pewhispanic.org/files/reports/85.pdf

Siasoco, R. V. (1999). *Defining hate crimes: No longer a black and white issue.* Retrieved from http://www.infoplease.com/spot/hatecrimes.html

U.S. Census Bureau. (2012). *The 2012 Statistical Abstract: The National Data Book.* Washington, DC: U.S. Census Bureau. Retrieved from http://www.census.gov/compendia/statab/cats/population.html

Willoughby, B. (2003). *10 ways to fight hate on campus: A response guide for college activists.* Retrieved from http://equity.psu.edu/assets-1/Ten_ways_to_fight_racism_.pdf

Critical Thinking Questions

1. Discuss three reasons for the need to develop diversity skills and cultural competence.

2. List the six primary dimensions of diversity. Does the qualifier "immutable" fit each dimension? If not, explain.

3. Secondary dimensions are largely invisible characteristics. What image from nature has been used in diversity training to illustrate this concept? How useful is the imagery?

4. Are all stereotypes negative? What are sources of stereotypes?

5. Hate crimes are the result of extreme prejudice. Why are hate crimes thought to have "far-reaching effects"? Give an example of a hate crime.

6. Contrast the differences in the metaphors that describe America's diversity.

7. Consider America's changing demographics: what factors are contributing to the population shifts?

8. What role can technology play in increasing cultural competence in the global community?

9. How is "cultural competence" defined for today's global community?

10. In what practical ways do diversity skills enhance preparation for a career?

Name _____ Date _____

Acquiring Diversity Skills: Reflecting and Observing

As you move through the stages to acquire your cultural competence skills, you will discover many things about yourself and others. First, you will need to examine how the *primary* and *secondary* dimensions of diversity have affected you and your relationships with others. You can begin by asking yourself questions about your attitudes, beliefs, and values. Then, you will need to put on your critical lens and observe how the dimensions affect others.

Questions for Reflection

1. What aspects of the dimensions of identity were most emphasized while you were growing up? How? Which were least emphasized? How?

2. Which aspect of your identity are you most proud of? Why?

3. Recall the incident in your life when you first became aware of differences. What was your reaction? Were you the focus of attention or were others? How did that affect how you reacted to the situation?

Journal: Describe the development of your beliefs and attitudes toward difference (i.e., race, ethnicity, gender, class, religion, sexual orientation, abilities). Include how you believe they were shaped by factors such as your:

- Ethnic or racial heritage

- Gender and sexual orientation

- Socioeconomic group

- Region of the country

- Religious beliefs or affiliation

What kind of messages (spoken or unspoken) did you get about people who were different from you in those categories?

Practicing your skill: Have the conversation you have always wanted to have with someone different from you.

EXERCISE 11-2
Activities Related to Diversity

Name _____ Date _____

Visit the chapter 11 resources folder on the textbook website. View James Patrick Kinney's short film depicting the poem "The Cold Within," and list three reasons why the poem might be useful to stimulate discussions on diversity.

CHAPTER 12

Leadership, Ethics, and Citizenship

DIANE FOREHAND GRINDELL, M.Ed.

Chapter Goals

- Define leadership and discuss leadership principles

- Identify five leadership practices of college students

- Discuss the importance of ethics and ethical decision-making in the context of leadership

- Describe the importance of active citizenry

Chapter Overview

This chapter examines how leadership practices, active citizenship, and ethical decision-making enriches the college experience and prepares students for their vocational journey. To provide a context for the study of leadership, a definition of leadership is presented along with specific principles about leadership and the college student. Next, the chapter explores five leadership practices useful in identifying key leadership behaviors of college students. When engaging in leadership practices, college students must make ethical decisions that require substantial consideration throughout their academic and professional careers. To assist leaders with ethical decision-making, this chapter explores the process of making ethical decisions. Finally, student leadership skills are often developed through active citizenship. This chapter provides a definition of these terms and ways students can make a difference. After exploring this chapter, students will have a basic understanding of the concepts and skills required to begin their leadership development and become successful college student leaders, and ultimately, successful employees and citizens of the world.

What Is Leadership?

There are numerous definitions of the term "leadership." Komives, Lucas, and McMahon (2006) define a leader as "any person who actively engages with others to accomplish change" (p. 19). Leadership is people engaging with others to accomplish change. It is important to emphasize that leadership is not reserved for university presidents or corporate managers. Leaders are found in homes, civic organizations, businesses, schools, and yes, college campuses. Given this straightforward definition, one can easily see examples of leadership on campus, such as when a student takes the initiative to brainstorm ideas with a class group on a project, participates in a student organization, or volunteers to help others in the community. Leadership, actively engaging with others to accomplish change, is comprised of a set of principles and practices that can be continuously developed. To fully comprehend and engage in leadership, the principles and practices must be included.

Leadership Principles

Komives and Wagner (2009) argue that there are five principles of leadership. They believe these standards are important in creating effective leaders and are the foundation of leadership. The five principles are:

* Leadership is positive.

* Leadership is collaborative.

* Leadership is action-oriented.

* All students are potential leaders.

* Service is a powerful vehicle for developing students' leadership skills.

Leadership Is Positive

Leadership is about improving circumstances, knowledge, and/or results for individuals, groups, and organizations. Leaders focus on actions to make things better for others and do not cause harm. An example of a positive leader is Laura Stewart, a former Kennesaw State University student. In 2011, Laura launched a student organization, KSU Against Cancer, and successfully raised funds and negotiated with the American Cancer Society to bring a national fundraising event, Relay for Life, to the Kennesaw State University campus in April of 2012 (McCrary, 2012). Though Laura lost her own battle with cancer on October 25, 2012, her legacy of positive leadership continues for students, faculty, and the community at large through the now annual Kennesaw State University Relay for Life event. To learn more about Laura Stewart, visit the textbook website chapter 12 resources.

Leadership Is Collaborative

Leadership is about working with others to accomplish positive results. Collaborative leadership is the collective efforts of people sharing information, ideas, and time toward a common goal. Examples of collaborative leadership can be identified all over the college campus in clubs, service organizations, fraternities and sororities, student government associations, and even daily, in our classrooms. For example, Laura Stewart did not establish the KSU Against Cancer organization by herself. The student organization consists of several officers and an academic advisor working together for a common goal.

Leadership Is Action-Oriented

By definition, leadership involves people engaging with others to accomplish change. There are numerous theories about leadership that can be studied, yet one must actually take action to demonstrate leadership. In most KSU first-year seminars, students are asked to engage in a group project to help others. The students are responsible for selecting and implementing a project. Their work on these projects demonstrates how leadership is action-oriented. These leadership actions, called practices, will be discussed in more detail later in this chapter.

All Students Are Potential Leaders

People of all ages and walks of life have the capacity to work with others to accomplish positive change. Komives and Wagner (2009) believe any college student has the potential to become a leader. In fact, college students are often uniquely prepared to become leaders because they are collaborating with others to accomplish positive change on an almost daily basis. A true story may be the best way to illustrate the point about all students being potential leaders.

In the spring of 2003, three college students from southern California purchased some video equipment off eBay and headed into Sudan, the largest country in Africa, to shoot a documentary about the genocide in the Darfur region. Through a unique set of events, the three young men stumbled into northern Uganda, Sudan's neighbor, and found a shocking humanitarian

crisis. Children in northern Uganda were being kidnapped, tortured, and forced to serve in the rebel army in a civil war that spanned two decades. Determined to understand the crisis, and dumbfounded by the world's silence, these three college students shot a documentary, formed a non-profit organization called Invisible Children and began to develop programs to help both the children and their families. Invisible Children has raised millions of dollars to build schools and hire dozens of teachers and mentors in Uganda. The organization also held awareness and advocacy events that brought more than 70,000 individuals together to work for change. These leaders—these *college students*—made an incredibly positive difference in the world. To learn more about these leaders, spend a few minutes reading about Jason Russell, Bobby Bailey, and Laren Poole at www.invisiblechildren.com, or find out when the KSU chapter of Invisible Children is meeting this semester.

Drew Dudley of Nuance Leadership Development Services, Inc. extends the principle that all students are potential leaders even further with the view that people demonstrate leadership every day, either unintentionally or purposefully (Dudley, 2013). Drew explains this concept in his uplifting TED talk: Everyday Leadership, which can be accessed and viewed from the textbook website. This short video is an excellent reminder of the positive impact student leaders and all people can have when interacting with others.

Service Is a Powerful Vehicle for Developing Students' Leadership Skills

Service—providing assistance to others to make a positive difference—is the cornerstone of leadership. Many college students erroneously believe they are too young, too inexperienced, too stretched for time, and/or too financially constrained to make a meaningful difference in the world. However, providing service gives students great opportunities to make a difference for others, enhance their leadership skills, and discover more about their potential careers. Over the years, many universities have expanded the number of opportunities and ways to involve students in service activities. Most liberal arts institutions, including Kennesaw State University, seek to provide students with a holistic education that not only prepares them to be leaders in their chosen field but also engaged citizens in their societies and world. Universities provide students with opportunities to "serve the common good" in multiple ways.

The five principles of leadership and the formal and informal opportunities universities provide help clarify the guidelines students may utilize as they develop leadership skills during college and beyond. In addition, there are specific behaviors or practices of leadership that can be mastered as part of leadership development for college students.

Leadership Practices

There are leadership practices college students can cultivate as they work with others to implement positive change during and after their college years. Kouzes and Posner (2008) identified the leadership behaviors or "practices" of college students in formal and informal leadership roles. The five practices are:

- Model the way

- Inspire shared vision

- Challenge the process

- Enable others to act

- Encourage the heart

Each practice highlights actions student leaders have implemented and can apply throughout the college experience. A brief explanation of the practices confirms the assertion that all students have the potential to be positive, collaborative leaders.

Model the Way

The first practice, Model the Way, encourages leaders to identify what is important to them and set an example for others by acting in accordance with what they believe is important. Also central to this practice is the idea that leaders build credibility and effectiveness by doing what they say they will do. Examples of college students modeling the way include being prepared and attending class each session, taking on a leadership position in a student government organization, or conducting a volunteer service project.

Inspire a Shared Vision

The second leadership practice starts with leaders imagining a better future and creating a vision for a cause, project, team, or organization. A core component of this practice is that leaders must genuinely believe in their vision so they can then recruit others to assist in making the vision a reality.

There are many opportunities for college students to establish a vision and enlist others. Student leaders inspire shared visions when they participate in group assignments, service projects, clubs, and organizations. While researching for a group service project for his First-Year Seminar class, Andrew Chatwood discovered an organization called Falling Whistles, which promotes peace in the Democratic Republic of Congo. This organization began as an effort to protect small children in the region who were forced to become human targets by blowing whistles to signal the start of battles. Andrew became very passionate about this cause and emailed the organization to ask them to speak at Kennesaw State University. Once the organization agreed, Andrew convinced a small group of his classmates to work with him to make arrangements for their visit.

Challenge the Process

The third practice involves reviewing existing processes and questioning the status quo. In this practice, leaders look for ways to improve an idea or process, summon the courage to suggest ways to change it for the better, and then implement the changes suggested. While this practice sounds simple, it can be very difficult to change the ways people think about and conduct their work. The establishment of ABLE (Advocacy, Boldness, Leadership, and Empowerment), a registered KSU student organization dedicated to providing a place where students who are differently abled can voice their concerns and receive support, is an example of student leaders successfully challenging the process. As per this practice, the leaders of ABLE identified a way to make things better for differently abled students on campus.

Enable Others to Act

The fourth practice involves developing collaboration among a group and building an environment that encourages all participants to perform at their best. Clear project goals, well-defined roles for group members, and trust in the expertise and promises of fellow members are fundamental elements of this practice. Student leaders demonstrate the practice of enabling others to act as they work with others in formal and informal groups throughout the college experience. For example, Andrew Chatwood's vision of helping the Falling Whistles campaign was adopted by other KSU students, who then established a Falling Whistles student organization on campus.

Encourage the Heart

The fifth practice encompasses the acknowledgement of group members' contributions and celebrating the successes of the group. This practice of encouraging and thanking group members begins with having high expectations for all and celebrating as these expectations are met and exceeded. In November 2011, the actions of a group of KSU Seminar students John Lewis, Jon Fey, Christian Asher, Jeff Crawford, and Mark Yancey exemplified this principle. The students volunteered at Habitat for Humanity and purposefully

considered how they could utilize this principle. John Lewis reported that the group encouraged the heart of its members by thanking each other for their ideas and willingness to compromise. The group also shared encouraging comments with each other before, during, and after the project. When student leaders simply recognize the work of their team members and celebrate accomplishments, they are encouraging the heart.

Employing these five practices helps students to develop leadership skills and create exceptional results. In addition to utilizing the leadership practices, student leaders are often required to make ethical decisions. A discussion of the meaning of ethics and a process to make ethical decisions can assist students in formal and informal leadership roles.

What Is Ethics?

The word "ethics" conjures many ideas and can be challenging to define. It may be useful to determine what ethics is by discussing what it is not. Ethics is *not* just doing what is legal. "Legal" and "ethical" may be synonymous in many instances, but that is not always the case. Nor is ethics about religion. While many people derive their ethical standards from their religious beliefs, someone who is not religious can still be ethical. Finally, ethics is not a "one-size-fits-all" idea. Whole societies have ethical standards to which they hold, but ethics is also an individual concept.

So what is ethics? Ethics is a "branch of philosophy dealing with values relating to human conduct, with respect to the rightness and wrongness of certain actions and to the goodness and badness of the motives and ends of such actions" ("Ethics," n.d.). Ethics is about action, what one should and should not do. Note: It is not concerned with what one did as much as what one "ought" to do. In essence, ethics is how one ought to act based on one's deeply held beliefs about right and wrong.

In some ways, it would be easier if ethics were about doing what is legal or what one's religious beliefs, or one's family or society, taught them. If any of those scenarios were true, then making ethical decisions would be a result of memorizing the rules or looking them up in some list. Is it okay for John to lie to his roommate? He could just look that up. Is it acceptable for Sue to ask her brother to write that English paper she cannot seem to finish? Well, there's no law against it in the Georgia code.

Yet, this is not how ethical decisions are made. Ethics is more than a set of legal behaviors. Think of an example of a legal behavior that is not ethical. What about the Jim Crow laws of the South prior to the Civil Rights Movement? It was legal to keep African Americans out of restaurants, schools, and businesses that were reserved for "whites only," but it certainly was not ethical. What about an ethical behavior that is not legal? Political activists consistently break laws to protest governmental actions they believe are unethical. Whether it is an "anti-nukes" group trespassing on a nuclear facility or a peaceful sit-in where the group refuses to disperse at the orders of the police, the protestors believe that breaking the law is the right thing to do.

If there is no list of ethical decisions, how does one decide what to do when faced with an ethical dilemma?

Ethical Decision-Making

The Markkula Center for Applied Ethics at Santa Clara University provides a framework for making ethical decisions. This model, like any illustration, helps the complexity of an ethical decision appear in a more simplistic format. It helps one to "break down" the situation before jumping to conclusions, and it provides one with a mechanism to discuss his/her decision with others. The center's framework consists of five components:

- Recognize an ethical issue.

- Get the facts.

- Evaluate alternative actions.

- Make a decision and test it.

- Act and reflect on the outcome.

Recognize an Ethical Issue

College students must address ethical issues throughout their academic career. Ethical issues involve matters or problems that require one to choose between two or more alternatives based on what he or she considers to be the right or just thing to do. Clearly identifying the specific ethical dilemma and one's beliefs about it are key steps in making ethical decisions.

Get the Facts

Making sound ethical decisions involves getting all the facts about the situation in order to make an informed decision. This involves refraining from jumping to conclusions and thinking about more than just how the situation impacts you. Sometimes an ethical dilemma involves several people, and the end result may not make everyone happy. Obtaining as much information as possible about the situation will make it easier to ultimately select a reasonable solution or decision.

Evaluate Alternative Actions

After obtaining the facts, one must then evaluate the alternative courses of actions. Evaluating different options and related consequences encourages one to fully consider all actions prior to making a decision about the ethical issue. When evaluating the alternative actions and outcomes, one must carefully consider the context of the situation and the people involved. Again, getting all the facts surrounding the situation is crucial in order to assess the alternatives and select the best course of action.

Make a Decision and Test It

In some situations, it is difficult to determine whether you have made the best decision. The Markkula Center recommends putting your decision to the test: "If I told someone I respect—or told a television audience—which option I have chosen, what would they say?" ("A framework for ethical decision-making," n.d.).

Act and Reflect on the Outcome

After thinking about the situation, getting facts, evaluating outcomes, and making a decision, one must choose a course of action. Not every course of action will be pleasant or positive. Sometimes after making a difficult decision, it seems easiest to just forget about it. However, the Markkula Center recommends reflecting on the outcome of our decisions, examining what we have learned from the situation and utilizing this information for future decision-making.

KSU's Model of Ethical Leadership

Another model that supports the student leader is the KSU Model of Ethical Leadership. The KSU Model of Ethical Leadership emphasizes the importance of leaders being keenly aware of, and acting in accordance with their values. In 2006, a group of faculty and staff at Kennesaw State University developed an ethical leadership model that forms the foundation for some of the leadership training programs on campus. Built on the four principles of invitational leadership (respect, trust, intentionality, and optimism), as well as service, the KSU Model of Ethical Leadership shows the integral relationship of character, ethics, and leadership. All three must be present for an individual to be an ethical leader, defined as one who serves the common good by building relationships (Stillion, 2006).

The core of the KSU Model of Ethical Leadership is character, knowing thyself. The model asserts that it is only after the leader understands who they are, what values they hold, how and why they act and react towards others,

and why they want to lead can they begin to fully develop their leadership abilities. The KSU Model of Ethical Leadership breaks leadership into four categories: trailblazing, operating, developing others, and connecting with others. According to the model, the overall goal of an ethical leader is to serve the common good by building relationships. Figure 12-1 illustrates the KSU Model of Ethical Leadership.

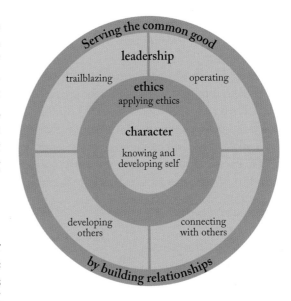

Figure 12-1. KSU Model of Ethical Leadership

In addition to the leadership principles, practices, and recommendations regarding ethics and ethical decision-making, it is important for student leaders to be familiar with common terms used to describe leadership and active citizenry.

Active Citizenry

One way to develop leadership skills is through active citizenry, which is comprised of volunteering, civic engagement, and social justice. Each of these components can be accomplished by the student leader during the college experience.

Volunteering

Volunteering is defined as "the policy or practice of volunteering one's time or talents for charitable, educational, or other worthwhile activities, especially in one's community" ("Volunteerism," n.d.). These activities usually provide students with the opportunity to deliver service to others or assist with some type of social problem. Volunteering can be a one-time commitment or a long-term activity.

Students at KSU have a number of opportunities to volunteer through Volunteer Kennesaw State University (VKSU). VKSU provides students the opportunity to volunteer with a number of different agencies in the metro-Atlanta area and will certify volunteer hours completed by KSU students. In addition, VKSU hosts volunteer fairs on campus each semester, at which students can interact with various community agencies and determine which one might align with their interests.

Civic Engagement

The American Psychological Association defines civic engagement as "individual and collective actions designed to identify and address issues of public concern" ("Civic Engagement," n.d.). The intent of civic engagement activities is to inspire students to discover those social problems that they find most compelling and fully seek to understand their complexity.

The focus on civic engagement has risen in the last few years due to the decline of civic involvement in college-aged students (Bridgman et al., 2004). Most recently, the *New York Times* and the American Association of State Colleges and Universities (AASCU)—an organization composed of 430 public colleges and universities, including KSU—partnered to sponsor the American Democracy Project (ADP) and the Political Engagement Project (PEP). Both initiatives promote greater civic and political engagement in traditional college-aged students ("American Democracy Project," n.d.; "Political Engagement Project," n.d.).

Social Justice

Bell (2007) defines social justice as "both a process and a goal" seeking to provide "full and equal participation in the development of a society where resources are equitably distributed and all members are physically and psychologically safe and secure" (p. 1). Like civic engagement, social justice may involve volunteering, but the intent is to inspire individuals to find opportunities to assist in developing an inclusive society that provides opportunity and safety for all people. The focus of these initiatives is to challenge students to address problems in a more holistic way, engaging in political and nonpolitical actions to bring about equality and justice. KSU offers a number of opportunities for students to participate in programs that promote social justice, and the Departments of Student Life and Student Development have organizations that promote awareness and inclusion of difference.

Volunteering, civic engagement, and social justice are three important components of active citizenry. Active citizenry allows the student leader to make choices about donating time and energy to specific causes or organizations. As a leader, involvement contributes to community improvement and leads to an enriched college experience.

Becoming a Leader

This chapter has provided a definition of leadership and the principles and practices of leadership, but how does one become a leader? Posner (2009) recommends participating in leadership programs on campus. Being on a campus with over 20,000 students may make this appear to be an impossible task. However, it is never too late to start. You could become an active member of the KSU Student Government Association (SGA). Within the KSU SGA, you could run for Freshman Senator or work as an SGA aide and learn more about the organization.

A great resource to start your leadership journey at KSU is the Center for Student Leadership (CSL). The CSL's mission is "to prepare students to become ethical leaders who are engaged in their campus and larger communities" ("Mission," n.d.). Within the CSL are several programs designed to help you become a leader, such as the Leaders IN Kennesaw (LINK), the President's Emerging Global Scholars (PEGS), the Lædan Program, the King-Casey Women's Leadership Experience, and the Peer Leader Program.

In addition, the Department of University Studies offers a certificate in Leadership Studies. This program is open to any student at KSU and involves taking five leadership courses that explore topics such as ethics in leadership, leadership in a global society, and leading in groups. Posner (2009) found that students who participate in these types of programs saw a significant increase in the development of leadership behaviors.

Summary

This chapter has provided you with a basic understanding of the concepts and skills required to begin leadership development and become successful college student leaders and ultimately, successful employees and citizens of the world. Winston Churchill once said, "We make a living by what we get, we make a life by what we give." So lead, give, and truly live!

References

A framework for ethical decision-making. (n.d.). *Markkula Center for Applied Ethics*. Retrieved from http://www.scu.edu/ethics/practicing/decision/framework.html

American Democracy Project. (n.d.). *American Association of State Colleges and Universities*. Retrieved from http://www.aascu.org/programs/ADP/

Bell, L. A. (1997). Theoretical foundations for social justice education. In M. Adams, L.A. Bell, & P. Griffin (Eds.) *Teaching for diversity and social justice* (2nd ed.). New York: Routledge.

Bridgman, M., Shreve, J., White, L., Heaviside, M., Dunshee, L., & O'Loughlin-Brooks, J. L. (2004). Encouraging civic engagement on college campuses through discussion boards. *Journal of Civic Commitment, 4*, 1–18.

Civic engagement. (n.d.). *American Psychological Association*. Retrieved from http://www.apa.org/education/undergrad/civic-engagement.aspx

Dudley, D. (2013, February 20). Drew Dudley: Everyday Leadership. [Video file]. Retrieved from http://www.ted.com/talks/drew_dudley_everyday_leadership.html

Ethics. (n.d.). *Dictionary.com Unabridged* (v 1.1). Retrieved from http://dictionary.reference.com/browse/ethics

Komives, S. R., Lucas, N., & McMahon, T. R. (2006). *Exploring leadership: For college students who want to make a difference* (2nd ed.). San Francisco, CA: Jossey-Bass.

Komives, S. R., & Wagner, W. (2009). *Leadership for a better world: Understanding the Social Change Model of Leadership Development* (2nd ed.). San Francisco, CA: Jossey-Bass.

Kouzes, J. M., & Posner, B. Z. (2008). *The student leadership challenge: Five practices for exemplary leaders*. San Francisco, CA: Jossey-Bass.

McCrary, E. (2012, February). "College student struck by cancer chooses to 'DO SOMETHING' to fight the disease by taking a leadership role in American Cancer Society's Relay For Life." *American Cancer Society South Atlantic Division Newsroom*. Retrieved from http://sacancernews.org/2012/02/college-student-struck-by-cancer-chooses-to-do-something-to-fight-the-disease-by-taking-a-leadership-role-in-american-cancer-societys-relay-for-life/

Mission. (n.d.). *Kennesaw State University Center for Student Leadership.* Retrieved January 22, 2011, from http://www.kennesaw.edu/csl/statements.html

Political Engagement Project. (n.d.). *American Association of State Colleges and Universities*. Retrieved from http://www.aascu.org/programs/adp/PEP/

Posner, B. Z. (2009). A longitudinal study examining changes in students' leadership behavior. *Journal of College Student Development, 50*, 551–563.

Stillion, J. & Boettler, L. (2006). *Serving the Common Good: Ethical Leadership through Building Relationships.* Kennesaw, GA: KSU Press Publications.

Volunteerism. (n.d.). *Dictionary.com Unabridged* (v 1.1). Retrieved from http://dictionary.reference.com/browse/ethics

The author would like to acknowledge and offer gratitude to Dr. Danielle Williams for her contribution to this chapter.

Critical Thinking Questions

1. Explain the Leadership Principles and give an example of each principle.

2. Describe how you have demonstrated one or more of the five practices of The Student Leadership Challenge.

3. Consider an ethical decision you have made in the past. Explain how you could have used the Markkula Center for Applied Ethics framework to make your decision.

4. Discuss a situation in which you behaved in accordance with your values. What was the situation? What values did you uphold?

5. Describe the actions you could take to become an active member of the KSU community.

EXERCISE 12-1
In-Class Ethical Case Studies

Name _____ Date _____

Please list all of the people in your group:

1. Review the following case study and answer the following questions.

   Joan would really like to utilize the newest version of Adobe Photoshop to create really interesting graphics for her KSU Seminar group presentation. She checks prices at the bookstore, computer stores, and several websites, but she cannot afford to purchase the software. Joan knows that her friend's mother is a graphic designer who uses Photoshop for her designs. Should she ask her friend to "borrow" the CDs from her mom's office, so Joan can load it on her personal laptop?

2. Using the Markkula Center model, explain the following:

   • What is the ethical issue?

   • What are the facts of this case?

   • What are the possible alternative actions?

   • Of the possible alternative actions, which one best addresses the situation?

   • How would you test it?

   • How can you reflect on the outcome of this situation?

CHAPTER 13
Becoming a Globally Competent Citizen
MICHAEL TODD SHINHOLSTER, M.B.A. AND KEN HILL, M.A.

Chapter Goals

*   Understand how global issues will play an ever-increasing role in your lives today and in the future

*   Explain the Global Engagement Certification program and its impact on your college experience

*   Examine the benefits of participating in a study abroad program

*   Summarize the seven Global Challenges and their impact on your lives both personally and professionally

Chapter Overview

Walt Disney considered the world to be "small," and Thomas Friedman chose to see the world as "flat." Disney viewed the world through the eyes of children, while Friedman views the world through the eyes of adults. Both are views of opportunity; however, times are changing. Our world is connected in ways that could never be imagined 20, 50, or 100 years ago. Financial markets are up and down, and an event on one side of the globe sends world leaders scrambling to calm the masses. People see the world through the eyes of opportunity, confusion, and panic. Now more than ever, we must face the fact that the world is part of our daily lives, and our lives are part of the daily world.

In this chapter, you will learn how your life can and will be affected by the world around you and how to prepare for it. Your competition is no longer the person seated at the desk beside you. It is more likely to be on the other side of the globe. We will explore KSU's Global Engagement Certification, study abroad programs, and AASCU's Global Challenges Initiative—a study in the major trends or key drivers of change that will shape our world

to 2030 and beyond. Lastly, we will look at the concepts of culture and values. Together, each of these will play an important role in helping you to understand the world in which we live and the opportunities presented to you here at Kennesaw State University.

Global Engagement Certification (GEC)

Kennesaw State University has focused on three global learning outcomes. They are global perspectives (knowledge), intercultural engagement (skills), and global citizenship (attitudes). By integrating these outcomes into your academic experience at KSU, you can graduate with a Global Engagement Certification (GEC) as well as your bachelor's degree, giving you a competitive advantage in the marketplace. KSU has established guidelines for all students, both undergraduate and graduate, to meet the three global learning outcomes while working toward their degree. Students may choose courses that have been approved by the Global Learning Coordinating Council that meet the requirements of the certification. Since KSU recognizes that all students must embrace global learning in order to succeed, all degree programs have been encouraged to develop courses at the junior and senior level (3000- and 4000-level courses) that are certified as global learning courses.

The Global Engagement Certification is free, and there are two options. Students who complete at least 12 hours of approved undergraduate global learning courses and study abroad for a total of at least four weeks are eligible for the certification. Students who complete at least 24 hours of approved courses and study abroad for at least eight weeks are eligible for the Global Engagement with Distinction. There is also a foreign language proficiency requirement for both certification options, but some KSU students have already met it through the foreign language classes they took in high school. Finally, there are short essays to complete as part of the application for either the basic certification or the certification with distinction. KSU students who obtain either certification are honored at Commencement; their transcripts also note the certification along with their degrees and any minors or certificate programs they completed. The Institute for Global Initiatives supervises the Global Engagement Certification program.

Study Abroad

Even if you do not complete the GEC, a study abroad experience will certainly benefit you and increase your knowledge of the world. KSU has a large, diverse set of study abroad opportunities and has a goal to increase enrollment in them each academic year. Study abroad programs give students the opportunity to see the world with their peers unlike any vacation would ever provide. By having first-hand experiences, students quickly embrace the importance of understanding diverse cultures, customs, and people while exploring the rich similarities. To assist students with the cost of study abroad programs, KSU has established a global learning fee that funds Global Learning Scholarships for all eligible students. For more information on the Global Engagement Certification, Study Abroad, and Global Learning Scholarships, access the KSU website links at the end of this chapter.

AASCU's Global Challenges Initiative

Political scientists, economists, sociologists, scientists, futurists, and other experts have developed thought-provoking theories to understand both the present and predict trends that will impact the future. Global experts at the Center for Strategic and International Studies (CSIS), a think tank based in Washington, D.C., developed a strategic look at planet Earth out to the year 2030. Known as the 7 Revolutions (7 Revs) project, CSIS argues that seven areas of change will have the most impact on what the world will look like in 2030. The revolutions are as follows:

1. Population
2. Resource Management
3. Technology
4. Information/Knowledge
5. Economic Integration
6. Security/Conflict
7. Governance

The CSIS 7 Revolutions project was created to identify and analyze the key policy challenges that policymakers, business executives, and citizens will face in the next 20 years. Because it was considered vital that higher education be included as a partner and to promote strategic thinking on the long-term trends that too few leaders take the time to consider, the senior leadership of the Washington D.C-based higher education organization Association of State Colleges and Universities (AASCU) has embraced these ideas and created a scholars group comprised of educators from nine institutions across the US. This group is committed to furthering the research, teaching, scholarship, and advocacy of the 7 Revolutions concept in universities and colleges across the country. As such, the scholars group has come together to create AASCU's Global Challenges Initiative. This effort mirrors the same fundamental ideas embodied in the original 7 Revolutions project. Proudly, Kennesaw State University is a contributing partner in the Global Challenges Initiative. As students, it is important to understand these seven areas of change because your generation will be the next leaders. By viewing the world through the lens of challenge, you will begin to understand how global issues impact you daily and that these key drivers of change offer both promise and peril.

Challenge 1—Population

In late 2011, the earth's population reached seven billion (National Geographic, 2012). It is anticipated that more than three billion people might be added to the human family over the next 50 years (U.S. Census Bureau, 2011). Additionally, various parts of the world will experience expansion and contraction during this period. For example, *The Economists' Pocket World in Figures* projects that India's population will surpass China's by 2050, and it will be approximately four times the size of the United States' population (2011). What are some of the other important trends that demographers foresee in conjunction with population? According to *Global Trends 2030*, a National Intelligence Council report (2012), migration, urbanization, and aging will also become significant variables in the decades to come. Some would contend that of all the dimensions recognized by AASCU's Global Challenge Initiative, population may arguably be the most critical. Why? Because it is inextricably linked to the other recognized challenges, especially resource management, economic integration, security/conflict, and governance.

Some questions should be asked:

- What are the basic characteristics that define the anticipated world population trends?

- How might these trends impact individual nation states and the global economy?

- What are the geopolitical implications of these trends?

- How do population shifts affect the quality of the environment, social and health structures, and on a larger scale, the ways humanity views and governs itself?

Because there are a variety of forces at play, prediction with any veracity is complex. However, we must attempt if we are going to anticipate and respond meaningfully to the population challenge, particularly the more critical aspects of population growth, global fertility rates, and urbanization and migration.

Population Growth: *Global Trends 2030* suggests that the world will simultaneously grow, decline, and diversify all at the same time (2012). Further, this report states that "Asia, Africa, and Latin America will account for virtually all population growth over the next 20 years." So, what does this mean in political, environmental and economic terms? We can readily see that these parts of the world are already struggling with extreme poverty, poor governance structures, and conflict or the threat of conflict. One might easily ask how they will they handle growth of that magnitude? That is indeed the crux of this challenge.

Global Fertility Rates: "Much of the developed world will face a static or negative population growth by 2030. In conjunction, the median and mean age of people in these countries will increase significantly" (Wilson, 2006, p. 6). What this means is that the world is aging, and the populations in countries like Japan and Germany are aging much faster than in developing countries like India and Brazil. Demographer Chris Wilson, in his article "The Century Ahead," went so far as to call the 21st century "a century of aging" (2006, p. 5). An aging population in the United States means fewer workers and more seniors who are utilizing entitlements such as Social Security and Medicaid (Wilson, 2006).

Urbanization and Migration: Projections suggest that over the next 20 years there will be a dramatic shift toward urban areas, and this will likely facilitate the development of greater than 20 mega cities, or population centers with greater than 10 million inhabitants. This may place strain on resources and place large populations in peril due to natural disasters. Alternatively, some social scientists argue that humans form closer relationships to one another and practice healthier lifestyles by living in cities (Glaeser, 2011).

As we look closer at the population revolution, it's important to examine the issues in terms of both developed and developing countries. Both constituencies are racing against time. As individuals, nations, even cultures and peoples, we will be drawn into either proactive engagement of the population dimension or be swept into the consequences of neglect. In many respects we are in "uncharted waters." There is no precedence in history, no time previously when nations have been so interconnected, so interdependent. This is the reality of globalization. Paul Hewitt (2002) said, "Comfortable ways of viewing the world seldom change overnight" (p. 9). Many adjustments are needed, and no panacea exists. It is doubtful that the policy changes, the shift of paradigm, or the way we filter and view our world can be implemented in the absence of crisis. "Consequently, the early twenty-first century could turn out to be every bit as tumultuous as the first half of the century just ended" (Hewitt, 2002, p. 10).

Challenge 2—Resource Management

Most recently, in November of 2011, the Bonn 2011 Conference concluded that the resources of food, water, and energy are integrally linked; they comprise a critical nexus in today's world (Federal Ministry for Economic Cooperation and Development, 2012). Does this come as a surprise? One might also begin to question how they might be tied to securities issues as well. It is doubtful that global resource experts or the average "layman" would challenge the importance of this triune in daily lives of citizens around the world. However, individuals born and raised in developed countries often take these resources for granted. For example, food seems to be abundant in America, and there's clean water available each time you turn on the faucet. While energy is discussed and debated quite often, especially when gas prices approach $4 a gallon, there appears to be enough energy for everyone to drive where they would like to go, heat their homes, and power their newest electronic gadgets. Nonetheless, food, water, and energy are critical resources both in America and around the world, and their relationships to other challenges, especially population, economic integration, and security/conflict, are paramount.

A recent report from Oxfam International, a global non-profit confederation of organizations working to end extreme poverty and injustice, noted that "world food prices reached a new historic peak in January 2011," placing the lives of millions in danger (Oxfam International, 2012a). There are multiple causes to the rise in food prices impacting consumers all around the world. In developing countries, however, where those in poverty spend between 50 to 80% of their meager incomes on food alone, the increased costs could be life-threatening (Oxfam International, 2012b). If the agricultural industries are struggling to stabilize food prices and produce enough food for the current population, how will those industries feed the estimated 9.2 billion who are expected to make up the global population by 2050? While some futurists predict a limit to the amount of food that can be produced to feed such a large population, others are confident in technology's ability to help farmers increase crop yields while developing new ways to grow food, such as hydroponics. Technology may not be able to help with challenges such as ocean depletion, land degradation, soil erosion, and desertification (Futurist. com, 2011). This is why leading up to the UN global climate talks in Durban, South Africa, at the end of 2011, "an independent global commission of eminent scientists released a set of

concrete recommendations to policymakers on how to achieve food security in the face of global climate change" (Meadu, 2011, para. 1).

A long-term strategy for food production must also address agriculture's relationships with both energy and water; it is obviously highly dependent on both of these resources. Food and energy, for example, have an interesting relationship. It takes energy to produce food—from the fuel in the tractors to the natural sunlight that helps the plants to grow—and food can also produce energy, like the corn in ethanol. As the demand for food increases, the agricultural industries' demands for energy will also increase. Will there be enough energy sources and a consistent supply to meet the demand?

Today's global engine runs on hydrocarbons (coal, oil, and natural gas), and there are very few experts predicting a change in the model in the next 20 years. The National Intelligence Council's *Global Trends 2030* (2012) examines the geopolitical chess game for energy resources that lies ahead. A potential "game-changer" may be the United States becoming more energy independent in light of newfound natural gas reserves and the use of hydraulic fracturing technology. This being said, the exploration of renewable energy certainly remains important as scientists continue to learn more about the environmental damage caused by hydrocarbons. It's not just about how much consumers are willing to pay at the pump for gas, but how much damage they are willing to cause the environment. As the *Economist* noted in a special issue, there are entrepreneurs who see green in "going green"; there is money to be made in alternative energy (*The Future of Energy*, 2008). If these entrepreneurs succeed, how cars are powered, homes are heated, and the sources of energy for the newest electronic gadgets may be somewhat different in 2030 than they are today.

If you took a quick poll and asked which of the three critical natural resources is most finite, many people would likely answer energy. They would be wrong. In fact, in 2006, the United Nations' Office for the Coordination of Humanitarian Affairs predicted that wars over water would increase as the demand for water increases (Integrated Regional Information Networks, 2006). The U.N. is not alone in predicting that both civil wars and cross-border conflicts will be fought over water, which is needed not only to sustain people but also agriculture and livestock. In fact, 70% of freshwater removed from its sources goes to agriculture. According to the World Water Council (2010), water is not just a future challenge. For some, it is a challenge today. Specifically, "more than one out of six lack access to safe drinking water, namely 1.1 billion people" (World Water Council, 2010, para. 2). Unless smart, strategic policies are developed and implemented, that number could increase rather than decrease in the coming decades.

The second trend in AASCU's Global Challenges Initiative model introduces both controversial and complex issues such as climate change, genetically modified crops, and water wars. It also reminds us that global issues impact each of us because we cannot survive without water, food, and energy.

Challenge 3—Technology

"Necessity is the mother of invention." This well-known phrase has been heard for generations as an explanation for innovation and creativity. Whether necessity was involved or not, advancements in technology can definitely be linked to curiosity. On December 17, 1903, the Wright brothers took to the air, claiming the honor of powered human flight. Did they fly because they had a need? The desire to take to the air was most likely the fulfillment of a childhood dream to fly as the birds rather than a true need. The benefits of powered flight were unveiled after the event. The advancement of mankind through technology continues to this day. Through advancements in computation, robotics, biotechnology, and nanotechnology, mankind continues to "take to the air" in so many industries.

Computational speed has continued to increase while the physical size of computing devices continues to decrease. Not only do computers process at speeds beyond comprehension, they have become mobile. Society is connected in the home, at the office, and on the go. Because of smartphones, laptops, and tablets, productivity can happen practically anywhere and at anytime. Mobility and ease of use have brought the world closer together. Technology is adjusting to the day-to-day rather than the day-to-day adjusting to technology. Many ideas for technological advances can be seen in movies filmed decades ago. One area of technology that appears to have taken cues from Hollywood is the area of robotics. From toys to surgical procedures, robots are engaged in activities as diverse as entertaining children to working on the production line to assisting in major medical procedures. In the town of West Point, Georgia, KIA Motors Manufacturing of Georgia is utilizing 244 robots in its welding shop. The robots appear to dance as they complete their tasks before passing parts along to another robot waiting to perform yet another task in the production of a KIA Sorento.

In March 2011, the International Space Station received a new addition to the team, Robonaut 2. The new robotic crew member will be able to work longer and handle tasks that may be too risky for human astronauts. What was yesterday's science fiction is truly becoming today's reality.

Biotechnology is an area where science and technology are unraveling the mysteries of the human genome. According to the Human Genome Project, roughly 25,000 genes and three billion chemical base pairs that make up the human genome have been sequenced (ORNL, 2011). The information and knowledge gathered will allow for advances in drug therapies, cleaner energy sources, and more accurate forensic testing. An area that will see great advances due to the research will be that of healthcare. Doctors will have the ability to test patients for cancer risks, heart disease, and mental disorders. The issue with being able to "predict" a patient's medical fate brings up medical ethics. Will insurance companies set higher insurance premiums for a customer whose tests "predict" a potential medical condition later in life? Should doctors inform patients of their fate as if they are holding a crystal ball? These questions have yet to be answered.

Nanotechnology is the final area within challenge 3. The field of nanotechnology refers to the study and development of structures that are smaller than 100 nanometers. The obvious benefit to the computer industry is the development of computers that are smaller than their predecessors. Smaller computer chips and components allow for the development of smaller and lighter technological devices without sacrificing performance. Researchers will be able to work on the molecular and cellular levels, allowing for the creation of micro-gears, nanotubes, and micro-machines. The National Science Foundation estimates by 2015, nanotechnology will have a $1 trillion impact on the global economy and employ two million workers (Nanoproject, 2011). This is an area of study worth watching in the years to come.

Challenge 4—Information/ Knowledge

As with each of the trends discussed in AASCU's Global Challenges Initiative, challenge 4 encompasses a wealth of issues. A great deal of it can be summarized by Tom Friedman's famous quote about the integration of technology and globalization that helped create the new information economy: "You no longer have to emigrate to innovate" (Friedman, 2005, para. 11). Indeed, professionals from around the world are able to participate in this new knowledge-based economy through the use of basic technology, which is certainly changing their lives. While Americans think of outsourcing computer help-desk jobs from one perspective, those who are moving out of poverty in India because of those new opportunities see it from a different perspective. As Friedman reminds his own children and students around the world, competition in the information economy is only going to increase.

Ideas are the hot commodity in this new economy. In fact, Rob Brazell (n.d.), founder of Overstock.com, said:

> "The primary product of the idea economy is ideas. You and I can and must produce ideas just as those who prospered in previous economies had to produce crops, manufactured goods and most recently services." (para. 5)

But what will happen with the information, knowledge, and ideas? Some important questions persist. How can one evaluate the veracity of the new information and ideas that are evolving? Will consumers be capable of using this new information make judgments on what is the best course of action—or what is right and wrong? And finally, will the plethora of knowledge, information, and ideas increase the complexity of decision-making?

Today, ideas are developed at a fast and furious pace because it is now possible for creators to collaborate across the globe. Ideas spread quickly thanks to what has been called "connectivity" by Friedman (2005) and the integration of open-source models like wikis and blogs. Think of how fast plans for protests in Egypt in early 2011 were spread to the population—and interested followers around the world—thanks to Facebook, Twitter, and other technological tools. There's a host of potential problems, however, that may arise from all of this connectivity. Has a virus ever infected your computer? Experience and common sense have taught us that as individuals, organizations, and even governments, we are exposed to the potentially nefarious intents and actions lurking in cyberspace on a daily basis. It will be up to legislators and government officials to ensure a balance between protection and free expression as ideas continue to spread at light speed.

Education is also an impact aspect of the fourth challenge. While colleges and universities have historically stressed the importance of lifelong learning, it is a survival skill in the 21st century. Dr. Larry Peterson, former dean of KSU's College of Science and Mathematics, used to welcome new students into the college by sharing with them that many of the careers they would choose in their professional lives had yet to be developed. It is a true statement not only in the sciences but in many industries. Welcome to the new information economy. Analysts at the Center for an Urban Future, a think tank in New York, predict that current students and the next generation of college students will have between 10 and 14 major career changes. It may be gratifying to learn that the Center for an Urban Future report also stressed the importance of a college degree in terms of succeeding in those careers: "College education is both the single biggest determinant in what an individual is likely to earn, and the biggest asset for self-determination in terms of the labor market. A college degree essentially confers upon its holder a measure of freedom in terms of what jobs he or she will take that high school graduates very rarely possess" (Fisher, 2005, para. 1).

The report also said that colleges and universities will have to utilize technology to a greater degree to prepare students for their 21st century careers. This is a sentiment shared by a 2010 article in the *Futurist* called "Global, Mobile, Virtual, and Social: The College Campus of Tomorrow" (Dew, 2010). It summarized six trends shaping the future of higher education: globalization, international standards, technology, the influx of adult learners, new roles for faculty members, and the changing role of the residential campus. In short, it predicts that tomorrow's college campus may be more virtual than today's campus, capable of serving changing student populations to meet the requirements of the global workforce. You may not be taking classes on your iPad, but there are educational researchers who predict that your younger sibling may use it for much more than entertainment while in college.

The future of education may change dramatically, but it is important to remember that data from the United Nations show that approximately 69 million children around the world still have no access to primary education (United Nations Summit, 2010). How can millions of children who never learn to read and write possibly compete in an information society as adults? Providing educational opportunities is a requirement for the "flatter" global economy that Friedman says is a foundation for the 21st century.

Challenge 5—Economic Integration

Throughout this chapter it should be apparent that each challenge affects the others. Economic integration is defined as "the elimination of tariff and non-tariff barriers to the flow of goods, services, and factors-of-production between a group of nations, or different parts of the same nation" (Business Dictionary, 2011, n.p.). The impact of economies not only has profound effects on how governments deal with their population and resources but can seriously influence conflict.

For decades the economy of the United States has been, and continues to be, the strongest in the world. And while the integration of world economies has not weakened America's power, it has enabled other nations to become more powerful. No longer do world leaders base economic policy decisions entirely upon the actions of the United States.

Several things have contributed to the global economic market. The technology boom has made it easier for more companies to become international. Today, someone living in one area of the world may be working for a corporation on another continent. Technology has not only integrated the marketplace, it has accelerated the spread of cultures around the world, and this, too, increases economic activity.

One of the ways economists assess economies is by studying the gross domestic product (GDP). GDP is defined as "the total market value of all final goods and services produced in a country in a given year, equal to total consumer, investment and government spending, plus the value of exports, minus the value of imports" (Investor Words, n.d., n.p.).

In the past few years five economies, the BRICSA (Brazil, Russia, India, China, and South Africa) economies, have been in the news. The BRICSA are both the fastest growing economies and largest emerging markets in the world. They account for almost three billion people, or just under half of the total population of the world. In recent times, the BRICSA have also contributed to the majority of world GDP growth (Economy Watch 2010).

According to various economists' projections, it is only a matter of time before China becomes the biggest economy in the world—sometime between 2030 and 2050 seems the consensus. In fact, Goldman Sachs believes that by 2050 these will be *the* most important economies, relegating the U.S. to fifth place. By 2020, all of the BRICSA countries should be in the top 10 largest economies of the world. The undisputed heavyweight, though, will be China—also the largest the creditor in the world (Economy Watch 2010). This would be a commanding global power shift. Economic integration is a very complex and commanding issue.

Challenge 6—Security/Conflict

Conflict is not a word with a generally positive connotation. Usually, conflict in one's own life falls on a continuum of "uncomfortable" at the very least and all the way to "destructive" at the other extreme. Yet, in the same way that conflict is an inevitable part of daily life, global conflict is an inevitable part of the world community.

Global conflict encompasses terrorism, war, weaponry, nuclear proliferation, genocide, and other human rights abuses including slavery, forced migration, internment, and torture. The aspects of conflict on the global scale can seem so overwhelming at times that individuals simply want to turn away. History is a reminder, however, that conflicts rarely solve themselves.

Political scientists, sociologists, conflict management experts, communication professors, and others have developed instructive theories and models to help us understand the origins of global conflict, the drivers that seem to perpetuate it, and the solutions that have worked in particular scenarios. It is challenging sometimes to apply those theories thoughtfully to the fast-paced issues that seem to spark global conflict. How many experts, for example, accurately forecasted the grassroots movements that toppled monarchies and dictators in the Middle East and northern Africa in early 2011? Think of some other global conflicts of the recent past keeping these questions in mind.

- Is this an example of a conflict that has the potential to have a positive impact on the world? Without being ethnocentric here, many would argue that the American Revolution was a conflict that impacted the world positively. Why? If one agrees that the United States has helped to further the ideals of equality, democracy, freedom, and independence, then the war that "gave birth" to the country was a conflict with a positive result. Many also agree that the Allies' ability to defeat fascism in World War II was a positive outcome.

- Is this an example of a conflict that has the potential to negatively impact the world? Pol Pot's reign of terror in Cambodia during the 1970s and 1980s not only resulted in a

genocide that killed more than two million Cambodians, but it devastated a country that was once an economic leader in Southeast Asia. The death and destruction of people, institutions, social structures, the government, and more are immeasurable.

- What kind of conflict resolution strategy would be useful to resolve this particular conflict? Just as individuals must employ constructive strategies to resolve conflicts in their families, work groups, and social networks, global conflicts require those same strategies—just on a significantly larger scale. How is stability ensured in Afghanistan? How can peace be achieved in the Middle East? What needs to be done, by whom, to end the systematic rape that continues in the Congo? Global conflicts rarely have easy "solutions," and intelligent, informed experts are likely to disagree on the appropriate strategy. The complexity of the conflict cannot overshadow the search for a resolution.

- What can I do to help bring an end to this global conflict? If you have the thought in your head that says something like, "I'm just a first-year student at KSU, so there's nothing I can do for Darfur," that needs to be reconsidered right now. Instead, reflect on Margaret Mead's famous quote: "A small group of thoughtful people can change the world. Indeed, it is the only thing that ever has." There is something you can do to help every global conflict. Maybe for Congo, it is educating yourself and others about the plight of women. Maybe for Afghanistan, it is voting your conscience in federal elections. For the Middle East, it is joining a student group on campus that promotes a peaceful resolution. Each conflict may require different actions from writing letters to the U.N. to promoting fair-trade products to reduce the market for those items made by slaves, but the key is "action." We are all impacted by global conflicts, even those that appear very remote to our daily lives. It is no longer possible to simply be a passive observer because our actions—and inactions—do have consequences.

Within the context of the seven global challenges examined within this chapter, scholars are most interested in the shifts of conflicts around the world. *Global Trends 2030* (2012), a National Intelligence Council report, explores the shift from interstate war (country against country) to intrastate conflicts (such as civil wars, terrorism groups, and organized crime). The combination of increasingly open economies and persistently authoritarian politics creates the potential for insurgencies, civil war, and interstate conflict. Many of these battles are fought for ideological reasons rather than more traditional reasons of enlarging territory. The "War on Terror" is an example of these ideological conflicts.

Challenge 6 also focuses on the dangers of weapons of mass destruction (WMD). The old paradigm of a country launching a nuclear attack on another country has been replaced, to a large degree, by the new paradigm of a single actor—such as a terrorist group—utilizing a nuclear weapon or a chemical attack. These new conflicts and the concerns regarding WMDs in the hands of small groups will necessitate that military leaders begin employing new strategies to combat this new style of conflict (NIC, 2012).

It is clear from the work of the National Intelligence Council and the office of the Director of National Intelligence, James Clapper, that because conflict, security, and the increasing reality of a multipolar world will, for the foreseen future, seemingly be with us, American leadership and creativity will be required to successfully navigate the turbulent waters in years ahead (NIC, 2012).

Challenge 7—Governance

The seventh key driver of change is that of governance. Whether by design or by chance, the topic of governance is the most likely area where mankind can make a true difference in the other six challenges. From population to conflict, mankind is the responsible party. Newton's third law of physics states that for every action, there is an equal and opposite reaction. This law can be expanded to governance. For every law, rule, or policy, there will be a consequence—intended or unintended. A good example of unintended consequences would be that of China's "One Child Policy" created in 1979. In order to control population growth, the government of China mandated that families would be limited to one child. While the intent of the plan was to slow population growth, the unintended consequence was an insufficient labor force to support the economic growth of the country and the aging population. This is just one of many examples of the power of governance. With a basic understanding of how governance can shape lives, it is possible to break it down further to see how citizens can and should be involved. The four main categories to review are: Corporate Citizenship, Civil Society, Corruption, and Megacommunities.

Corporate Citizenship: Corporations are beginning to realize the power they have in shaping and supporting the communities where they operate. This serving of the public good is known as corporate citizenship. From providing little league uniforms to aiding a community devastated by natural disaster, many corporations are in a better position to act than most governments in a time of need. In the past, corporate success was based on dividends paid to shareholders. Annual reports would boast how costs were reduced and revenues were increased, leading to greater profits. Times have changed!

Consumers are seeking green-minded corporations. They want to see corporations involved in community-based activities. When a company does embrace the importance of corporate citizenship, everyone benefits. Now, companies are producing Corporate Citizenship Reports in addition to Annual Reports. The advantage of a Corporate Citizenship Report is that it gives a complete picture of a corporation's fiscal health as well as its social health. A fine example of corporate involvement is Coca-Cola's Haiti Hope Project. Following the January 2010 earthquake in Haiti, Coca-Cola committed to fostering long-term development and growth by creating a sustainable mango juice industry. It is possible that this investment could contribute more to the country than foreign-government aid could ever provide. What socially conscious corporations do you support?

Civil Society: Nongovernmental organizations (NGOs) are groups that work to promote a specific cause. From human trafficking to disaster relief, NGOs work to bring attention to various issues around the globe. These organizations are able to fill a void where some governments may not have resources to do so. Without NGOs, many developing countries would not have access to healthcare, food, water, or education. Think about a cause that is important to you. Do you know of a group that focuses on that cause here at home or around the globe? Consider finding out more about them and becoming involved.

Corruption: What comes to mind when you see this word? However you define it, corruption only benefits a few by taking advantage of many. Extortion, fraud, and bribery are all examples of governmental corruption. Throughout history into present day, leaders and governments have used their power to control the masses. Sudan, especially the Darfur region, is an excellent example of a corrupt government taking advantage of its people. Darfuris are still living in refugee camps almost a decade after their own government began driving them from their lands. The situation remains dire, although little is said about it on nightly news.

Megacommunities: As the world becomes smaller, we become more interconnected. These increasing connections require larger oversight due to the various groups and governments working together. The United Nations is probably the best-known example of a megacommunity. It gives countries the opportunity to work within a framework similar to a governmental structure. When the international financial crisis hit in 2009, the G-8 and G-20 countries came together to discuss how to better manage the crisis. Why was this necessary? Economic integration! What happens in China will create a ripple in the U.S., and what happens in the U.S. will create a ripple across Europe. Other examples of megacommunities include NATO, the African Union, the International Monetary Fund (IMF), and the World Trade Organization (WTO). As the world becomes even more interconnected, these organizations will have greater and greater influence around the globe.

Culture and Values: An Eighth Challenge?

This chapter of *Foundations of Academic Inquiry* has focused on seven global challenges that are radically changing our world today. The impact of these challenges will likely be even greater over the next 20–30 years. Since the concept of 7 Revolutions was introduced by the Center for Strategic and International Studies in 1992, the importance of issues such as population, resource management, technology, and the integration of global economic systems have become indisputable. Clearly, change as the only constant has become commonplace. But what magic lies in these seven challenges? Might there be other emerging challenges that have been neglected? As we evolve *globally*, it is likely that other key drivers will emerge that should not be overlooked. Indeed, the **culture** and **values** of different countries or civilizations may well be the eighth global challenge.

Whether you consider **culture** and **values** as global challenges or simply contextual issues around which the other challenges play out, an understanding of these two concepts is important. First, what is **culture** and why is it relevant? In *When Cultures Collide*, Richard Lewis (2006) citing Geert Hofstede, a contemporary Dutch organizational researcher, defined culture in the following terms: "the collective programming of the mind" (p. 17). Similarly, it is the full range of human behavior and beliefs that characterize a group—politically, socially, or ethnically. It is what we believe and practice, how we make and assign meaning—our institutions, our religion, our language, our food and the traditions that bind us together. On a deeper level, culture is connected to morality and what we consider right and wrong. Simply put, culture defines us. It is who we are.

Secondly, **values** represent one component of culture. Values are the things important to us—what we believe in and hold dear. Some common examples of values include: life, liberty and the pursuit of happiness, independence, democratic institutions, and ethical leadership. It is how we define these values that make issues controversial. What other values do you have? Considering the larger model of Western and Eastern values, is it conceivable that cultural groups and societies may differ on what they believe, what they practice and consider of value?

In his seminal work, *The Clash of Civilizations* (1996), former Harvard professor Samuel Huntington asserts that future conflict will be driven by cultural differences. Clearly establishing the concept of civilizational identity, Huntington states that "a civilization is the highest cultural grouping of people and the broadest level of cultural identity maintained by a unique group" (1993, p. 24). Further, each civilization has its own distinct culture which is defined by a "common history, religion, customs, institutions, and by the subjective self-identification of that group" (p. 24). Huntington goes on to identify nine contemporary civilizations: Western, Orthodox, Islamic, African, Latin American, Sinic, Hindu, Buddhist, and Japanese.

Huntington further recognizes that in addition to the challenges of culture and civilizational difference, the concept of values and value systems cannot be ignored. Similarly, in *Contemporary International Relations: Sixth Edition* (2002), Daniel S. Papp, KSU's President, recognizes six important global value orientations that are apparent in today's world: individualism versus collectivism, materialism versus spiritualism, modernization versus traditionalism, centralization versus decentralization, political democracy versus authoritarianism or totalitarianism, and moral value versus opposed moral value. These values and the way that different cultures interpret them often play out on societal levels both domestically and internationally.

A couple of important questions should be presented and discussed.

- Admitting these concepts of values and civilizational differences, is conflict inevitable?

- Do values and the defining characteristics of a culture change?

Huntington and Papp differ. While it is Papp's belief that culture and values can change over time (Papp, 2003, p. 470), Huntington says that culture and civilizational characteristics rarely change, if at all (Huntington, 1993, p. 24). Unfortunately, both would seem to agree that values-centered conflict is, in fact, essentially inevitable.

What Do You Think?

History is full of good illustrations that provide evidence that culture and values have been at the heart of conflict between societies or groups for centuries. In fact, our own state of Georgia is at the heart of a good example that is indeed a sad story. It is the story of the Cherokee Indian Nation and its conflict with the United States government. Commonly, we know this story as the *Trail of Tears*. Here, a Native American tribe, living in Georgia, who were relatively advanced in many ways—they built roads, schools, churches and had a representative government—were physically displaced from the world that they had built with their own hands and inhabited for centuries. Herded like animals approximately one thousand miles to what is now Oklahoma, they were relocated to the most paltry and inadequate facilities. This, because their culture was different from the "white man" that was settling the North American continent.

Doubtless, an event such as this suggests the potential for contention and conflict that lies ahead with regard to culture and values and the important role they play in our world today.

Summary

In today's interconnected world, we are aware of events around the globe, just as we are aware of events down the street. Through KSU's encouragement of Global Learning for Engaged Citizenship, it is our goal to provide you with a true global mindset or worldview. Having a truly global worldview is important to both critical thinking and cultural understanding. Without knowing about the world around you and how global issues affect your day-to-day life, you may be at a true disadvantage compared to your counterparts around the world. Remember the following as you progress through your college career:

- Take advantage of the opportunities offered to you in the Global Engagement Certification program

- Plan to study abroad early in your college career

- Learn how the trends addressed in AASCU's Global Challenges Initiative can and will affect your life now and in the future

- Understand the influence of culture and values on human behavior and perspective

There is a world overflowing with opportunity—be a part of it! Choose to become a globally competent citizen.

KSU Links to Explore

Study Abroad
http://www.kennesaw.edu/studyabroad/

Scholarship Opportunities for Study Abroad and Work Overseas
http://www.kennesaw.edu/studyabroad/financial.html

Global Engagement Certificate
http://www.kennesaw.edu/globalengagement/

Get Global
http://www.kennesaw.edu/getglobal/

References

Achieve Universal Primary Education. (2010, September). Retrieved from http://www.un.org/millenniumgoals/pdf/MDG_FS_2_EN.pdf

Brazell, R., (n.d.). Retrieved from http://www.theideaeconomy.com/

Burgess, A. (2010). *Pocket world in figures: 2011 edition*. London: Profile Books.

Business Dictionary. (2011). Retrieved from http://www.businessdictionary.com/definition/economic-integration.html

Commission on Sustainable Agriculture and Climate Change (2011). Achieving food security in the face of climate change. Retrieved from http://ccafs.cgiar.org/news/commission-sustainableagriculture-and-climate-change/global-commission-charts-pathway?page=1

Dew, J. (2010). Global, mobile, virtual, and social: The college campus of tomorrow. *The Futurist*, 46–50.

Economy Watch. (2010, June). *The BRIC Countries: Brazil, Russia, India, China*. Retrieved from http://www.economywatch.com/international-organizations/bric.html

Federal Ministry for Economic Cooperation and Development (2012). *The water, energy and food security nexus: Solutions for the green economy*. Bonn 2011 Conference. Retrieved from http://www.water-energy-food.org/documents/bonn2011_nexussynopsis.pdf

Fisher, D. (2005, October). Center for an urban future. *A workforce vision for continuing education*. Retrieved from http://www.nycfuture.org/content/articles/article_view.cfm?article_id=1128&article_type=3

Friedman, T. L. (2005, April). It's a flat world after all. *The New York Times*. Retrieved from http://www.nytimes.com/2005/04/03/magazine/03DOMINANCE.html?pagewanted=print&position

Futurist.com. (n.d.). *What is the global future of agriculture?* Retrieved from http://www.futurist.com/articlesarchive/questions/future-of-agriculture/ p 277

Glaeser, E. (2011). Triumph of the city: How our greatest invention makes us richer, smarter, greener, healthier and happier. New York: Penguin Press HC.

Hewitt, P. (2002). The end of the postwar welfare state. *The Washington Quarterly, 25*(2), 7–16.

Huntington, S. (1993). The clash of civilizations. *Foreign Affairs, 72*(3), 22–29.

Integrated Regional Information Networks. (2006, September). *Water is running out: How inevitable are international conflicts?* Retrieved from http://www.irinnews.org/InDepthMain.aspx?InDepthId=13&ReportId=61029

International Energy Agency. (2008). *World energy outlook executive summary*. Retrieved from http://www.worldenergyoutlook.org/docs/weo2008/WEO2008_es_english.pdf

Investor Words. (n.d.). Retrieved from http://www.investorwords.com/2153/GDP.htm

Jackson, R., & Strauss, R. (2007, July). The geopolitics of world population change. *CSIS Commentary*. Washington, D.C. CSIS Publication. http://www.csis.org/files/media/csis/pubs/070710_jackson_commentary.pdf

KSU. *Get Global*. (2007). Retrieved March 14, 2011, from http://www.kennesaw.edu/getglobal/definition.shtml

Lewis, R. (2010). *When cultures collide. Third Edition*. Boston: Nicolas Brealey Publishing.

Meadu, V. (2011). *Global commission charts pathway for achieving food security in the face of climate change. Retrieved from* http://ccafs.cgiar.org/news/commission-sustainable-agriculture-and-climate-change/global-commission-charts-pathway

National Geographic (2012). *7 Billion*. Retrieved from http://ngm.nationalgeographic.com/7-billion

National Intelligence Council (2012). *Global trends 2030: Alternative Worlds*. Retrieved from www.dni.gov/index.php/about/organization/global-trends-2030

Nanoproject. (2011). Retrieved from http://www.nanotechproject.org/news/archive/successful_commercialization_depends_on/

ORNL. (2011). Retrieved from http://www.ornl.gov/sci/techresources/Human_Genome/home.shtml

Oxfam International (2012a). *Global food prices in 2011: Questions & answers*. Retrieved from http://www.oxfam.org/en/campaigns/agriculture/food-price-crisis-questions-answers

Oxfam International. (2012b). *Food prices: A looming crisis?* Retrieved from http://www.oxfam.org/en/campaigns/agriculture/food_prices

Papp, D. (2003). *Contemporary international relations: frameworks for understanding. Sixth Edition*. New York: Addison Wesley Longman.

The future of energy. (2008, July). *The Economist*. Retrieved from http://www.economist.com/node/11580723

United Nations Summit. (2010). Retrieved from http://www.un.org/millenniumgoals/pdf/MDG_FS_2_EN.pdf

U.S. Census Bureau. (2011). Retrieved from http://www.census.gov/ipc/www/idb/worldpopgraph.php

Wilson, C. (2006). The century ahead. *Daedalus*, Winter 2006, 5–8.

Worldwatch Institute. *Vital signs*. (2011). Retrieved from http://vitalsigns.worldwatch.org/vs-trend/world-population-growth-slows-modestly-still-track-7-billion-late-2011

World Water Council (2012). Retrieved from http://www.worldwatercouncil.org/index.php?id=25

Critical Thinking Questions

1. What does it mean to be a globally engaged citizen? Why is KSU interested in you becoming one?

2. How do each of the seven global challenges impact the key issues of ethics, leadership, and citizenship that you explored in chapter 12?

3. Which challenge is likely to have the greatest impact on your intended career?

4. Challenge 4 discusses the importance of lifelong learning. What skills and abilities can you learn in college to make you more competitive as new careers are being developed?

KSU TRADITIONS

Kennesaw State University was once regarded as a community college. Even though the institution attained university status in June 1996, the institution did not change the identity it proudly held as a community! Kennesaw State University is a community, and you, as a student, play an integral part. The other members of our campus community are administrators, faculty, and staff.

Our campus community is really no different from other communities you may know. However, we can assess the quality of the experiences of the members of our community by using as a basis the six principles that Ernest Boyer identifies in his work, *Campus Life: In Search of Community* (The Carnegie Foundation, 1990).

- A college community is an educationally *purposeful* community, a place where faculty and students share academic goals and work together to strengthen teaching and learning on campus.

- A college or university is an *open* community, a place where freedom of expression is uncompromisingly protected and where civility is powerfully affirmed.

- A college or university is a *just* community, a place where the uniqueness of the individual is honored.

- A college or university is a *disciplined* community, a place where the individuals accept their obligations to the group and where well-defined governance procedures guide behavior for the common good.

- A college or university is a *caring* community, a place where the well-being of each member is sensitively supported and where service to others is encouraged.

- A college or university is a *celebrative* community, one in which the heritage of the institution is remembered and where rituals affirming both tradition and change are widely shared.

The KSU Alma Mater

Kennesaw, dear Kennesaw,

Nestled in the Georgia pines,

What a special place you hold,

Treasured in this heart of mine.

For the candles you set burning,

Lighting paths of love and learning,

For the gifts you have given me,

Kennesaw, I will cherish thee.

Kennesaw, dear Kennesaw,

Fairest of the Southland's fame,

Sons and daughters gathered here,

Stand to praise thy lovely name.

For the friendships that were made here,

For the dreams we dare to dream here,

Kennesaw, we will cherish thee,

Kennesaw, we will cherish thee.

INDEX